AF760215

International Claims Commissions

ELGAR INTERNATIONAL LAW

Editorial Board: Fausto Pocar, *University of Milan, Italy and ICTY, The Hague, the Netherlands*, Christian Tams, *University of Glasgow, UK*, Nigel D. White, *University of Nottingham, UK*, Jacob Katz Cogan, *University of Cincinnati, USA* and Hilary Charlesworth, *Australian National University*

This important series will present high quality monographs that analyse current thinking and research across the field of international law, rigorously examining key concepts as well as provoking debate and questions for further research. Some volumes will draw on insights from disciplines other than law, such as economics and politics, in an attempt to arrive at a genuinely inter-disciplinary perspective. Seeking to attract original thinking and new, challenging research, proposals are encouraged that primarily engage with new and previously under-developed themes in the field, or alternatively offer an innovative analysis of areas of uncertainty in the existing law.

Titles in this series include:

Epistemic Forces in International Law
Foundational Doctrines and Techniques of International Legal Argumentation
Jean d'Aspremont

International Claims Commissions
Righting Wrongs after Conflict
Lea Brilmayer, Chiara Giorgetti and Lorraine Charlton

International Claims Commissions

Righting Wrongs after Conflict

Lea Brilmayer

Howard Holtzmann Professor, Yale Law School, USA

Chiara Giorgetti

Associate Professor of Law, Richmond Law School, USA

Lorraine Charlton

USA

ELGAR INTERNATIONAL LAW

Edward Elgar PUBLISHING

Cheltenham, UK • Northampton, MA, USA

© Lea Brilmayer, Chiara Giorgetti and Lorraine Charlton 2017

All rights reserved. No part of this publication may be reproduced, stored in a retrieval system or transmitted in any form or by any means, electronic, mechanical or photocopying, recording, or otherwise without the prior permission of the publisher.

Published by
Edward Elgar Publishing Limited
The Lypiatts
15 Lansdown Road
Cheltenham
Glos GL50 2JA
UK

Edward Elgar Publishing, Inc.
William Pratt House
9 Dewey Court
Northampton
Massachusetts 01060
USA

A catalogue record for this book
is available from the British Library

Library of Congress Control Number: 2017931775

This book is available electronically in the **Elgar**online
Law subject collection
DOI 10.4337/9781785363825

MIX
Paper from
responsible sources
FSC® C013056

ISBN 978 1 78536 381 8 (cased)
ISBN 978 1 78536 382 5 (eBook)

Typeset by Columns Design XML Ltd, Reading
Printed and bound in Great Britain by TJ International Ltd, Padstow

Contents

About the authors

Lea Brilmayer is the Howard Holtzmann Professor of International Law at Yale Law School. There, she teaches various international law courses as well as Conflict of Laws. Between 1998 and 2010 she served as lead counsel for the State of Eritrea in several public international law arbitrations at the Permanent Court of Arbitration in The Hague. One of these was the mass claims compensation commission of *Eritrea v. Ethiopia*, in which she worked with Lorraine Charlton and Chiara Giorgetti.

Lorraine Charlton is Knowledge Management Counsel at the National Office of Latham & Watkins LLP. In this capacity, she oversees internal publications related to financial regulation. Prior to rejoining Latham in 2014, Ms. Charlton was a staff attorney in the Office of International Affairs at the Securities and Exchange Commission.

For several years in the mid-2000s, Ms. Charlton served as Deputy Legal Advisor to the Office of the President of Eritrea. She represented the Eritrean government before the Eritrea–Ethiopia Claims Commission at the Permanent Court of Arbitration in The Hague. She also managed the Office of the Legal Advisor in Asmara, Eritrea, and conducted evidence-gathering fieldwork throughout the country.

Before joining the Office of the Legal Advisor, Ms. Charlton worked as an associate in New York and Brussels for Cleary Gottlieb, and then in London for Latham & Watkins. Her work was concentrated in international securities offerings.

Ms. Charlton received her J.D. from New York University. She clerked for Judge Charles P. Sifton of the United States District Court for the Eastern District of New York.

Chiara Giorgetti is Associate Professor of Law at Richmond Law School in Virginia, where she teaches and writes in the areas of public international law, international arbitration, international dispute resolution, and statehood. She also serves as the Faculty Director of the School of Law's LL.M. Program. She has published over a dozen articles and authored or edited four books.

Prior to joining the Richmond Law faculty in 2012, Professor Giorgetti practiced international arbitration in Washington DC, and Geneva, Switzerland, and worked extensively with the United Nations in New York and Somalia. Her practice includes representing sovereign states at the United Nations Claims Commission, the Eritrea–Ethiopia Claims Commission and the Eritrea–Ethiopia Boundary Commission.

Professor Giorgetti holds a law degree from Bologna University School of Law, a M.Sc. in Development Studies from the London School of Economics and Political Sciences, an LL.M. and a J.S.D. from Yale Law School. She clerked at the International Court of Justice in The Hague.

Acknowledgements

Lea Brilmayer owes a great debt to the students enrolled in her fall 2014 seminar on International Legal Theory, which addressed problems relating to international compensation commissions. The discussions in class and the paper drafts were invaluable contributions to an early version of her thinking about the subject. Among the students providing valuable research and writing were: Abigail Graber and Maeghan Mikorski (overview and historical precedents); Tara Davenport and Celso Perez Carballo (institutional advantages and disadvantages); Chris Nason (costs and funding); Karun Tilak (jurisdiction); Shlomit Stein (jurisdictional time frame); Gautam Bhatia (diplomatic representation); Kristine Beckerle (individual claims); Robert James (party structure); Rebecca Buckwalter Poza (evidence) and Shouvik Bhattacharya (remedies). She has also been fortunate to have spectacular research assistance by students at Yale. These include Daniel Hessel, Stephanie Krent, Jack Whitely, Erin Biel and Delbert Tran. She has been more fortunate, still, to have her husband Bill Horne, who is simply spectacular in all respects.

Dear friends: I owe you the experience of a lifetime, and an unusually fortunate one at that. H, your support and friendship carried me through thick and thin and there is no one like you. Y, you'll never read this, so why bother with thanks (even though deserved)? C, you are an incomparable colleague and an intellectual challenger worthy of a professorship. I, the confidence that you placed in me changed my life. Nothing could mean more to me.

In 2002, Lorraine Charlton took a six-month sabbatical from her career as an international capital markets lawyer to work on a public international arbitration. Five years later, she returned to the international capital markets, but not without a deep appreciation for the community of people who work to bring stability, justice and peace to the aftermath of an armed conflict.

She will be forever grateful to Lea Brilmayer for offering that first opportunity to work on her team and for the increasing levels of trust placed in her and for the friendship offered over the years. Working with

Lea and Chiara on this book has been every bit as interesting, challenging, and rewarding as expected – and then some! Ms. Charlton thanks both for their many helpful suggestions and encouragement. She also owes a particular debt to Pamela Fiawoo, the Latham & Watkins law librarian who laid her hands on any book requested and kept the lending libraries at bay when all those books were well past their due dates.

Ms. Charlton also offers all her love to Amanda, Celia and Theo, who have received less attention than they deserved and gave her the time and solitude needed to get it done. Especially Amanda, who continues, after all these many years, to cheerfully make sure she never, ever puts two spaces after a period.

I am immensely grateful to Lea Brilmayer – for her generous, careful and fun mentorship for many years. Working on this book together is the cherry on top.

I am also grateful to Lea and to Lorraine for making writing this book such a rewarding, collaborative and enjoyable experience, and for their dedication to the project, for their suggestions, for keeping all the deadlines and for their sense of humor. You go girls!

At Richmond Law, I am grateful for the research assistance by Charles Davidson, Klementina Pavlova, Malcolm Savage, Cassandra Powell, Mahan Ashouri and Azar Mahmoudi. In addition, Samantha Fleming, Clay Campbell, Ally DeBoer and Caleb McCallum provided excellent editorial review. I would also like to thank two masterful librarians, Alexis Fetzer and Jason Zarin, for all their help.

Lastly, I owe an endless debt of gratitude to my husband Andre, and my children Alexander and Charlotte – *ecco i miei gioielli.* CG

Abbreviations

CAFQ	Committee on Administrative and Financial Questions
CIL	Customary International Law
COP	Conference of the Parties
CRPC	Commission for Real Property Claims of Displaced Persons and Refugees in Bosnia–Herzegovina
CRT-I	Claims Resolution Tribunal for Dormant Accounts in Switzerland I
CRT-II	Claims Resolution Tribunal for Dormant Accounts in Switzerland II
EEBC	Eritrea–Ethiopia Boundary Commission
EECC	Eritrea–Ethiopia Claims Commission
FCSC	Foreign Claims Settlement Commission
GCCF	Gulf Coast Claims Facility
GFLCP	German Forced Labor Compensation Program
HPCC	Housing and Property Claims Commission
HVAP	Holocaust Victim Assets Program
ICC	International Criminal Court
ICHEIC	International Commission on Holocaust Era Insurance Claims
ICJ	International Court of Justice
ICTR	International Criminal Tribunal for Rwanda
ICTY	International Criminal Tribunal for Yugoslavia
IMCC	International Mass Claims Commissions
IOM	International Organization for Migration
IUSCT	Iran–US Claims Tribunal
KPA	Kosovo Property Agency
M&A	Monitoring and Assessment
OAU	Organization of African Union

PCA	Permanent Court of Arbitration
PCC	Property Claim Commission (Kosovo)
PD	Prisoner's Dilemma
POW	Prisoner of War
TRC	Truth and Reconciliation Commission
UNCC	United Nations Compensation Commission
UNCITRAL	United Nations Commission on International Trade Law
UNCLOS	United Nations Convention on the Law of the Sea
UNFCCC	United Nations Framework Convention on Climate Change
UNHCR	United Nations High Commissioner for Refugees
UNMIK	United Nations Interim Administration Mission in Kosovo
UNRWA	United Nations Relief and Works Agency for Palestine Refugees in the Near East

Introduction: international mass claims commissions: "build-it-yourself" justice?

Why might states or international institutions support the creation of mass claims commissions? Presumably because mass claims commissions achieve results that cannot be accomplished in any other way.[1] The paucity of international adjudicative institutions with compulsory jurisdiction means that there are no standing bodies with jurisdiction and managerial competence that can match the accomplishments of which claims commissions are able.

Or are thought to be able – the states and statesmen that create them are not always realistic. Whether in retrospect a particular commission deserved the confidence that was entrusted to it is not always clear, to put the matter politely. But claims commissions must be compared to the alternative, which in the international sphere means no remedy at all. And this may be the reason that their failings are often viewed more charitably than these commissions would otherwise deserve. Claims commissions, however imperfect, are created to fill a void that has become increasingly troublesome in international relations.

We focus mainly on three relatively recent cases: the Iran–US Claims Tribunal, the United Nations Compensation Commission and the Eritrea–Ethiopia Claims Commission. What the claims commissions considered here all have in common is that they were established to determine appropriate compensation for large-scale injuries from violence involving violations of international law.[2] All were designed to be more efficient at adjudicating a larger number of more varied claims than any existing international court could manage. Claims commissions are thought to be better equipped to tailor their procedures, substantive law and remedies to the specific needs of the parties to the particular dispute – hardly a small accomplishment. The conflicts and the types of claims that they

---

[1] See Chapter 2 for a discussion of the advantages and disadvantages of resolving mass claims through a claims commission.

[2] Each of these programs is described in detail in Chapter 1.

have addressed have been varied – traditional wars between states, violent revolutions and genocides – and the decision-making structures that the parties have created to resolve their legal claims were as varied as the upheavals that made them necessary. What makes claims to almost infinite flexibility plausible is that claims commissions are *ad hoc*.

We can illustrate what this means by recounting the tale of a hypothetical dispute between two bordering states, Alpha and Beta. Alpha alleges that Beta invaded it to establish a puppet government that would guarantee Beta privileged access to Alpha's valuable natural resources. Beta was also allegedly entertaining hopes that it might eventually annex Alpha's entire territory through the puppet government's connivance, and, indeed, it tried to do that. Alpha believed itself to be the aggrieved party, but it responded, alleges Beta, with legal violations of its own; mistreatment of its ethnic Beta minority, deliberate shelling of civilians in Beta, violations of Beta's diplomatic immunities and so forth. Tens of thousands of innocent civilians were injured on both sides.

An ordinary domestic dispute would be resolved more or less as follows. Whichever side wanted more to obtain a legal resolution would search out the most appropriate legal institution (probably a trial court) already in existence. The steps to be followed would be roughly these:

1. Dispute resolution mechanisms already exist (courts) with standing judges and procedures.
2. Beta and Alpha's dispute arises.
3. The aggrieved party files in appropriate pre-existing court.
4. The forum applies its own procedural law.
5. Court determines/selects the appropriate law, remedy.
6. Appeal filed by dissatisfied party.
7. Final remedy is enforced.

But Beta and Alpha's conflict is not a domestic dispute, and the parties are probably states, over whom domestic courts typically have no jurisdiction.

Another alternative might be to search for an existing international court, such as the International Court of Justice, which has compulsory jurisdiction in certain instances. The order in which the events occur match stages one through five. But there may not already be such a structure in existence; indeed, there probably won't be. The existing international adjudicative institutions are strictly limited in jurisdiction and subject matter, and their capabilities are limited as well. If claims are to be heard, a new institutional solution must be devised. The answer is "build-it-yourself" justice.

The difference that this makes is enormous. The downside is that the parties may be unable to agree on any legal resolution at all; most international conflicts do not generate mechanisms for creating a body to hear claims for violations of international law, after all. But an obvious upside also exists: Because the commission is created after the dispute arises, it is possible to tailor the structure and the competence to the specific numbers and types of damages claims that are anticipated. And the new commission proceeds with the parties' agreement – a fairly substantial sign of international legitimacy. This is a subject worth studying!

The result is a different progression of the steps in the dispute resolution process, particularly the point at which the adjudicative mechanism is established and then constituted.

1. Dispute between Beta and Alpha arises.
2. Beta and Alpha agree to end the conflict and settle their claims legally.
3. A commission is established by the parties' agreement.
4. The commission is constituted by the parties choosing the members, who select a chair.
5. The commission follows the peace agreement where it specifies substantive and procedural rules.
6. Where the agreement does not address certain questions, the commission decides.
7. The commission resolves the facts and law for the competing claims.
8. Typically, no provision is made for appeal.
9. There may or may not be provision for enforcement.
10. Upon completion of the task, the commission disbands.

As this list suggests, the steps in the post-decision process are also different from the stages in domestic courts (compare stages 6 and 7 of the first example to stages 8 and 9 of the second). The latter typically have appellate bodies to review their decisions and the power of the state to enforce them. International claims commissions typically have neither.[3]

---

[3] Issues arising out of crafting a suitable remedy and enforcing it are discussed in Chapter 7.

The most important of these differences is that commissions are created after the dispute arises; those drafting the instrument that creates the commission can take the characteristics of the dispute into account and tailor the new commission's provisions to a dispute's unique characteristics. Even the judges are chosen by the parties with an eye toward suitability and expertise in the particular subject matter. This, essentially, is the functional meaning of the phrase "*ad hoc.*" Standing institutions – those already in existence before the dispute arose – obviously lack this flexibility.

The chapters below spell out the numerous ways in which the *ad hoc* character of claims commissions makes a difference. One enduring difference affects the framing of almost every legal issue there identified. A discussion of claims commissions cannot focus exclusively on existing law, the way that a treatise on international maritime or intellectual property law would do. On many of the issues that we discuss, there *is* no existing law but only determination of what the parties provided in their peace agreement. A book on claims commissions therefore fulfills an important purpose even where it simply identifies issues that may arise in the course of the proceedings. When put on notice, the parties can choose either to address the issues in their consent to arbitration, or leave the question open for the commission to decide.

We started this Introduction by asking what claims commissions have to offer that accounts for the parties' willingness to create them. As will be shown in the chapters that follow, the costs and benefits are not merely theoretical. There is one underlying motive for establishment of claims commissions that has not been mentioned yet, however, and it may be the real reason that some of them are established. That reason is their ability to contribute to the termination of conflict between the parties by channeling the parties' energies into pursuit of their (real or supposed) *legal* rights. Even while honestly striving for a negotiated end to violent international upheaval, the parties will probably not be positioned to formulate and prove their legal demands for compensation. Creation of a claims commission effectively "kicks the can down the road" so that peace need not wait until mass claims are resolved. The parties can start to rebuild their countries and the lives of their inhabitants. Once the hostilities have halted, they are difficult to resume; halting the fighting temporarily can therefore bestow significant benefits. This is certainly a substantial benefit to the parties and to the international communities, and, even when unspoken, may be the most important benefit of all.

1. What are international mass claims commissions?

International mass claims commissions (IMCCs) represent a unique and important form of international adjudication established to consider claims resulting from significant international war-related and traumatic historical events.[1] Their principal, but not sole, aim is to determine compensation to individuals and states for certain losses, damages and injuries.[2]

This chapter begins by analysing the common features of IMCCs. It then clarifies the differences between IMCCs and similar domestic and international mechanisms that may share some, but not all, of the characteristics of IMCCs. Finally, this chapter offers an historical overview of IMCCs and an initial introduction to the most relevant modern examples of IMCCs that form the core of this book's analysis.

We offer a detailed study of this important, though hitherto understudied, mechanism. Indeed, this book seeks to study analytically the fundamental procedural and substantive characteristics of IMCCs with the aim of providing a blueprint for future use.

WHAT ARE IMCCS?

IMCCs are *ad hoc* bodies and their structure, jurisdiction, procedure and ability to remedy vary considerably. Indeed, there is no uniform, formal definition of IMCCs. They make up an eclectic and unique group,

---

[1] *See, generally,* Howard Holtzmann and Edda Kristjánsdóttir (eds), *International Mass Claims Processes: Legal and Practical Perspectives* (Oxford University Press, 2007). The book addresses such matters as funding, balancing arbitral and administrative approaches, key elements in drafting rules of procedure, establishing standards of proof, defining the respective functions of arbitrators and the secretariat and utilizing computer technology. *See also* David Caron, "International Claims and Compensation Bodies," in Cesare Romano, Karen Alter and Yuval Shany (eds), *Oxford Handbook of International Adjudication* (Oxford University Press, 2014).

[2] For a detailed analysis of the reasons to create IMCCs, see Chapter 2.

characterized by important shared characteristics. First, IMCCs are binding dispute resolution mechanisms; second, they are structured and act like judicial bodies; third, they are created after an event of international relevance; fourth, they are international law instruments; fifth, they engage the responsibility of states; and sixth, they are *ad hoc* institutions. Each of these elements is explored below.

IMCCs Are Binding Dispute Resolution Mechanisms

IMCCs are, first and foremost, binding dispute resolution instruments. Decisions made by international commissions are judicial decisions and are binding on all parties. IMCCs are not mediation or conciliation mechanisms, nor do they serve as advisory or review bodies. The instruments that create them typically contain a clause that makes their decisions binding on the relevant parties, who are, therefore, obligated under international law to respect and enforce them. The 2000 Algiers Agreement that created the Eritrea–Ethiopia Claims Commission (EECC), for example, states that decisions and awards of the commission are "final and binding" and that "the parties agree to honor all decisions and to pay any monetary awards rendered against them promptly."[3] Similar provisions exist in the instruments that created other IMCCs.[4] By creating IMCCs, parties aim at providing final compensation to a defined set of legitimate claimants that have suffered harm.[5]

The fact that IMCCs are binding dispute resolution mechanisms does not, of course, mean that they are *only* binding dispute resolution mechanisms. Indeed, parties create international claims commissions for a variety of reasons. Thus, international claims commissions are also instruments that serve to transition from turmoil to peace. IMCCs are often part and parcel of a more comprehensive peace process.[6] Parties also seek to have a third, neutral body deciding claims that are politically and domestically sensitive.

---

[3] Art. 5 (17), Peace Agreement between Eritrea and Ethiopia, signed in Algiers on 12 December 2000, 13 December 2000, A/55/686 and S/2000/1183.

[4] Art. IV of the Claims Settlement Declaration that created the Iran–US Claims Tribunals, for example, provides that "All decisions and awards of the Tribunal shall be final and binding." See also paras. 16–19 of UN Security Council Resolution 687 (1991) of 8 April 1991, UN Doc S/RES/687 (1991), that created the United Nations Compensation Commission.

[5] See Chapter 4 for an analysis of who are the claimants and what are the different claims.

[6] See Chapter 2 for a detailed discussion.

Moreover, the creation of IMCCs generally also fulfills a variety of functions. In addition to providing satisfaction to parties involved through the payment of compensation and rectifying harms suffered by diverse groups, IMCCs provide a form of closure after a violent event. Often, they also help by providing a narrative and historical record for all the parties involved.[7]

IMCCs Are Structured and Act as Judicial Bodies

IMCCs are structured and act as judicial bodies, though each with its own variations. This is in direct correlation with the fact that they are binding dispute mechanisms, as explained above. Thus, IMCCs incorporate the essence of the principles of fair trials in their proceedings. They are neutral and impartial bodies, and decisions are taken by an odd number of independent and impartial adjudicators deciding by majority and in a timely fashion.[8]

Claims commissions are also structured to result in fair proceedings, where evidence can be presented equally by the parties and evaluated fairly by the tribunal. Thus, parties are usually represented by counsel. Proceedings most often include both a written and an oral phase, and hearings are open to the parties and their representatives, though they are most often held *in camera*.[9]

IMCCs Are Created in the Aftermath of an International Upheaval

IMCCs are created as a consequence of an underlying action or event involving at least two states that provoked a set of related claims, which the states themselves decided needed to be remedied. Historically, they have been created in the aftermath of an international violent upheaval, such as an armed conflict or a revolution, though the underlying event does not necessarily need to be violent.

Thus far, these events have included revolutions, like the 1979 Islamic Revolution in Iran, which overthrew the US-supported Shah and had significant economic repercussion for US businesses and US government contracts. They have also included wars, such as the 1998

---

[7] See David Luban, Julie R. O'Sullivan and David P. Stewart, *International and Transnational Criminal Law* (Aspen, 2014).

[8] For an analysis of the structure of the commissions and of the decision makers, see Chapter 3.

[9] On the issue of evidence, see Chapter 6, on the issue of party representation see Chapter 5.

Eritrea–Ethiopia war, which resulted in substantial loss of life, personal injuries and damages to property in both Eritrea and Ethiopia. Another event that resulted in the creation of an international claims commission was the territorial invasion of Kuwait by Iraq in 1991, which caused significant personal injuries and considerable damage to the property, environment, and natural resources of many states in the region.

The creation of an international claims commission mechanism is often also part and parcel of the peace process that all parties undertake to restore peace and trust after a significant crisis. IMCCs also aim to provide a form of closure and possible settlement between disputing parties who are often emerging from years of tense and violent relations.

IMCCs Are Created by International Agreements

IMCCs are international law bodies created by international agreement. The kind and format of each international instrument can vary substantially. For example, the Eritrea–Ethiopia Claims Commission was established by a bilateral agreement between Eritrea and Ethiopia, signed in 2000 and witnessed by the President of Algeria and the US Secretary of State. The United Nations Compensation Commission (UNCC) was created by a resolution of the UN Security Council in the aftermath of Iraq's invasion of Kuwait.[10] The Iran–US Claims Tribunal was established through agreements expressed separately by Iran and the United States – which at the time did not have diplomatic relations – to the government of Algeria and collected in the Declaration of the Government of Algeria.[11]

Because they are international bodies, IMCCs also share many of the structural characteristics of international organizations: they are regulated under international law, they generally apply international law, and they employ mostly international staff.

The international nature of claims commissions is also important *per se*. In fact, in the aftermath of international turmoil, the involved parties often do not trust any party's domestic systems. They often seek a neutral and *super partes* entity that is capable of providing a venue for reconciliation and dialogue. An international setting offers these reassurances.

---

[10] UNSC Res 687 (1991) of 8 April 1991.

[11] Declaration of the Government of the Democratic and Popular Republic of Algeria Concerning the Settlement of Claims by the Government of the United States of America and the Government of the Islamic Republic of Iran (Claims Settlement Declaration), 19 January 1981.

IMCCs Engage the International Responsibility of States

IMCCs engage the responsibility of the state as a sovereign entity and a subject of international law. Thus, they only engage the responsibility of states for violations of international law. This means that they only review claims for damages, loss and injuries to individuals, states and international organizations that result from an international wrongful act of a state, consisting of either an action or an omission, which constitutes a breach of an international obligation of the state itself and is attributable to the state under international law.[12] Under the structure created by an IMCC's processes, states pay compensation to determined entities, which will usually include individuals and may also include other states, international organizations and private sector entities.

Importantly, IMCCs are not concerned with any criminal responsibility of individuals that could arise from the same events. Criminal responsibility is generally dealt with separately, through a separate and distinct process. In the aftermath of the Yugoslav conflict and the Rwanda genocide, for example, the Security Council created by its own resolutions the International Criminal Tribunal for Yugoslavia (ICTY) and the International Criminal Tribunal for Rwanda (ICTR). These international tribunals were tasked with prosecuting individuals for specific violations of international criminal law.

IMCCs Are *Ad Hoc* Institutions

Another important characteristic of IMCCs is their *ad hoc* nature. IMCCs are created for the specific purpose of resolving claims arising from a particular dispute or defined category of disputes. They are created after a violent event occurred and are dissolved after their functions are completed.

Thus, they are retrospective, backward-looking institutions with a docket that is fixed at the time of their creation.[13] IMCCs are, therefore, also different from standing international courts, such as the International Court of Justice, which have a prospective and open docket, unknown to

---

[12] See Articles 1 and 2 of the Draft Articles on the Responsibility of States for International Wrongful Acts, Text adopted by the International Law Commission at its 53rd session, 23 April – 1 June and 2 July–10 August 2001, and submitted as Official Records of the General Assembly, Fifty-sixth Session, Supplement No. 10, A/56/10.

[13] *See generally* David Caron, "Towards A Political Theory of International Courts and Tribunals," (2007) 28 *Berkeley Journal of International Law* 401.

the parties when they agree to submit themselves to the jurisdiction of those entities.

THE UNIQUE NATURE OF IMCCS

IMCCs are distinct and unique instruments in international law. However, there are several other international and domestic mechanisms that may share some of the characteristics or elements of IMCCs.

IMCCs, for instance, are different from domestic mass claims processes such as US class actions in the sense that they are *ad hoc* systems. IMCCs may also employ mass claims procedures but do not necessarily do so. For example, while some of the claims adjudicated by the UNCC used mass claims methodologies, neither the Iran–US Claims Tribunal nor the EECC have availed themselves of such procedures.

This book focuses only on IMCCs. The section below distinguishes IMCCs from other possibly similar instruments, namely mixed claims commissions, domestic claims processes, international criminal courts and tribunals, and truth and reconciliation commissions.

IMCCs and Mixed Claims Commissions

IMCCs share many of the characteristics of mixed claims commissions. Mixed claims commissions are *ad hoc* bodies created by an international agreement after an international conflict or internal disturbance, with the aim of settling claims between nationals of different states, between nationals of one state and the other state or between states themselves.[14] Mixed claims commissions engage in formal proceedings, and their decisions are final and binding.

Unlike international claims commissions, mixed claims commissions only include commissions created by the states involved and created by treaties between states (generally treaties relating to arbitration and conciliation). Thus, mixed claims commissions do not include commissions set up by international organizations, such as the UNCC, which was created by a resolution of the United Nations Security Council. Mixed claims commissions represent, therefore, a subset of IMCCs.

---

[14] Rudolf Dolzer, "Mixed Claims Commissions," *Max Planck Encyclopedia of Public International Law*, (Oxford University Press, last updated May 2011).

IMCCs and Domestic Claims Processes

IMCCs differ also from compensation mechanisms established by one state only, even those established on the basis of an international agreement. Indeed, domestic compensation mechanisms are numerous. In the United States, for example, the Foreign Claims Settlement Commission (FCSC), an agency of the Department of Justice, settles claims that US nationals have against foreign governments. The jurisdiction of the FCSC is conferred by Congress, through an international claims settlement agreement or at the request of the secretary of state. Its funds derive from either Congressional appropriations, international claims settlements or from liquidation of foreign assets in the United States. Completed FCSC claims programs include claims against the Federal Republic of Germany, Bulgaria, Romania, Poland and Albania.[15] Although international in origin, these claims are fully addressed and resolved in the domestic context by a US governmental agency.

Claims commissions are also established to deal with wholly domestic events. For example, in the aftermath of the 2010 Deepwater Horizon oil spill in the Gulf of Mexico, British Petroleum, which owned the damaged oil rig, established the Gulf Coast Claims Facility (GCCF), a $20 billion fund to settle claims for natural resource damages, state and local response costs, and individual compensation arising from the oil spill. These are entirely domestic claims that may use mass claims procedures but share little else with IMCCs.

IMCCs and International Criminal Courts and Tribunals

IMCCs only engage the responsibility of states for violations of international law as a sovereign entity and a subject of international law. IMCCs do not adjudicate criminal responsibility of individuals that may arise from the same events.

In recent years, separate international *ad hoc* mechanisms have been established by the international community to deal with criminal responsibility. For example, the ICTR and the ICTY were set up by the UN Security Council to judge those individuals most responsible for gross violations of international criminal law, including the crime of genocide, crimes against humanity, war crimes and grave breaches of the Geneva

---

[15] For more on the Foreign Claims Settlement Commission, see https://www.justice.gov/fcsc. In addition, Chapter 3 touches on the role of the FCSC in resolving a subset of claims settled and outsourced to it by the Iran–US Claims Tribunal.

Conventions, which establish basic principles of international humanitarian law. The ICTY and ICTR could impose prison terms, up to life imprisonment, on those found guilty. Their jurisdiction was limited to individuals only and did not include any review of acts of states. Further, neither the ICTY nor the ICTR provided any monetary compensation to victims.

At times, these mechanisms are created in parallel with other claims commissions, but remain separate. For instance, several real-property claims processes ran in parallel to the ICTY. These included the Commission for Real Property Claims of Displaced Persons and Refugees in Bosnia–Herzegovina (CRPC), established by the 1995 Dayton Peace Agreement. The CRPC was headquartered in Sarajevo and had a mixed composition of nine members: six internationals appointed by the President of the European Court of Human Rights, and six nationals, two appointed by the Republika Srpska and four appointed by the Federation of Bosnia and Herzegovina. The CRPC dealt only with mass property claims resulting from the disintegration of Yugoslavia.[16]

IMCCs and Truth and Reconciliation Commissions

International Truth and Reconciliation Commissions are typically created after a violent international or domestic event that significantly impacted a state. The fundamental functions of these commissions are to provide an instrument of reconciliation and closure to the parties involved, through a process of dialogue, and to create an historical record. IMCCs are adjudicative bodies and are therefore inherently different from Truth and Reconciliation Commissions.

The last few decades have seen the establishment of several International Truth and Reconciliation Commissions. For example, the government of South Africa created a Truth and Reconciliation Commission (TRC) after the abolition of apartheid. The TRC served largely as a reconciliation mechanism and created an important historical record of the abuses that occurred during apartheid. Hearings were mostly held in public and were often televised. Witnesses who were identified as victims of gross human rights violations were invited to give statements about

---

16 Hans van Houtte, "Mass Property Claim Resolution in a Post-War Society: The Commission for Real Property Claims in Bosnia and Herzegovina" (1999) 48 *International and Comparative Law Quarterly* 625–638. The operational structure of the CRPC is discussed in more detail in the second section of Chapter 3.

their experiences. At the same time, perpetrators could also give testimony and ask for amnesty from both civil and criminal prosecution. This served an important, cathartic function and also helped to create a record and historical narrative.

Similarly, Argentina created the National Commission on the Disappearance of Persons after the Dirty War and the military dictatorship that ruled Argentina from 1976 to 1983. This Commission documented human rights violations committed during that period and established an important record. The work of the Commission also resulted in the trial of some of the military commanders for war crimes. Similar commissions were established in Uganda, Guatemala, El Salvador and the Philippines, among other places.

CLAIMS COMMISSIONS IN HISTORY

The history of IMCCs is rooted in post-conflict compensation mechanisms, and their subsequent development altered the presumption that their only useful function was to extract compensation from the vanquished to the victors for war damages.[17] As such, IMCCs largely replaced arbitration by single persons (generally a head of state) and mixed arbitral tribunals, and they introduced judicial elements in the resolution of the dispute, in terms of procedure, due process and the right of all parties to be heard.

This section looks at international claims commissions from an historical perspective. It first offers a short exploration of past claims commissions and then examines the contemporary model of IMCCs.

An Overview of Past Claims Commissions

Historically, IMCCs saw their first iteration in the 1794 Jay Treaty between the United States and the United Kingdom, which established two commissions to resolve claims of British merchants against the United States and those of US ship-owners against the UK.[18]

In the nineteenth and twentieth centuries, claims commissions became a leading method of peaceful settlement of international disputes. Indeed, in that period, affected states created more than 90 claims commissions after wars or revolutions in order to decide claims arising from either

---

17 Dolzer, "Mixed Claims Commissions."

18 Treaty of Amity, Commerce, and Navigation, Between His Britannic Majesty and the United States of America, 1794 (Jay Treaty).

international or domestic conflict during which aliens suffered damages.[19] For example, claims commissions were created to settle claims against France after the Napoleonic Wars. Claims commissions were also established in 1839, 1854, 1859 and 1868 (after Mexico's independence) to settle claims between the United States and Mexico over territory and taxation, as well as claims from private citizens. Claims settlements commissions were established in many instances in Latin America, including in Chile, Venezuela and Peru. For example, the 1903 joint commission between Panama and the United States was created to compensate property claims arising out of the establishment of the Panama Canal.[20] The commission was composed of four members, two appointed by the President of the United States and two appointed by the President of Panama. In case of disagreement of the commission, an umpire was appointed by the two governments to render a final decision.[21]

Claims commissions were also created to decide damages arising out of World War I. The Treaty of Versailles, which ended the war, provided for the creation of a reparations commission to establish the amount Germany would be required to pay France, the United Kingdom and the other Allied Powers. Additionally, the United States negotiated a separate reparation agreement in the Treaty of Berlin, which established a Mixed Claims Commission to provide compensation for both sovereign and, importantly, individual claims. A similar agreement was reached by the United States with Austria and Hungary through the Tripartite Claim Commission.

An additional set of claims commissions was set up between the United States and Mexico to deal with longstanding claims. The American–Mexican Claims Commission (the General Commission) was created by treaty to adjudicate claims by US and Mexican citizens for losses suffered due to the acts of one government against nationals of the other. It lasted from 1924 to 1934. A Special Commission was also created by the two countries to resolve claims pertaining to the Mexican Revolution. The commissions were not entirely successful, but Mexico and the United States eventually settled all claims in 1934.

The use of mixed claims commissions declined after World War II, as countries were wary of the effects that payment of heavy reparations had

---

19 C. Romano, "A Taxonomy of International Rule of Law Institutions" (2011) 2 *Journal of International Dispute Settlement* 264.

20 Convention Between the US and Panama (Panama Canal), 1903, see especially Arts. VI and XV.

21 See Dolzer, "Mixed Claims Commissions."

had on Germany: The substantial reparations provided in the Treaty of Versailles were seen as one of the indirect causes of World War II. Reparations after World War II were negotiated bilaterally with Germany, and no general claims commission was established.[22]

Contemporary IMCCs

Up until the latter half of the twentieth century, most agreements establishing mixed claims commissions were concluded between the United States, on one side, and either Latin American or European states on the other or among European states. Asia, Africa and the Middle East were largely absent and did not use this mechanism.[23]

The resurgence of the claims commission mechanisms occurred with the establishment of the Iran–US Claims Tribunal in 1981, followed by the United Nations Compensations Commission in 1991, and the Eritrea–Ethiopia Claims Commission in 2000. Each entity is briefly described below.

The development of modern IMCCs, which are the focus of this book, clearly drew from the experience of the past. The essence of the post-conflict dispute resolution mechanisms was maintained, while new judicial elements were introduced. Contemporary claims commissions also involved a much larger variety of regional actors.

The Iran–US Claims Tribunal

The Iran–US Claims Tribunal is the first modern example of an international claims adjudication program.[24] It was created in 1981, through indirect negotiations between Iran and the United States, to adjudicate individually complex commercial and international law cases totaling tens of billions of dollars. Despite a challenging mandate and a tense

---

22 Dolzer indicates three bilateral claims commissions: the Arbitral Commission on Property, Rights and Interests in Germany; the Conciliation Commissions Established Pursuant to Art. 83 Peace Treaty with Italy (1947) and the Property Commissions Established Pursuant to Art. 15 Peace Treaty with Japan (1951).

23 See Dolzer, "Mixed Claims Commissions."

24 For an excellent overview, see Jeremy K. Sharpe, "The Iran–United States Claims Tribunals," in C. Giorgetti (ed.), *The Rules, Practice and Jurisprudence of International Courts and Tribunals* (Martinus Nijhoff Publishers, 2012). See also Richard Lillich (ed.), *Iran–United States Claims Tribunal 1981–1983* (Charlottesville, VA: UP of Virginia, 1985).

political climate, the Iran–US Claims Tribunal has successfully resolved over 3,900 claims and is still hearing cases in The Hague.[25]

The creation of the Iran–US Claims Tribunal was part of the settlement of the hostage crisis that followed the Islamic Revolution in Iran, which culminated in 1979 with the ousting of the Shah and the establishment of the Islamic Republic of Iran. In the period leading to the crisis, the United States was a key ally to the Shah and had provided critical support to his regime through trade, investment and military equipment. The decline in popular support for the regime of the Shah resulted in rising anti-American sentiment. In early 1979, the Shah left Iran and the government of his successor, Ayatollah Ruhollah Khomeini, began a nationalization process that included the banking, insurance and oil sectors. US nationals in Iran faced increasing difficulties, and, by the summer, around 45,000 Americans living in Iran had fled the country. On 4 November 1979, the situation further deteriorated when a group of Iranian militants seized the US Embassy in Tehran and detained a number of diplomats and consular officers.

As it became clear that the militants enjoyed the support of the new Iranian government, the United States responded by taking a series of retaliatory actions, including severing diplomatic relations, imposing economic sanctions and freezing Iranian assets held in the United States. Following Iraq's unexpected invasion of Iran in 1980, Algeria acted as a broker and mediator to resolve the deadlocked situation and negotiate a peace agreement. On 19 January 1981, the Algerian government issued two declarations (known as the Algiers Accords), one signed with Iran and one signed with the United States, which was composed of several documents containing legally binding provisions.[26] The General Declaration contains the main commitments of the parties, including the liberation of the US hostages, the transfer of some frozen assets back to Iran and the termination of litigation in the US courts in favor of arbitration. The Claims Settlement Declaration established the Iran–US Claims Tribunal, headquartered in The Hague.

The Iran–US Claims Tribunal is still operating as an independent arbitral body and is composed of nine judges: three from the United States, three Iranians and three judges (including the President) from other countries appointed by the party-appointed members (or, if they

[25] For more information, see the Tribunal website at: https://www.iusct.net/Pages/Public/A-About.aspx.

[26] The Algiers Accords, including the General Declaration, are available at: http://www.iusct.net/General%20Documents/1-General%20Declaration%E2%80%8E.pdf.

cannot agree, by the Tribunal's appointing authority). The Tribunal decides cases by majority of either one of the three member Chambers or by the full Tribunal. Article V of the Claims Settlement Declaration provides that the Tribunal shall "decide all cases on the basis of respect for law, applying such choice-of-law rules and principles of commercial and international law as the Tribunal determines to be applicable, taking into account relevant usages from the trade, contract provisions and changed circumstances."[27]

The jurisdiction of the Tribunal includes private claims of US nationals against Iran and of Iranian nationals against the United States arising out of debts, contracts, expropriations or other measures that affected property rights. Claims under $250,000 are defined as small claims. About 2,800 small claims were filed (the great majority from US nationals), and they were settled by a lump-sum payment by Iran to the United States of $105 million. About 1,000 large claims were filed and decided by 2003. Overall, the Iran–US Claims Tribunal has awarded more than $2.5 billion to US nationals and companies.[28] The Iran–US Claims Tribunal also has jurisdiction over official claims between Iran and the United States based on contractual arrangements for the purchase and sale of goods and services. Washington has filed 24 cases and Tehran has filed 53 cases. Seventy-two of those claims have been decided. The remaining pending cases are all by Iran against the United States.

In its procedures, the Tribunal uses the arbitration rules of the United Nations Commission on International Trade Law (UNCITRAL), as modified by the parties and the Tribunal. The cost of running the Tribunal is split equally between the two parties. Under the Algiers Accord, Iran agreed to place $1 billion in an account as security for payment of Iran–US Claims Tribunal awards against Iran, and to keep that account at $500 million until all awards against Iran are satisfied. This unique mechanism simplifies the enforcement of awards and makes payments possible.[29]

The Iran–US Claims Tribunal is the longest-running international commission in history and has many achievements. Despite the persistence of a tense relationship between Iran and the United States, the Tribunal has resolved by binding arbitration the great majority of the disputes that it was mandated to resolve. The awards have been respected

---

[27] Art. 5 Claims Settlement Declaration, available at: http://www.iusct.net/General%20Documents/2-Claims%20Settlement%20Declaration.pdf.

[28] See the overview of the tribunal by US State Department, available at: http://www.state.gov/s/l/3199.htm.

[29] A general discussion of remedies and compliance is found in Chapter 7.

and enforced, although its slow pace and the difficult relations between Iran and the United States have impacted the work of the Tribunal.[30] However, the Iran–US Claims Tribunal remains an example of a successful international claims commission. It also sets a useful example for the creation of future IMCCs and provides initial guidance for possible structure and procedure of future similar mechanisms.

The United Nations Compensation Commission

In the wake of the successful creation of the Iran–US Claims Tribunal, the United Nations decided to create a compensation commission to process and pay claims compensation for a variety of losses resulting from Iraq's invasion of Kuwait in August 1990. The task was monumental: between 1991 and 2005, the commission processed about 2.7 million claims seeking more than $350 billion in compensation.[31]

As with other IMCCs, the roots of the creation of the United Nations Compensation Commission (UNCC) are found in a violent international event. On 2 August 1990, Iraq invaded Kuwait and started a seven-month occupation of the country. The invasion and occupation caused great destruction to property and natural resources, resulted in the death and injury of thousands of Kuwaitis and foreign civilians and some 300,000 foreign workers fled Kuwait. A UN-sanctioned military intervention led by the United States deployed in January and February 1991 to reverse the occupation. Memorably, Iraqi troops set alight more than 600 Kuwaiti oil wells when leaving the country, causing enormous environmental and economic damage.

The UNCC was created in the aftermath of Iraq's invasion as a subsidiary organ of the UN Security Council by Resolution 687 of the Security Council. The Resolution contained the basic framework for the establishment and the jurisdiction of the UNCC, providing that, as a

---

[30] See Lee Caplan, "Challenges of Arbitrators in the Iran–US Claims Tribunals," in C. Giorgetti (ed.), *Challenges and Recusals of Judges and Arbitrators in International Courts and Tribunals* (Brill, 2015), see also Sharpe, "The Iran–United States Claims Tribunals."

[31] For an overview of the UNCC, see David Bederman, "The United Nations Compensation Commission and the Tradition of International Claims Settlement" (1994) 27 *New York University Journal of International Law and Politics* 1–42. See also Timothy J. Feighery, "The United Nations Compensation Commission," in C. Giorgetti (ed.), *The Rules, Practice and Jurisprudence of International Courts and Tribunal* (Martinus Nijhoff Publishers, 2012) and Timothy J. Feighery, Christopher S. Gibson and Trevor M. Rajah (eds), *War Reparations and the UN Compensation Commission – Designing Compensation After Conflict* (Oxford University Press, 2015).

result of its unlawful invasion and occupation of Kuwait, Iraq was "liable under international law for any direct loss, damage, including environmental damage and the depletion of natural resources, or injury to foreign Governments, nationals and corporations."[32] It also created a special Fund to be financed by a percentage of the value of Iraq's petroleum and petroleum-products exports. The Fund permitted the payments of all the claims and covered all the cost of the UNCC.[33]

The UNCC was given unusually extensive jurisdiction, which included claims for individuals who were forced to leave Iraq or Kuwait as a result of the invasion, individual claims for serious personal injury or death, and individual claims for losses. This jurisdiction also included claims by corporations and other private or public enterprises, claims from governments in the region (including Iran, Saudi Arabia, Syria, Jordan and Kuwait) and international organizations.[34] Overall, about 2.7 million claims were filed with the Commission, with an asserted value of $352.5 billion. The Commission concluded the processing of claims in 2005. Out of the claims filed, it awarded compensation of about $52.4 billion to approximately 1.5 million successful claimants.[35] The UNCC has so far paid $47.8 billion in compensation. The remaining amount of $4.6 billion pertains to a single claim awarded to Kuwait for the production and revenue losses resulting from damages to Kuwait's oil-fields assets.

The administration of such a vast program required the establishment of a large administrative structure, which was comprised of three organs.[36] The Governing Council, whose membership mirrored that of the Security Council, was the principal organ responsible for the general policy and legal framework. It also reviewed and finally approved the reports and recommendations on claims made by the commissioners. The commissioners, nominated by the UN Secretary-General upon recommendation of the executive secretary of the UNCC, sat in panels of three members to consider and render recommendations on claims in specific categories. Finally, the Secretariat, headed by the executive secretary, supported the work of both the Governing Council and the commissioners. The Secretariat was headquartered in Geneva, Switzerland, and, at its peak, numbered 250 staff.

---

32 UNSC Res 687 (1991) of 8 April 1991, UN Doc S/Res/687.

33 See also UNSC Res 692 (1991) detailing the funding procedures. Issues of funding and costs are discussed in depth in Chapter 7.

34 For a detailed explanation of the kinds of claims received as well as an analysis of the claimants, see Chapter 5.

35 For specific awards, see the website of the UNCC at: http://www.uncc.ch.

36 For a general discussion of the structures of IMCCs, see Chapter 3.

The legacy of the UNCC is substantial, and it processed a large number of claims in a relatively short time. It was the first example of a successful mass claims procedure that provided compensation on a priority basis to thousands of foreign workers who had to flee the region. The UNCC was, however, very much objected to by Iraq, which saw it as an unreasonable imposition by the international community.[37] This remained true until 2003, when a US-led coalition invaded Iraq and deposed Saddam Hussein. The new coalition-backed government collaborated more with the UNCC. This period of greater cooperation coincided with the resolution of larger and more complex claims. Iraq had more extensive access to counsel and decisions were taken after all parties were heard. Certainly, claims processing was facilitated by the fact that Iraq's liability for losses was already established in Resolution 687 and the creation of the fund for the payment of awards. Still, the professionalism and hard work of the UNCC allowed for the mostly smooth administration of a complex situation.

The Eritrea–Ethiopia Claims Commission

The most recent example of an international claims commission is the Eritrea–Ethiopia Claims Commission (EECC), created in 2000 as part of the peace agreement between the two countries. The EECC closely resembled an international tribunal, though it was tasked with administering claims arising from the violation of international law, including humanitarian law, by Eritrea and Ethiopia.[38]

Between 1998 and 2000, Eritrea and Ethiopia fought a ruinous boundary war that resulted in a significant loss of life, personal injury and economic damage. Approximately 70,000 combatants died, and 35,000 people were displaced by the war. The conflict ended in June 2000, thanks to a ceasefire agreement negotiated with the assistance of the United Nations, the Organization of African Unity (OAU) (now, the African Union), the United States and others, which was signed in Algiers.[39] The agreement was followed by a permanent peace agreement,

---

[37] See Michael E. Schneider, "The Role of Iraq in the UNCC Process with Special Emphasis on the Environmental Claims," in Timothy J. Feighery, Christopher S. Gibson and Trevor M. Rajah (eds), *War Reparations and the UN Compensation Commission – Designing Compensation After Conflict* (Oxford University Press, 2015).

[38] *See, generally,* Sean D. Murphy, Won Kidane and Thomas R. Snider, *Litigating War: Mass Civil Injury and the Eritrea–Ethiopia Claims Commission* (Oxford University Press 2013).

[39] Agreement on Cessation of Hostilities, signed in Algiers on 18 June 2000.

also signed in Algiers, on 12 December 2000. The agreement terminated the hostilities between the two countries and established a neutral Boundary Commission to delimit and demarcate the borders between Eritrea and Ethiopia.[40] Article 5 of the Agreement also established a Claims Commission to decide "through binding arbitration all claims for loss, damage or injury by one Government against the other and by nationals (including both natural and judicial persons) of one of the parties against the Government of the other party or entities owned or controlled by the other party" that were related to the conflict and resulted "from violations of international humanitarian law, including the 1949 Geneva Conventions, or other violations of international law."[41]

The EECC was established under the auspices of the Permanent Court of Arbitration (PCA), which served as its registry, maintained the Commission's files and managed communications between the Commission and the parties. The EECC used the staff of the PCA on a part-time basis instead of retaining its own staff. The EECC consisted of five commissioners: Eritrea and Ethiopia appointed two commissioners each. The fifth, the presiding commissioner, was selected by the four party-appointed commissioners. The Algiers Agreement mandated the EECC to adopt its own rules of procedure based on the 1992 PCA Arbitration Operational Rules for Arbitration Disputes Between Two States. After consultation with the parties, the Commission adopted its Rules of Procedure in October 2001. The parties agreed to split the costs of the Commission equally. The Commission was based in The Hague and could at its discretion hold hearings and conduct investigations in the territory of the parties or in any other location as it deemed appropriate. Under the Algiers Agreement, claims had to be filed by 12 December 2001 (one year after the signing of the Agreement). The Commission was instructed to attempt to finalize proceedings within three years after the claims-filing period, though the deadline was extended and the final decision was issued in 2009.

The EECC issued its first decisions on jurisdiction and procedure in 2001, several partial awards on the merits from 2003 to 2005, and final awards on damages in August 2009. Decisions were required to be made by majority, but were, in almost all cases, made unanimously. In its partial awards, the EECC dealt with a variety of issues, including the

---

[40] Agreement between the Government of the State of Eritrea and the Government of the Federal Democratic Republic of Ethiopia, 12 December 2000, transmitted to the Secretary General of the United Nations and President of the Security Council as UN Doc A/55/686 and S/2000/1183.

[41] Art. 5, Algiers Agreement.

treatment of prisoners of war, internees and civilians, the legality of certain means and methods of warfare, the treatment of diplomatic premises and personnel, and the looting, seizure and unlawful destruction of private property. The damage awards ordered the payment of compensation of about $161 million to Eritrea and about $2 million to Eritrean nationals. The EECC awarded about $174 million to Ethiopia.

The EECC's accomplishments are significant. The Commission was tasked with the assessment of very complex and delicate claims originating from the law of war. It did so carefully and expeditiously. The work of the Commission also contributed to the maintenance of the peace between Eritrea and Ethiopia, as the two parties – though still in a tense relationship – have not since resumed the conflict.

Still, the EECC was not immune from criticism. The most controversial act was its decision to issue an award on *jus ad bellum*, which it found Eritrea had violated.[42] This decision was criticized as overstepping the Commission's mandate because Article 3 of the Algiers Agreement provided for the investigation of the origins of the conflict by an independent and impartial body to be appointed by the Secretary-General of the OAU, in consultation with the Secretary-General of the UN and the two parties.[43] Not surprisingly, once the Claims Commission purported to resolve the issue, the OAU body was never brought into existence. Additionally, the awards have yet to be paid, though neither party is adamantly demanding payment, which substantially undermines the very reason for creation of the Commission. The situation is vastly complicated by the refusal of one of the parties (Ethiopia) to adhere to the decision made by the Boundary Commission – it also was, by the Algiers Agreement, declared to be "final and binding".

Other international compensation commissions

Other modern international compensation commissions include:

Commission for real property claims of displaced persons and refugees in Bosnia–Herzegovina (CRPC) The CRPC was established by the General Framework Agreement for Peace in Bosnia–Herzegovina and the former Republic of Yugoslavia (the Dayton Accord). Its purpose was adjudication of individual claims to property or occupancy rights after the

---

[42] EECC, Partial Award – *Jus Ad Bellum* – Ethiopia's Claims 1–8, issued on 28 April 2004.

[43] Christine Gray, "The Eritrea/Ethiopia Claims Commission Oversteps Its Boundaries: A Partial Award?" (2006) 17 *European Journal of International Law* 699.

armed conflict in Yugoslavia, which had resulted in an estimated 2.2 million refugees and displaced persons.[44] The CRPC was headquartered in Sarajevo and at one point had 320 staff members. It had a mixed composition of nine members: six internationals appointed by the President of the European Court of Human Rights; and six nationals, two appointed by the Republika Srpska and four appointed by the Federation of Bosnia and Herzegovina. The CRPC dealt only with property claims resulting from the disintegration of Yugoslavia.[45] Indeed, it was created to ensure legally binding decisions to guarantee the rights of those who had lost property during the conflict by either enabling them to return home or to receive compensation for their loss.[46] The decisions of the commission were reviewed by the Supreme Court of Kosovo or another competent court. Remedies available included eviction, placing the property under administration, auction and compensation. The CRPC operated for seven years. It heard nearly 300,000 claims, benefitting an estimated one million people.[47] It was funded mostly by contributions from the European Union and the United States.[48]

Housing and Property Claims Commission (HPCC) The HPCC was established, like the CRPC, in part of the former Yugoslavia for the purpose of adjudicating individual claims to property or occupancy rights in the wake of armed conflict.[49] The HPCC was created by regulation 1999/23 of the United Nations Interim Administration Mission in Kosovo (UNMIK), which at the time administered Kosovo.[50] The HPCC was given exclusive jurisdiction to "settle private non-commercial residential property disputes" until the Special Representative of the UN Secretary-General in Kosovo, who headed UNMIK, determined that local courts

---

44 Article VII of Annex 7, Bosnia and Herzegovina–Croatia–Yugoslavia: General Framework Agreement for Peace in Bosnia and Herzegovina Ann. 7 art. VII, Dec. 14, 1995, 35 ILM 75, 139.

45 van Houtte, "Mass Property Claim Resolution in a Post-War Society."

46 van Houtte, "Mass Property Claim Resolution in a Post-War Society," 91. Claimants did not have to establish that the alleged dispossession was caused by the conflict; Dayton Accord, Art. XI.

47 See Commission or Real Property Claims of Displaced Persons and Refugees, End of Mandate Report (1996–2003), available at: http://www.pict-pcti.org/publications/Bibliographies/EMR-Part1-CoverExec1-Summary-EMR.pdf.

48 CRPC, End of Mandate Report.

49 Reparation Mechanisms at 89.

50 On the Establishment of the Housing and Property Directorate and the Housing and Property Claims Commission, UNMIK Reg. No. 1999/23, UNMIK, § 2, UN Doc UNMIK/REG/1999/23 (1999).

could carry out the same mandate. The Commission was composed of three members, two of whom, including the chair, were international staff, and one is a national of Kosovo. It acted as a mass claims processing mechanism.[51] The HPCC was originally given jurisdiction over three types of claims: "claims by natural persons (a) whose rights to residential real property were revoked on the basis of discriminatory legislation, (b) who entered into informal transactions of residential property after 23 March 1999, or (c) who owned property prior to March 24, 1999 and involuntarily lost possession of the property."[52] It was replaced in March 2006 by the Property Claims Commission (PCC),[53] which has operated since December 2008 under a law passed by the Assembly of Kosovo.[54] UNMIK Regulation 2006/10 on the "Resolution of Claims Relating to Private Immoveable Property, including Agricultural and Commercial Property" (as amended) mandated the PCC to resolve "conflict-related claims resulting from the armed conflict that occurred between 27 February 1998 and 20 June 1999," including ownership claims and claims involving property use rights with respect to private immoveable property including agricultural and commercial property, where the claimant is not able exercise those rights.[55] The deadline for receiving claims expired on 3 December 2007. Claims filed since that date fall within the jurisdiction of Kosovo domestic courts.[56] During its work, the commission heard more than 29,000 claims.

Holocaust claims Holocaust claims refer to the collection of claims arising from the Holocaust committed by Germany during the Nazi regime. It includes claims of restitution of funds and compensation from,

---

[51] See http://www.kpaonline.org/kpcc.asp.

[52] UNMIK Reg. No. 1999/23, § 1.2(a)–(c).

[53] Final Report of the Housing and Property Claims Commission, Housing and Property Claims Commission 9, 30 n97 (2007), available at: http://www.pca-cpa.org/showfile.asp?fil_id=626. Resolution 2006/10 established the Kosovo Property Agency (KPA), which consisted of a Supervisory Board, Executive Secretariat, and a Property Claims Commission (PCC). UNMIK, Reg. No. 2006/10, § 3.

[54] Reparation Mechanisms, 90; Amending UNMIK Reg. 2006/50 on the Resolution of Claims Relating to Private Immovable Property, Including Agricultural & Commercial Property (Law No. 03/L-079) (Kos.).

[55] On the Resolution of Claims Relating to Private Immovable Property, Including Agricultural and Commercial Property, UNMIK/REG/2006/10 of 4 March 2006, UN Doc. UNMIK/REG/2006/10 (2006) available at: http://www.kpaonline.org/hpd/pdf/UNMIK%20Regulation%202006-10%20(2).pdf.

[56] Reparation Mechanisms, 92–93.

among others, Swiss banks for money held in accounts, life insurance claims that were in place before the Holocaust and from German corporations that benefited from the forced slave labor of the Holocaust victims.[57]

CONCLUSION

This chapter introduces IMCCs as a unique and important form of international adjudication, established to consider claims resulting from significant international war-related and traumatic historical events. IMCCs are an eclectic group but share important characteristics. This chapter provides an analysis of these characteristics, as well as a brief historical overview of the main IMCCs. In the following chapters, we focus our attention on three commissions: the Iran–US Claims Tribunal, the United Nations Compensation Commission, and the Eritrea–Ethiopia Claims Commission.

The resurgence of IMCCs comes in conjunction with the acceptance of the need to adjudicate claims related to armed conflicts. It is increasingly becoming the norm that in post-conflict societies, individual remedies can contribute to a lasting peace. Indeed, an international dispute resolution body created with the active participation of all relevant parties can create a solution seen as building trust between adversaries and ensuring the compensation of innocent victims.

The creation of a heterogeneous system of claims commissions also complements the proliferation of international courts and tribunals as one

[57] The resolution of Holocaust claims includes a complex system of claims commissions including: Austrian General Settlement Fund; Austrian Fund for Reconciliation, Peace and Cooperation; Belgian Jewish Community Indemnification Commission; Claims Resolution Tribunal (CRT I & II); French Commission for the Compensation of Victims of Spoliation Resulting from the Anti-Semitic Legislation in force during the Occupation; German Forced Labor Compensation Program (GFLCP); German Foundation "Remembrance, Responsibility and Future"; Holocaust Victim Assets Program (HVAP); The International Commission on Holocaust Era Insurance Claims (ICHEIC); The Netherlands' Foundation for Individual Bank Claims Shoah; The Netherlands' Holocaust Foundation for Individual Insurance Claims; The Netherlands' Shoah Foundation for Individual Securities Claims and the Conference on Jewish Material Claims Against Germany. Each of these institutions addressed a specific type or category of claim. See PCA website, Mass Claims Processes Relating to the Holocaust, at: https://pca-cpa.org/en/services/arbitration-services/mass-claims-processes/. (The most important Holocaust claims are the CRT I & II).

further option for post-conflict reparations. Other mechanisms include truth and reconciliation commissions and domestic proceedings.

The chapters that follow critically assess the main constitutive and procedural characteristics of claims commissions and highlight lessons learned from past practice.

2. Why a claims commission?

International law offers no formal definition of international mass claims commissions.[1] But there is not much disagreement in practice about what they look like and what they are for.[2] A post-conflict mass compensation claims commission is a particular kind of arbitral tribunal. Set up to award compensation for economic and bodily injuries suffered in the course of some particular transboundary conflict, claims commissions engage the responsibilities of states and act as mechanisms for binding dispute resolution.[3] The purpose of a claims commission is to render

---

1 Our proposed definition, given in Chapter 1, is as follows:

> [T]here is no uniform, formal definition of IMCCs. They make up an eclectic and unique group, characterized by important shared characteristics. First, IMCCs are binding dispute resolution mechanisms; second, they are structured and act like judicial bodies; third, they are created after an event of international relevance; fourth, they are international law instruments; fifth, they engage the responsibility of states; and sixth, they are *ad hoc* institutions.

2 By the term "IMCC" we mean an "international mass claims compensation commission." The parameters of such a commission are dealt with in greater detail in Chapter 1 and Chapters 4 and 6, dealing with party structure and methods of claim presentation. By using the word "mass" we do not mean to indicate any particular method for aggregating claims, but only that there is a large number of claims, large enough that the situation calls for some kind of pragmatic accommodation to make the adjudication manageable.

3 There are many kinds of arbitration, but all are drawn together by a single characteristic: arbitration's "do-it-yourself" nature. An arbitral tribunal is, first and foremost, an *ad hoc* decision-making body rather than a standing institution such as a domestic court or an international tribunal such as the International Court of Justice. It is established by the parties; its personnel are chosen by the parties; and its costs are paid for by the parties. *See* Christine Gray and Benedict Kingsbury, "Developments in Dispute Settlement: Inter-state Arbitration Since 1945" (1992) 98 *BritishYearbook of International Law* 102–103 ("[A]lmost all arbitration tribunals have in practice been *ad hoc* tribunals established by special agreement"). For the agreements that created mass claims commissions, *see, e.g.*, Declaration of the Government of the Democratic and Popular Republic of Algeria Concerning the Settlement of Claims by the Government of the United States of America and the Government of the Islamic Republic of Iran, 19 January 1981 (IUSCT Algiers Accord); Agreement Between the Government of

legally binding compensation awards to victims of internationally unlawful activity and to do so in a way that reflects to the greatest degree possible the processes and outcomes agreed on by the parties.

The increased use of such commissions, relative to the pre-World War II era, reflects a broader ascendance of human rights law and principles. In the past, a victorious state might demand reparations from a vanquished enemy regardless of whether or not the vanquished enemy had violated international law, simply because it had been defeated in battle.[4] But the current broad consensus that military success does not excuse violations of international law means that the defeated state is as likely as the victorious state to file claims.[5] Guarantees of respect for individuals apply whether or not their sovereign was a "bad actor" in the conflict and whether or not their state emerged victorious. As such, individuals from the vanquished state are just as entitled to claim compensation as their counterparts from the victorious state. This premise of modern international humanitarian/human rights law is central to understanding the formation and operation of IMCCs and the remedies that the commission may impose in order to fully satisfy its central task: compensation.

We have taken as illustrative examples three quite different commissions: the Iran–US Tribunal (IUSCT), the United Nations Compensation Commission (UNCC), and the Eritrea–Ethiopia Claims Commission (EECC).[6] The last of these – the EECC – follows fairly closely the

---

the Federal Democratic Republic of Ethiopia and the Government of the State of Eritrea, 12 December 2000 (EECC Agreement).

[4] *See, e.g.*, Jean Pictet (ed.), *Commentary to Geneva Convention I for the Amelioration of the Condition of the Wounded and Sick in the Armed Forces in the Field* (International Committee of the Red Cross, 1952) 373; Yves Sandoz, Christophe Swinarski and Bruno Zimmermann (eds), *Commentary to Protocol Additional to the Geneva Conventions of 12 August 1949, and Relating to the Protection of Victims of International Armed Conflicts (Protocol I)* (International Committee of the Red Cross, 1987) 1053–58.

[5] An arguable counterexample is the UNCC. As will be discussed in detail in Chapter 4, Saddam Hussein was forced to agree to a claims commission funded by Iraqi oil revenues. The commission was asymmetric; Iraq was required to pay money judgments for its violations of international law, but there was no vehicle for Iraqis to sue nationals of other countries.

[6] None of this to say that all IMCCs are created equal. Each of the three IMCCs discussed in this book had certain unique features and, indeed, unique functions. Warren Christopher, a deputy secretary of state who negotiated the Iran–US claims agreement, and Richard M. Mosk, who served as a judge on the Iran–US Claims Tribunal (IUSCT), have noted that the Tribunal in many ways resembled "a judicial system" as much as "an arbitral body." *See* Warren Christopher and Richard M. Mosk, "The Iranian Hostage Crisis and the

traditional statist model in which states, acting as representatives of their nationals, collect and aggregate claims for presentation to the Commission. As we will see, this way of structuring the litigation undercuts a commission's ability to award compensation to the individual victims – the very people whom the commission was formed, ostensibly, to compensate. The proceeds of the award all go to the state, or are used to set-off the amount that the commission awarded to the opposing side. The statist model compromises compensation for individuals and prioritizes protection for the interests of states; it should not come as a surprise that concern for individual rights, and the search for adjudicative protection of those rights, is in tension with a statist model of compensation.

The IUSCT and the UNCC are more innovative in their structure and operation; the extra complications in their design resulted in a more cumbersome and lengthy claims process, but, at the same time, one that comes much closer to providing actual compensation. Both of these tribunals have been at work for much longer than their original proponents expected and also for much longer than the EECC was in business. The pace is necessarily slower when claims are given individual attention. The costs of these two tribunals have also been much higher than expected, likely because their work has gone on so long.[7] But in both cases the mechanisms created to fund their work were well-enough thought out that the tribunals have managed to continue to operate and to pay out claims.

All three of these commissions were designed to resolve the same sort of disputes as judicial bodies do. But an IMCC is not a standing court

---

Iran–U.S. Claims Tribunal: Implications for International Dispute Resolution and Diplomacy" (2007) 7 *Pepperdine Dispute Resolution Law Journal* 165, 172. The UN Claims Commission was in some senses less judicial than political and more inquisitorial than adversarial. *See generally* Frances E. McGovern, "Dispute System Design: The United Nations Compensation Commission" (2009) 14 *Harvard Negotiation Law Review* 171. Indeed, the UN Secretary-General's Report that helped pave the design for the UNCC acknowledged that "[t]he Commission [was] not a court or an arbitral tribunal before which the parties appear," but rather "a political organ that perform[ed] an essentially fact-finding function of examining claims, verifying their validity, evaluating losses, assessing payments and resolving disputed claims." The Report further noted that "[i]t is only in this last respect that a quasi-judicial function may be involved." Secretary-General, *Report of the Secretary-General Pursuant to Paragraph 19 of Security Council Resolution 687*, ¶ 20, UN Doc S/22559 (2 May 1991) (Report of the Secretary-General on UNCC).

[7] *See* discussion of costs of running a claims tribunal in Chapter 5.

acting under the auspices of a particular state government; it is a tribunal established by the parties for achieving "build-it-yourself" justice.[8] Those who are contemplating the possible formation of a claims tribunal, therefore, face a preliminary question of great importance: should a tribunal even be created? This question obviously does not arise with standing judicial bodies, whose existence predates the occurrence of the claim.[9] And a positive answer should not be taken for granted.

There are at least two parts to this question about whether to bring a claims tribunal into existence. First, would such a tribunal (if created) be authoritative; that is, would it have legitimacy in the eyes of the parties and the international community? Second, is it worth the commitment of financial and human resources for the parties to create a claims commission, or should the parties attempt to resolve their disputes in some other way? The first question deals with authority, legitimacy and jurisdiction; the second relates to policy, cost-benefit analysis and state preferences. It is not possible to generalize with confidence about answers to these questions – the answers depend in part on the preferences of the state creators of particular IMCCs, who are likely to differ among themselves in interests and beliefs. Instead, we outline some of the major pros and cons that ought to be considered as a general matter in deciding whether the game is worth pursuing.

LEGITIMATE AUTHORITY: CONSENT THEORY AND COMPENSATORY JUSTICE

IMCCs are not official standing government bodies such as the United States Supreme Court, nor are they standing adjudicative institutions of the international legal community, such as the International Court of Justice. They are *ad hoc* tribunals created by, and owing their existence to, the litigants. Indeed, this fact is essential to their authority because the

---

[8] *See* note 3 and accompanying text for a discussion of the *ad hoc* nature of these tribunals.

[9] Of course, claimants preparing to go before standing tribunals must also answer the same question: is the cost of filing and pursuing a claim outweighed by the value of the potential outcome? If the answer is no, they should not file a suit. But in the IMCC context, the costs include not only filing and pursuing a claim, but also negotiating the creation of a tribunal, selecting arbitrators and funding the tribunal. Thus, there will be a much higher threshold for determining that a proceeding under an IMCC will be beneficial.

parties who would be bound are precisely the ones that set up the commission in the first place.

This theoretical tenet, basic to what might be called the *consent* theory of legitimacy, derives from central principles of international law that privilege state consent over almost every other value. A different theory of legitimacy, *compensatory justice*, focuses on the moral and legal imperative of providing compensation for the victim of an unlawful act.[10] Although both the consent and the compensatory justice explanations contribute to the analysis of what makes claims commissions legitimate, neither theory standing alone is completely satisfactory. Rather, each fills the logical gaps left by the other so that, when combined, a reasonably adequate explanation for the authority of claims commissions emerges.[11]

Party Consent as a Source of Legitimacy

Party consent is the most obvious of the various possible responses to a challenge to an IMCC's authority; the commission is legitimate if it was established by the parties' consent and in accordance with procedures mandated by their agreement.

Strengths of the party consent explanation of legitimacy

Consent is a strong argument for the legitimacy of an IMCC for the same reasons that it is a strong argument for legitimacy of domestic contracts, domestic arbitration agreements and international treaties.[12] International law attaches great importance to questions of legitimate authority; as the international community lacks a centralized coercive enforcement power,

10 *See, generally* Dinah Shelton, *Remedies in International Human Rights Law*, 3rd ed. (Oxford University Press, 2015) 19–20, discussing the theory and purpose of remedial or compensatory justice.

11 In short, the two concepts go hand-in-hand, and each complements the legitimacy of the other. As this chapter argues, state consent alone cannot legitimize IMCCs absent some remedial or compensatory effect. Likewise, a remedial or compensatory effect without state consent comes perilously close to outmoded victors' justice and cannot legitimize IMCCs in a global legal order that relies so heavily on consent.

12 Indeed, consent is such a foundational concept in international law that Judge José Cabranes has remarked, "If the idea that consent by sovereign states is a *sine qua non* of the creation of 'law' rings hollow – I would welcome the opportunity to be informed of what other bedrock principles govern the development of international law." José Cabranes, "International Law by Consent of the Governed" (2007) 42 *Valparaiso University Law Review* 119, 122.

consensus is essential.[13] Treaty law requires explicit consent to make it authoritative; customary international law lowers the standard for what counts as consent but still focuses on what the parties agreed to implicitly.[14] International law, generally, is dependent on community acceptance if it is to have its intended effect, and the same is true of claims commissions.

Consent is an attractive standard in many respects. The ability to make an enforceable commitment to a contract, an arbitration agreement or a treaty is a very valuable power; it enables a state to enter into relationships of mutual advantage by providing legal assurances to the other contracting powers that it will carry out the agreement's provision. Since *ad hoc* tribunals are created by agreement between the parties (usually in a written instrument such as an arbitration agreement or its equivalent), whether consent was given will in almost every instance be easily provable. By signing and ratifying an arbitration agreement, the parties deliberately make their consent as clear and unequivocal as possible.

Explanations in terms of party consent have implications for how the tribunal members can be expected to fulfill their mandate. Most importantly, if consent is the source of the commission's authority to issue binding awards, the commission should steer clear of assuming jurisdiction where the parties' consent is absent or uncertain. The commission's jurisdiction should be exercised conservatively because mistakenly asserting jurisdiction where the parties have not agreed is not simply erroneous; it is illegitimate. A mistake in the direction of wrongly assuming jurisdiction is more serious than a mistake in the direction of wrongly failing to assume jurisdiction.

A body like a claims commission stands little chance of effectuating its decisions if the parties and the world community view it as illegitimate. Legitimacy is key to acceptance of a tribunal's decision by the international community, and is therefore essential to increasing the likelihood

---

[13] For a longer discussion of why the theory of consent serves to legitimate international institutions, see Matthew Lister, "The Legitimating Role of Consent in International Law" (2011) 11 *Chicago Journal of International Law* 663.

[14] For example, Judge Cabranes asserts that although consent is less foregrounded in customary international law (CIL), it still provides the theoretical justification for the application of CIL. Consent of an individual state can be found through the "affirmative policy decisions, actions, and practices in the international arena indicating intent to be bound." Consensus can be found through the requirement that "states must universally engage in that practice out of *opinio juris* – that is, out of a sense of *legal obligation* rather than merely as an act of courtesy or grace." Cabranes, "International Law by Consent of the Governed," 132.

that awards will be implemented.[15] For relatively uncommon or novel types of decision-making bodies such as mass claims commissions, legitimacy is not a luxury but a necessity.

Weaknesses of the party consent explanation of legitimacy

Although generally attractive, the consent explanation has certain glaring logical gaps. It does not mean, for one thing, that after the awards are announced, the dissatisfied party is legally entitled to reject some or all of a commission's rulings on the grounds that (in its view) jurisdictional requirements were not satisfied. Typically, a commission is entitled under the agreement that established it to resolve challenges to its own jurisdiction. A clause in the agreement stating that "the Commission's decisions shall be final and binding" will have that effect, as will a clause recognizing what is often referred to as "jurisdiction to determine jurisdiction."[16]

If objections are made to the self-evident circularity of this "jurisdiction to determine jurisdiction" formula, then, of course, a response to this challenge is readily available. While circular, the party that is now complaining agreed to that circular formulation when the commission was originally established. More pragmatically, the tribunal *needs* to be able to rule on its own jurisdiction if it is to produce binding decisions. Without giving the tribunal authority to resolve challenges to its own authority, every jurisdictional challenge would stop the tribunal dead in

---

15 *See* Thomas Franck, *The Power of Legitimacy among Nations* (Oxford University Press, 1990).

16 *See, e.g.*, Eritrea–Ethiopia Claims Commission, Rules of Procedure art. 27(1), at 12 (2000), available at: http://archive.pca-cpa.org/Rules%20of%20Procedure65f4.PDF?fil_id=140 ("The Commission shall have the power to rule on objections that it has no jurisdiction. A plea that the Commission does not have jurisdiction shall be raised not later than in the Statement of Defense."); Iran–United States Claims Tribunal, Tribunal Rules of Procedure art. 21(1), at 25 (1983), available at: http://www.iusct.net/General%20Documents/5-TRIBUNAL%20RULES%20OF%20PROCEDURE.pdf ("The arbitral tribunal shall have the power to rule on objections that it has no jurisdiction, including any objections with respect to the existence or validity of the arbitration clause or of the separate arbitration agreement."). Unlike the EECC and IUSCT, the UNCC governing documents do not explicitly grant the UNCC jurisdiction to rule on jurisdictional conflicts; given the one-sided nature of the proceedings, Iraq had little choice in challenging claims that were submitted to the UNCC for consideration.

its tracks.[17] There is no other decision maker available to a commission that can resolve jurisdictional challenges – or at least, no decision maker that is less dependent on the notion of "jurisdiction to determine jurisdiction" – so rejecting this logic has the unfortunate consequences of making finality impossible.

But other logical defects persist; despite the intuitive appeal of this approach, a consent-based theory of legitimacy is not entirely satisfactory. For example, although one hears sometimes that involuntariness is a basis for invalidating a treaty, it is quite difficult to find cases where that logic is taken seriously.[18] Quite to the contrary, it is commonplace for states to sign agreements in what can only be understood as a situation of duress.[19] The phrase "victor's justice," whereby the party occupying the militarily dominant position on the ground when the fighting is over unilaterally dictates the terms of a peace agreement, is pejorative; but the phenomenon is commonplace enough to be recognized, if ruefully, as a fact of life.[20]

Saddam Hussein's acquiescence in the establishment of the United Nations Claims Commission at the end of the first Gulf War provides a clear example.[21] With Iraq under allied occupation in substantial part, and with the allies' armies positioned to continue on to Baghdad and unseat

[17] At first blush, it might seem bizarre to grant a tribunal with ostensibly limited jurisdiction the authority to rule on its own jurisdiction. However, such a grant is a necessary quirk. In the absence of authority to rule on its own jurisdiction, an IMCC would be mired in infinite regress: every time Alpha filed a claim against Beta, Beta would challenge the tribunal's jurisdiction and there would be no mutually agreed upon entity to resolve the jurisdictional dispute, essentially prohibiting any substantive decision on the merits of Alpha's claim.

[18] *See* Robert Kolb, *The Law of Treaties: An Introduction* (Edward Elgar, 2016) 91 ("[I]t may be emphasized that there are few instances of practice where the [Vienna Convention on the Law of Treaties] provisions of invalidity have been invoked.").

[19] The Vienna Convention, for example, provides that a treaty is void if it has been "procured by the threat or use of force in violations of the principles embodied in the Charter of the United Nations." Vienna Convention on the Law of Treaties art. 52, May 23, 1969, 1155 UNTS 331.

[20] Allowing victors to determine the metes and bounds of peace treaties or subsequent claims commissions is, of course, very far from what most would consider "justice." It is an oxymoron, much like "jumbo shrimp" or "dorm food."

[21] The United Nations Compensation Commission Handbook, for example, noted that while Hussein's consent to the UNCC was "clearly … obtained through the threat or use of force," it was nevertheless legal because the Security Council Resolution did not violate the United Nations charter. Marco Frigessi di Rattalma and Tullio Treves, "Introduction: The United Nations Compensation

Saddam Hussein's regime, agreement to form a commission to compensate victims of the Kuwait invasion was hardly consensual on Iraq's part. Consent is often illusory when states sign international agreements.[22]

Consent certainly seems to be an important ingredient of legitimacy – where true consent exists this is a good reason for treating an agreement as enforceable and the creation of a claims commission as legitimate. But as the example of Iraq's "consent" to the formation of the UNCC suggests, true voluntariness is not a *necessary* condition. A state's legal decisions (such as whether to sign a particular treaty) can be patently coerced without affecting in the least the binding nature of an international agreement. Some other consideration must be doing the hard work of explaining why agreements of this sort are considered authoritative. We turn now to possible additional reasons why a commission might be thought authoritative.

Compensatory Justice as a Source of Legitimacy

A second line of reasoning supporting the legitimacy of claims commissions might be called the "compensatory justice" explanation. This explanation is most persuasive where there is no alternative forum with the competence to resolve these claims, for that is when a new compensatory justice mechanism must be created. Typically, in such situations, the parties must create a new tribunal if their legal claims against one another are to have a hearing. Supported by the substantive authority of the legal norms that the defending party transgressed, the parties set up a commission to entertain cases that could not be heard in any other way. This is justified as an application of the jurisprudential theory of compensatory (or remedial) justice.

Commission: Problems and Prospects," in *United Nations Compensation Commission Handbook* 31 (UN, 1999) 31.

[22] One scholar has gone so far as to propose applying the contracts doctrine of adhesion to treaties in recognition of the immense power imbalances among states signing international agreements with a specific focus on the TRIPS agreement. Donald P. Harris, "Carrying a Good Joke Too Far: TRIPS and Treaties of Adhesion" (2006) 27 *U Pa J International Econ L* 681. Another scholar, James D. Fry, suggested that historical imbalances in power, affecting treaty ratification as well as interpretation, create a system in which "consent in the context of treaties is not 'frontally assaulted but cunningly outflanked'." James D. Fry, "Legitimacy Push: Towards a Gramscian Approach to International Law" (2008) 13 *UCLA J International L and Foreign Aff* 307, 331.

Strengths of the compensatory justice explanation

The theory of compensatory justice requires compensation for individuals who were injured unlawfully. Dinah Shelton has explained that "[t]he primary function of corrective or remedial justice is to rectify the wrong done to a victim, that is, to correct injustice."[23] The theory underpinning such remedies dates at least to Aristotle; compensatory justice "aim[s] to place an aggrieved party in the same position as he or she would have been had no injury occurred."[24]

Compensatory justice explains the legitimacy of claims commissions in terms of their consistency with and support for substantive international law. An IMCC's authority to impose a remedy derives from the substantive rules of international law that it relies on. A valid substantive claim, according to this argument, is both a necessary and a sufficient condition for a right to compensation. Once the substance of the injury is established (it can be argued) additional authority to impose a remedy is not required.

A defendant found to be a perpetrator of acts unlawful under international law can argue that requiring payment of compensation is unfair, but as a practical matter this argument is likely to raise little sympathy for the defendant's attempt to avoid the consequences of his or her illegal conduct. If the defendant violated substantive norms of international law, it cannot plausibly "cry foul" when required to remediate the violation.

Weaknesses of the compensatory justice explanation

One glaring weakness of the compensatory justice explanation is that it would seem, in principle, to justify imposition of the will of any group strong enough to impose its view of the law simply because that group cited as justification a (real or supposed) substantive transgression of international law. Such a justification would completely sidestep the challenge, "why are *you* the one to impose *your* view of what international law requires?" We ordinarily assume that both the substance of a norm of international law and the identity of the party seeking to impose its views would have to be justified before an international enforcement action was legitimate.

Another problematic aspect of the compensatory justice explanation is that claims commissions, in many if not most instances, provide very little compensation even to victims who successfully prove an injury

---

23 Shelton, *Remedies in International Human Rights Law*, 19–20.
24 Shelton, *Remedies in International Human Rights Law.*

unlawfully caused by the defending state. If claims commissions' legitimacy and authority are traceable to their role in promoting compensation for the wrongfully injured, then any systematic cause of incompetence at promoting compensation has the effect of undermining the commission's reason for existence. Yet, as we will demonstrate below, the fact that powerful influences are systematically aligned against the possibility of compensation in many claims commission proceedings, making the award of individual compensation improbable if not impossible, has not been treated as depriving the commission of legitimacy.

The problem is not simply, as might be imagined, that injured claimants will find it difficult to amass the evidence of harm and the proof that the defendant was responsible.[25] That is certainly a problem, but it is a different problem. All adjudication has an element of randomness or "noise" that frustrates a tribunal's efforts to find the facts accurately and efficiently.[26] What we are referring to, rather, is a tendency of claims commissions to fail to ensure compensation even though the claimant was proven to be worthy.

The justification for international mass claims commissions is strongest when both consent-based and compensatory-justice-based explanations coincide. Claims commissions reflect a combination of the two. It could be argued that they combine through some sort of a "sliding scale"

---

[25] And it is not only the claimants who are hampered by lack of evidence. Although creation of a claims commission is designed primarily with the victims' rights in mind, it is also possible for defendants to be hampered in their production of evidence. It is all too easy for false claims to be made, and all too difficult for the innocent target to disprove them. The UN Office of the High Commissioner on Human Rights underscores the difficulties in their training materials on corroboration of human rights accusations. Tactics include always seeking independent corroboration from family members, neighbors and friends, as well as accounting for victim or witness bias in giving statements. Human rights organizations face these difficulties every day as they investigate claims in the field. *See* UN Office of the High Commissioner for Human Rights, *Training Manual on Human Rights Monitoring*, Professional Training Series No. 7 (UNHCR, 2001), available at: http://www.unhcr.ch/html/menu6/2/training.htm. Finding such evidence for every alleged victim is extremely challenging for parties during the compressed timeline of a claims commission.

[26] Evidentiary rules, the possibility that evidence may be unobtainable, the unavailability of witnesses and the temperament of factfinders, parties and attorneys all introduce some amount of chance into adjudication. F.E. Guerra-Pujol sees so much randomness in the US judicial system that he actually tested the hypothesis that litigation outcomes are as random as coin tosses. *See* F.E. Guerra-Pujol, "Chance and Litigation" (2011) 21 *Boston University Public Interest Law Journal* 45.

– the more compelling the showing of consent, the less is required in strength or urgency of the substantive rights at stake (and vice versa). The precise way that they combine is left for those scholars who take such theories as their primary focus. Enough has been said here to move on from challenges to legitimacy to the question of why or when we find it desirable as a matter of policy to establish a claims commission.

CLAIMS COMMISSIONS: PROS AND CONS

The legitimacy of the contemplated commission's decision-making is not the only preliminary consideration in establishment of an IMCC. Assuming that its authority has been justified, questions still remain about whether it is actually a good thing – attractive and advantageous to the parties. Most post-conflict situations do not give rise to claims commissions; considering the frequency with which international conflicts arise, the number of IMCCs that are created is quite small.[27] Presumably the states that could have but did not form IMCCs concluded that it was not a good choice – but why would that be?

Of the possible reasons for choosing *not* to set up a claims commission, several are particularly plausible. First, there may be other ways of dealing with the dispute that do not require setting up a new tribunal; second, IMCCs are massive and unwieldy with little guarantee of accuracy in finding facts or law; and third, there is, in any event, likely to be no money at the end of the day to pay the award. This third consideration is particularly intractable when a symmetric commission – one where both sides have claims against the other – results in awards being given to both parties, with the bottom line being a set-off and neither claimant receiving enough money to pay the injured victims their compensation.

This third reason reduces to a conclusion that IMCCs frequently accomplish nothing. The goal is to compensate the victims of unlawful wartime conduct, but in some cases no compensation is paid at all – a fact that certainly should have been predicted from the outset. In circumstances like these, *ad hoc* commissions are hardly more than vast black holes into which money gets sucked at frightening speed. We will

---

[27] This does not mean that the two questions are identical, however; the fact that a claims commission would be legitimate in some particular situation does not mean that it is in the parties' interest. As we shall see, there are as many reasons that IMCCs are potentially disastrous as there are reasons for expecting the resolution to be successful.

return shortly to the question of why faltering confidence about the likelihood of payment may be warranted.

Alternative Methods of Resolving Mass Disputes

The desirability of establishing a claims commission depends in part on whether there are alternative approaches that would be at least as satisfactory. If there are, then the claimants are that much less likely to set out to establish a new mass claims commission. If there are none, then any defects in the claims commission process are more excusable.

As we identify and assess the most plausible alternatives, it is immediately clear that claimants looking for a forum in which to litigate their international law complaints have few options. There is likely to be no standing international court that is suitable for mass claims proceedings, and the *ad hoc* courts that do exist are tailored to particular conflicts and unlikely to have authority to add new cases to their jurisdiction. Domestic courts might in theory fill the void, but they are rarely set up to handle international mass claims cases. And turning to the theoretical question of establishing a new standing court for mass claims specifically, we find intractable practical problems. Mass claims compensation cases simply have nowhere to go.

Standing international courts

There are in existence standing international courts with fairly expansive subject matter jurisdiction, which can hear a broad range of cases. Most of the time, however, there is no tribunal with jurisdiction, or even with suitable procedural rules. It is unlikely that any of these could serve as a forum for mass claims cases.

Lack of jurisdiction Some adjudicative bodies, such as the International Court of Justice (ICJ), could simply lack the jurisdiction to get involved.[28] The ICJ is open to all United Nations member states, derives

---

[28] The ICJ can "hear any legal dispute concerning international law." UN Office of Legal Affairs, *Handbook on Accepting the Jurisdiction of the International Court of Justice*: Model Clauses and Templates 8, A/68/963 (2014) (ICJ Jurisdiction Handbook) ("The Court can hear any legal dispute concerning international law."). Nevertheless, with the exception of a narrow subset of specific issues, the ICJ must derive jurisdiction from the consent of parties to the dispute. *See* Statute of the International Court of Justice art. 36, at http://www.icj-cij.org/documents/?p1=4&p2=2. In short, as global law and politics

jurisdiction from those states' consent and is charged with hearing legal disputes concerning international law.[29]

At the ICJ, consent may be expressed through unilateral declarations, through treaties or through special agreements. The first way is for a state to express its recognition of the ICJ's jurisdiction unilaterally, as compulsory in the event of any dispute with another state that similarly recognizes compulsory jurisdiction of the ICJ as a general matter. Seventy-two states, including Japan, Italy and the United Kingdom, have agreed in advance to compulsory jurisdiction over international law disputes generally and on a reciprocal basis.[30]

The second is by signing a treaty. The treaty can cover a particular subject matter and therein designate the ICJ as the juridical entity to adjudicate disputes arising out of that treaty. Parties could also sign a treaty specifically for the purpose of dispute resolution, designating the ICJ as the juridical entity to adjudicate specific classes of disputes (or any dispute) arising between the signatories. Over 300 treaties currently grant the ICJ jurisdiction.[31] Finally, parties may enter into a special agreement *ad hoc* to grant the ICJ jurisdiction over a particular dispute; 17 cases have been brought this way since the ICJ's inception.[32] None of the cases that the Court has decided has resembled those heard by mass claims commissions.

Regional courts of general jurisdiction are no more suitable for hearing mass claims cases than the International Court of Justice. The Court of Justice of the European Union, for example, serves as a forum for claims against EU institutions by member states (and vice versa), for claims disputing the validity or interpretation of EU policies and treaties, and other specific instances outlined in the Treaty on the Formation of the European Union.[33] The Economic Community of West African States

---

currently stand, the ICJ lacks authority to assert jurisdiction over the type of issues with which MCCs deal.

[29] ICJ Jurisdiction Handbook ("The Court can hear any legal dispute concerning international law.").

[30] International Court of Justice, Declarations Recognizing the Jurisdiction of the Court as Compulsory, http://www.icj-cij.org/jurisdiction/index.php?p1=5&p2=1&p3=3.

[31] ICJ Jurisdiction Handbook, 15–16.

[32] ICJ Jurisdiction Handbook, 25.

[33] The European Court of Justice derives its jurisdiction from several different treaties. *See* European Parliament, European Union Competences of the Court of Justice of the European Union, http://www.europarl.europa.eu/atyourservice/en/displayFtu.html?ftuId=FTU_1.3.10.html (summarizing these treaties and their grants of jurisdiction).

Court of Justice maintains jurisdiction over cases where member states have allegedly failed to meet their obligations under Community law.[34] While the jurisdiction of these courts is wide-ranging, their powers are tied to disputes arising from treaties and regional policies only, making it unlikely that they would justify asserting jurisdiction over mass claims.

Another category of cases is those decided by standing human rights courts. They likewise assert jurisdiction only over the predefined set of disputes that they were created to deal with. Regional agreements setting out human rights protections work through investigative commissions and adjudicative courts established by treaty or convention. These courts typically only have jurisdiction to hear disputes arising out of the interpretation and application of that underlying treaty or convention.[35]

Procedural unsuitability Lack of jurisdiction is only the first problem; it is far from the only one. Another difficulty is procedural unsuitability. For example, although some Conventions, like the European Convention on Human Rights, allow individuals to bring claims in human rights courts, the majority limit claims to intergovernmental organizations and ratifying states.[36] Because of such standing requirements, it is unlikely that a regional human rights court would be competent to hear many post-conflict claims.

Moreover, none of these existing courts possesses the capacity to manage mass claims proceedings. The ICJ was designed for answering questions of international law[37] and has little competence at deciding disputed facts (especially large numbers of them). The ICJ generally does not take testimony from live witnesses at hearings, and it has no experience dealing with large masses of claim forms or other technical

---

34 Community Court of Justice, Economic Community of West African States, Jurisdiction, http://www.courtecowas.org/site2012/index.php?option=com_content&view=article&id=10&Itemid=10.

35 *See, e.g.,* Organization of American States, American Convention on Human Rights Art. 61, Nov. 22, 1969, OASTS No. 36, 1144 UNTS 123 [hereinafter American Convention on Human Rights]; African Union, Protocol to the African Charter on Human and Peoples' Rights on the Establishment of an African Court on Human and Peoples' Rights Art. 3, June 10, 1998, OAU/LEG/MIN/AFCHPR/PROT.1 rev.2 (1997) [hereinafter African Union Protocol]; Council of Europe, Convention for the Protection of Human Rights and Fundamental Freedoms Art. 32, Nov. 4, 1950, ETS 5, 213 UNTS 221 [hereinafter European Convention on Human Rights].

36 European Convention on Human Rights art. 34. *But see* American Convention on Human Rights art. 61 and African Union Protocol art. 5.

37 UN Charter art. 38, ¶ 1. s.

materials.[38] It is hard to envision how mass claims would be fitted into the standard procedures of the ICJ.

Pre-existing *ad hoc* international adjudicatory bodies

Even less probable as an alternative forum are existing *ad hoc* claims commissions. Certainly, they would have experience in dealing with large amounts of data, relevant statistical techniques, and a variety of procedural devices designed to make adjudication expeditious and accurate. But the scope of existing tribunals would already have been defined at the point that they were created, and it would be quite a surprising coincidence for any of them to have the possibility of expansion.

For example, when the Algiers Accords ended the Iranian hostage crisis, the jurisdiction of the IUSCT that was established covered only certain kinds of disputes between the United States and its nationals and Iran and its nationals. The substance of the dispute had to have the appropriate nexus to the events in Tehran at around the time of the Iranian revolution.[39] It would not have been possible to take advantage of that tribunal for litigating other sorts of mass claims cases, at least not without a formal agreement among all of the parties to expand its jurisdiction.

Domestic courts

Finally, some sort of recovery might in theory be available in domestic courts. The theory of "universal jurisdiction" would allow prosecution to proceed anywhere, if the offense is truly heinous; but few states have followed up on this possibility by attempting to prosecute conduct that had nothing to do with their own territory.[40] In the United States, the

---

[38] The ICJ's rules do contemplate live witness testimony, although it is quite rare. International Court of Justice, *International Court of Justice Handbook* (2013), 56–58, available at: http://legal.un.org/avl/pdf/rs/other_resources/manual_en.pdf.

[39] *See* IUSCT Algiers Accord.

[40] Restatement (Third) of Foreign Relations Law of the United States § 404 (American Law Institute 1987).

> § 404. Universal Jurisdiction to Define and Punish Certain Offenses
>
> A state has jurisdiction to define and prescribe punishment for certain offenses recognized by the community of nations as of universal concern, such as piracy, slave trade, attacks on or hijacking of aircraft, genocide, war crimes, and perhaps certain acts of terrorism, even where none of the bases of jurisdiction indicated in § 402 is present.

Alien Tort Statute provides jurisdiction to federal courts for torts committed by aliens "in violation of the law of nations."[41] Despite the expansive language of this provision, however, the statute has been restrictively construed.[42]

Another example is Spain. For almost 20 years, Spanish law authorized jurisdiction for genocide, terrorism and treaty violations that Spain is obligated to prosecute – regardless of the connection between the conduct (or perpetrator) and Spain.[43] However, in 2014, the law was amended to limit jurisdiction to situations in which the defendant is a Spanish citizen, a resident of Spain or a foreigner in Spain whose extradition has been denied by Spain.[44] If victims do have domestic causes of action, the judgment would be enforceable, but only to the extent that the defendant state has assets in the forum – or is willing to work with the forum state to execute the judgment. Rarely are these conditions met.

Toward a standing mass claims commission?

The claims commissions that have existed to this day have all been *ad hoc* commissions possessing jurisdiction only over disputes relating to particular conflicts. The scope of existing commissions' authority is strictly defined by the legal instruments that created them; these instruments are unlikely to cover new international conflicts arising at some later point. Therefore, if no provision is made to create a dedicated

---

41 Ursula Tracy Doyle, "The Evidence of Things Not Seen: Divining Balancing Factors from Kiobel's 'Touch and Concern' Test" (2015) 66 *Hastings Law Journal* 443, 445.

42 For example, a group of Nigerians permanently living in the United States could not use the statute to bring a claim against a corporation that allegedly aided and abetted the Nigerian government in committing human rights violations, including beating, raping, killing and falsely arresting civilians. The Court found that the ATS does not "provide a cause of action for conduct occurring in the territory of another sovereign" where that conduct does not "touch and concern the territory of the United States … with sufficient force to displace the presumption against extraterritorial application." *Kiobel v. Royal Dutch Petroleum Co.*, 133 S. Ct. 1659, 1663, 1669 (2013).

43 Wolfgang Kaleck, "From Pinochet to Rumsfeld: Universal Jurisdiction in Europe, 1998–2008" (2009) 30 *Michigan Journal of International Law* 927, 955–58.

44 Elizabeth LaForgia, "Spain Parliament Approves Proposal to Curb Universal Jurisdiction" *Jurist* (12 February 2014), available at: http://www.jurist.org/paperchase/2014/02/spain-parliament-approves-proposal-to-curb-universal-jurisdiction-powers.php.

international claims commission, victims simply get no compensation – regardless of the merits of their claims.

It might be argued that there *ought* to be some standing institution with general jurisdiction comparable to the ICJ but procedurally suited to entertaining mass compensation cases. Would it be worthwhile to create such a tribunal?

Here, one recalls the genesis of the International Criminal Court (ICC). For many decades, international criminal cases were brought only before *ad hoc* criminal tribunals – the Nuremberg Trial was brought before the International Military Tribunal, and the Tokyo War Crimes Trial brought before the International Military Tribunal for the Far East. More recently, we have witnessed the formation of adjudicative bodies such as the International Criminal Tribunal for the Former Yugoslavia, the Extraordinary Chambers in the Courts of Cambodia, the International Criminal Tribunal for Rwanda, and the Special Court of Sierra Leone. Each of these tribunals can claim successes and failures, and proponents of a special standing criminal court found as much to be said in favor of the idea as opponents found to say against it. But over the long run, it became clear that there were advantages to the creation of a standing international criminal court.

The advantages were spelled out by M. Cherif Bassiouni, who argued strongly for the creation of the ICC. Bassiouni asserted that a standing tribunal has several benefits over *ad hoc* prosecution. First, by turning to a permanent court system instead of creating an *ad hoc* tribunal, parties can save considerable time, crucial because obtaining evidence of war crimes becomes more difficult as time goes on.[45] Second, instituting permanent judges and set procedures reduces the opportunities for political manipulation, which Bassiouni asserted plagued most *ad hoc* tribunals.[46] Finally, with adequate funding, Bassiouni suggested that the open-ended nature of an international tribunal would allow it to find, investigate and punish a greater number of war criminals.[47]

---

45 M. Cherif Bassiouni, "From Versailles to Rwanda in Seventy-Five Years: The Need to Establish a Permanent International Criminal Court" (1997) 10 *Harvard Human Rights Journal* 11, 60.

46 Bassiouni, "From Versailles to Rwanda," 60–61.

47 Bassiouni, "From Versailles to Rwanda," 15–18 (noting how political pressures "prevailed over the pursuit of justice" when the international community failed to prosecute Turkey for its large-scale killing of Armenians during World War I); *Id.* at 59 (for a similar discussion of Rwandan prosecutions). *See also* Beth Fain, "The International Criminal Court: An Eminent Impact on a Hesitant United States" (2004) 35 *Texas Tech Law Review* 163, 166.

Other commentators agree, arguing that, given the stature and permanence of standing courts, norms of international law might develop more cohesively and consistently with a standing than with an *ad hoc* tribunal.[48] In addition, a standing international court might be better placed to deter crimes against humanity through the threat of individual punishment.[49] In 2001, the ICC was created by widespread adoption of the Rome Statute.[50]

It is not difficult to see how these arguments might also apply to the creation of a standing international claims commission. As with the ICC, a standing claims commission might promote more consistent substantive and procedural rules through the application of precedent, greater efficiency through the repeated use of the same tribunal facilities, lower costs from paying tribunal members by fixed salary rather than hourly rates, the development of a qualified bar with special experience appearing before the tribunal, and so forth.

The effect on decision-making might be substantial. A standing tribunal might mean increased prestige for both the tribunal members and the tribunal staff, leading to the recruitment of higher caliber individuals to serve as judges. Professional judges might bring about a higher level of expertise, simply by virtue of greater experience dealing with mass compensation issues, resulting in a higher quality of published opinions. Full-time judges might be more likely to decide cases on principle, rather than by compromising in an effort to achieve legitimacy through unanimity. It is quite plausible that full time judges (as opposed to party-appointed arbitrators) would not feel beholden to one of the parties for having selected him or her as an arbitrator. *Ad hoc* tribunal members might be concerned about losing future "repeat business" as arbitrators if perceived not to be especially skilled at promoting the interests of the appointing state.[51] Moving to a system of full-time judges might therefore enhance the commission's neutrality.

---

[48] Fain, "The International Criminal Court," 167; American Bar Association Section of International Law and Practice et al., *Recommendation of the Standing Committee on World Order Under Law Task Force 2* (1998) (ABA Recommendation).

[49] Hon. Francis T. Murphy, "United States Should Ratify Treaty for International Criminal Court" (1999) 71-Apr. *New York State Bar Journal* 86; *ABA Recommendation* 2.

[50] United Nations, Rome Statute of the International Criminal Court, 17 July 1998, 37 ILM 1002 (1998), 2187 UNTS 90.

[51] Yuval Shany, for example, has noted that "the very concept of party-appointed adjudicators may be anathematic to traditional notions of judicial

These considerations are somewhat speculative; it is difficult to say whether, and by how much, standing judges would be better than *ad hoc* judges. But the considerations pushing in the opposite direction are speculative, too. *Ad hoc* claims commissions might be preferable because they provide complete flexibility to accommodate special circumstances. And it is possible that the quality of full-time tribunal members would actually be lower that the quality of *ad hoc* judges; if they were paid less while having to commit to a full-time position hearing mass claims cases, it might be more difficult to recruit first-class arbitrators.[52]

Mass claims proceedings are quite diverse, and it might be difficult to capture all the different possible kinds of cases in the jurisdictional statement of a single standing arbitral tribunal. The calculations of which sort of tribunal would do a better job – *ad hoc* or standing – are likely to be highly fact-specific and somewhat subjective. And given the variety of fact patterns that a commission might need someday to confront, no single formula is likely to answer the general question: are standing or *ad hoc* tribunals better for handling mass claims?

---

impartiality" and that "this problem is further compounded by the tendency of parties to select arbitrators with whom they had previous professional contacts." Yuval Shany, "Squaring the Circle? Independence and Impartiality of Party-Appointed Adjudicators in International Legal Proceedings" (2008) *30 Loyola Los Angeles International and Comparative Law Review* 473, 473–74. Shany, however, asserts that the loss of some independence is not necessarily bad and argues for looser, rather than stricter, ethical standards for party-appointed arbitrators, 489. *See also* Fabien Gélinas, "The Independence of International Arbitrators and Judges: Tampered With or Well Tempered?" (2011) *24 New York International Law Review* 1.

[52] After all, IMCCs can cover an astoundingly broad number of topics. Claimants can include "individuals, companies, nongovernmental organizations, and even government." Claims can be based on "real property, personal injury, business losses, environmental harm, forced labor, or demands for public apology." Unifying conflicts might be "a war, revolution, terrorist attack, state- or corporate-cause environmental disaster, or other significant tragedy." Christopher Gibson, "Recent Books on International Law" (2009) 103 *American Journal of International Law*, 193 (reviewing *Redressing Injustices Through Mass Claims Processes: Innovative Responses to Unique Challenges* (Permanent Court of Arbitration ed., New York: Oxford University Press 2006) and *International Mass Claims Processes: Legal and Practical Perspectives* (Howard M. Holtzmann, ed., New York: Oxford University Press 2007)). Another scholar succinctly stated that "every mass claims process is different from the next." Pierre A. Karrer, "Mass Claims Proceedings in Practice: A Few Lessons Learned" (2005) 23 *Berkeley Journal of International Law* 463, 463.

For present purposes, the question need not be addressed: no such institution currently exists. The closest that we now have is a standing institution that supplies practical support for arbitrations, including mass claims proceedings: the Permanent Court of Arbitration (PCA).[53] In the somewhat analogous world of commercial and investment arbitration, there are institutions that play a similar role.[54]

But the PCA, which hosted the Eritrea–Ethiopia Claims Commission, is far from an actual tribunal like the ICJ, with a standing bench, existing procedural rules, its own funding and so forth. The possibility that a mass compensation analog of the International Court of Justice might some day be created is not much of an argument against the creation of *ad hoc* claims commissions today. The most likely result of not creating an *ad hoc* mass compensation commission is failure to supply any adjudicative mechanism at all, leaving matters (in other words) at the *status quo*.

Doing Nothing: The Status Quo as an Alternative

Historically, the preferred legal response to the problem of war-time mass claims has been to do nothing. There were until recently no standing international courts to speak of. And although arbitration was a possibility, the financial, political and logistical costs associated with trying to set up a mechanism for adjudicating liability in those technologically challenged times would have been prohibitive. Moreover, until the last half of the last century, international law took a rather more permissive view of allowable tactics in war; many things that are considered unlawful now would not at that point have been cause for compensation – even if compensation had been the usual practice for other legal violations (which, generally speaking, it was not).

To a lesser degree, the same considerations still apply today. Although great strides have been made in spelling out what conduct is permissible

---

53 Indeed, some have argued for the development of a Permanent International Claims Commission, to function like the PCA with an emphasis on supplying expert commissioners and creating standard procedural rules for processing mass claims. *See* Menno T. Kimminga, "Towards a Permanent International Claims Commission for Victims of Violations of International Humanitarian Law" (2007) 25 *Windsor Yearbook Access Justice* 23, 28.

54 For example, the International Centre for Settlement of Investment Disputes (ICSID), the International Arbitration Chamber of Paris, and the Arbitration Institute of the Stockholm Chamber of Commerce all serve similar functions. World Bank, ICSID, https://icsid.worldbank.org; International Arbitration Chamber of Paris, http://www.arbitrage.org/en/; Stockholm Chamber of Commerce, Arbitration Institute, http://www.sccinstitute.com/.

during international conflict and what is not, the mechanisms for enforcement are still underdeveloped. Mass claims cases are still unwieldy and costly, and the international courts and tribunals that currently exist (while better prepared to hear large cases than the courts and tribunals of earlier times) are still not well-equipped for such an assignment. The lack of standing institutions means that for every case that is to be adjudicated, a new agreement to arbitrate would have to be negotiated; a new tribunal would have to be formed; new procedural rules would have to be agreed on; and so forth. This pace would be unsustainable.

Mass claims commissions are not the right answer for every conflict in which unlawful conduct is involved. It is only in limited circumstances that positive factors outweigh the negative, and claims commissions emerge as a suitable solution. In other cases, doing nothing may be the wisest course of action. In terms of speeding the healing process, many people in the affected community might prefer letting bygones be bygones. The processes of investigating contested facts, interviewing witnesses and inducing them to testify (let alone exposing them to hostile cross examination by opposing counsel at a hearing) were not designed with the well-being of victims and witnesses first and foremost in mind.

In any event, every situation for which a claims commission is proposed must be evaluated individually. We do not propose an arithmetically precise formula as we list some of the relevant criteria below, but only a series of considerations that might be factored into the decision what to do in a particular case.

Inaction: easy and cheap

The immediate practical appeal of doing nothing is obvious: It is easy and cheap.[55] The costs of arbitration are discussed at greater length in Chapter 5; but even without precise figures, it is clear that claims commissions are expensive, in terms of both financial outlays and human capital.

Typically, each party pays a proportionate share of claims commission expenses, together with its own legal expenses.[56] While the former is not

---

55 The funding of claims commissions is discussed at greater length in Chapter 5. In general, the costs of setting up a claims commission, paying a substantial group of attorneys to investigate, aggregate and advocate for the claims of nationals, and ultimately paying arbitration fees as well as awards could easily add up to a cost much higher than that of paying off citizens' claims directly.

56 Art. 3, IUSCT Algiers Accord.

insignificant, the latter can be more substantial. Wealthy states are likely to have in-house legal departments, often with legal talent of great sophistication; in any event, they can find the resources to attract top-notch support from high-powered law firms and academic departments. Less-developed countries are at a systematic disadvantage in litigation (as they are, of course, in any other resource-intensive enterprise). For them, it may be better to avoid litigation altogether rather than to enter into a contest lightly armed and on a distinctly non-level playing field.

The chance of a large recovery might be thought sufficient to lure the more reluctant of the parties into court. But while the possibility of a large payout might provide an incentive for countries to pursue the claims commission solution, this strategy is a gamble. They also undertake the risk of losing in a big way. Willingness to take that gamble is likely to be a function of how much confidence the party has in its case. It is reasonable to expect that the party with the weaker claim would be less interested in obtaining a definitive legal determination than the party with the stronger claim. But few states would be so confident in their chances of prevailing that the possibility of losing would cause no hesitation. The status quo is familiar, while arbitration tends to make everyone risk averse.

Even where a state successfully proves its claim, its recovery may be canceled out by payments it must make to another state[57] or to its claimants, or never realized due to difficulty in executing the award.[58] Given the many factors in play, it should not be surprising that states often prefer to avoid litigation when they can. If a state is even moderately risk-averse, or is disinclined to spend large amounts of money

---

[57] Ultimately, the Eritrea–Ethiopia Claims Commission awarded Eritrea $164 million for its claims and the claims of its nationals and awarded Ethiopia $174 million, canceling out all but $10 million. EECC, Final Award – Eritrea's Damages Claims § 9 ¶ 21, issued 17 August 2009; EECC, Final Award – Ethiopia's Damages Claims § 7 ¶ E, issued 17 August 2009.

[58] The UNCC used resources from Iraqi Oil Exports. Report of the Secretary-General on UNCC ¶ 16–17. The IUSCT relied on frozen Iranian assets in the custody of the United States. IUSCT Algiers Accords ¶ 2–3. In both cases, the Western Powers coordinated their legal strategies and effectively froze the assets of the defendant government. *See* Stephen Kalin, "Kuwait Defers Iraq's Final War Reparation Payment Until 2017," *Reuters* (29 October 2015), available at: http://www.reuters.com/article/us-mideast-crisis-iraq-kuwait-idUSKCN0SN1DW20151029; Stephanie Nebehay, "Iraq Wins One-Year Reprieve on Gulf War Reparations Due to Crisis," *Reuters* (18 December 2014), available at: http://www.reuters.com/article/us-mideast-crisis-iraq-un-idUSKBN0JW1DH20141218.

pursuing a small reward, it would probably be better off to avoid claims commissions altogether and to resign itself to the status quo.

Avoiding interference with development aid

There is another financial reason why states might prefer not to get involved in claims litigation. Bilateral or multilateral aid organizations sometimes help out after war, providing immediate physical support to refugees, money and technical assistance to rebuild infrastructure and help for the victims of combatants' unlawful conduct. Would they be as ready to come quickly with aid if it were generally assumed that damage caused unlawfully by the state's opponents was the legal responsibility of the states that caused it in the first place? Might they instead take their scant development assistance to a state where damage was caused by drought or epidemic?

A claims commission, as with other forms of litigation, has the potential to expose the worst about the states or people who form the subject matter of the litigation. Given that one or both of the states in question may have a long relationship with generous bilateral donors, it might seem that the better strategy would be to stick with the entity with the proven track record.

Other legitimate reasons for avoiding litigation

We alluded to the reluctance that victims and witnesses often have when speaking to outsiders about things that are not discussed publicly in many cultures. Even matters that are not considered taboo for public discussion may be too painful to revisit: the terror and pain of invasion by a hostile army, the fear of revisiting memories of physical abuse, grief over loss of loved ones, and destruction of childhood homes and family gravesites. Some contemporary international law scholars take such costs as essentially one of the chief reasons for creating claims commissions in the first place, on the belief that reliving wartime experiences publicly in the context of a judicial proceeding can have a cathartic effect. This is sometimes called the "expressive value" theory.

A central accomplishment of a claims commission (according to the expressive value theory) is to provide citizens whose international legal rights have been violated with official recognition of those violations and a chance to air their grievances. It is said that people care about recognition of the validity of their claims, with vindication of their rights, in theory, being important even if not accompanied by an actual award of money damages. Process is valued even when substantive rights cannot be compensated.

Ideally, a claims commission provides a neutral forum capable of identifying meritorious complaints. If nothing else, victims may value the expressive opportunities provided by claims commissions. Many scholars have discussed the possibility that expressing values through international tribunals will change international norms and modify behaviors.[59] Tom Ginsburg and Richard H. McAdams found empirical support for these theories and of the expressive power of adjudication in the international context.[60]

But it should be kept in mind that these benefits accrue to the international community *writ large*; they do not focus on compensating victims. And, given the personal cost and difficulty of providing testimony to tribunals, victims may not feel benefitted at all by the opportunity to share their private stories publicly with groups of hostile attorneys representing the country that one was only recently at war with. Claims commissions do not purport to be expressive vehicles for reconciling narratives of mass conflict. Instead, they claim to be tools for remunerating the victims of international law violations. When victims expect the latter, but only receive an imperfect version of the former, it is unclear whether they will look on their experiences as worth the effort and pain of coming forward.

There are some tribunals where a particular population is given a chance to tell their stories for the historic record, without the chance for compensation. Truth and reconciliation commissions (TRCs) have been created most famously in South Africa, but also in places as diverse as Liberia,[61] Peru,[62] and Greensboro, North Carolina.[63] Some states, like East Timor, have even coupled criminal prosecution with TRCs.

Many scholars, especially those who believe in the expressive value of criminal and international tribunals, are optimistic about truth and

---

59 *See, e.g.*, Saira Mohamed, "Deviance, Aspiration and the Stories We Tell: Reconciling Mass Atrocity and the Criminal Law" (2015)1 *24 Yale Law Journal* 1628.

60 Tom Ginsburg and Richard H. McAdams, "Adjudicating in Anarchy: An Expressive Theory of International Dispute Resolution*" (2004) 45 William and Mary Law Rev*iew 1229.

61 Truth and Reconciliation Commission of Liberia, available at: http://trcofliberia.org/.

62 United States Institute of Peace, Truth Commission: Peru 01, available at: http://www.usip.org/publications/truth-commission-peru-01.

63 Greensboro Truth and Reconciliation Commission, Executive Summary, available at: http://www.greensborotrc.org/exec_summary.pdf.

reconciliation commissions.[64] But those of a very practical bent are unlikely to be influenced by arguments about pure expression of one's injuries. It is doubtful, all around, whether the personal value of expression is substantial enough, in most circumstances, to warrant the creation of a tribunal with the sort of time consuming and costly adjudicative capacity of a claims commission. It is submitted that "expressive value" is best kept separate from claims commissions that are tasked with identifying and calculating the value of wartime violations of international law.

Most international legal violations end up without any forum for making a compensation claim. This does not mean that the victims are left entirely without any remedy, but simply that there is no *adjudicative* remedy. Political or diplomatic remedies are still possible. If compensation is important to the state parties, they may try to negotiate some form of reparations,[65] or each state may provide funding to assist its own nationals.[66] These states will then have the last word on which of their claimants would be compensated, under what conditions and in what amount. Compensation becomes a matter of domestic politics and not international law.

To this point we have focused mainly on the "con" side of claims commissions. Before arriving at conclusions, however, it is necessary also to think systematically about the benefits that come from the

---

[64] Martha Minow's *Breaking the Cycles of Hatred: Memory, Law, and Repair* (Princeton University Press, 2002) provides a good overview of arguments in support of non-prosecutorial mechanisms like TRCs. John Braithwaite has also written extensively about the conditions under which TRCs can be successful in his 25-year project to track mass conflicts from 2005 to 2030, *Peacebuilding Compared*. He has published four books thus far, on Timor-Leste, the Solomon Islands, Bougainville and Indonesia, through the Australian National University Press Library. His work is available at: http://press.anu.edu.au/publications/series/peacebuilding-compared.

[65] For example, Germany paid significant amounts of money in reparations in the wake of World War II, including to Jews who were displaced. *See* Ariel Colonomos and Andrea Armstrong, "German Reparations to the Jews after World War II," in Pablo de Greif (ed.), *The Handbook of Reparations* (Oxford University Press, 2006). More recently, several countries, including the United States, United Kingdom, Canada, the Netherlands, Australia and Poland, have made payments to Afghan civilians injured by military hostilities in Afghanistan. *Amsterdam International Law Clinic, Monetary Payments for Civilian Harm in International and National Practice* 11–15 (2013), available at: http://civiliansinconflict.org/uploads/files/publications/Valuation_Final_Oct_2013pdf.

[66] Afghanistan, for example, maintains funds to offer support to civilians injured by military hostilities there. Amsterdam International Law Clinic, 15–16.

formation of claims commissions. Just as IMCCs have substantial costs, under the right circumstances they can have substantial benefits. This is particularly true when the calculations are careful to include the impact on the international community, as well as the impact on individual claimants.

Reasons for Litigating: Systemic Values

Just as there may be reasons arguing against the creation of a commission to adjudicate the legal consequences of a particular conflict, there also may be reasons that litigation should be encouraged. The international community has an interest in peaceful dispute resolution that is reinforced by the parties' choice to pursue peaceful legal means rather than continuing the conflict. Pursuit of an arbitral remedy provides a means of communication between the parties should the threat of open conflict revive. Just compensation is a value in and of itself, it also carries with it a deterrent effect on future violators as well as a requirement of disgorging possible unjust enrichment.

Importantly, the needs and values of the international system are not always congruent with the self-interest of one or more of the claimants. Whether systemic values should be taken into account over the objections of the claimants is open to dispute. Here, we merely list a series of systemic considerations that may be implicated in the establishment of claims commissions. How much weight particular factors should be given depends on the political, social and economic context in which the determination will be made. Whether the game is worth the candle depends, therefore, on context.

Reinforcing the value of the rule of law

The discussion above considers the "downside" of claims commissions, viewed in isolation from the anticipated benefits that drive states to agree to their creation. Viewed this way, the case for a claims commission does not seem particularly compelling. But such a view is incomplete. It fails to take into account the positive ethical value of constituting a tribunal to determine violations of international law. To refocus the process of justification as resting on the unlawfulness of the defendant's acts – as international justice seems to require, given that this is a compensation commission – there must be some systematic method for determining legal fault. This is the rough equivalent of a claims commission.

Quite apart from the success or failure of particular commissions, the act of subjecting a conflict to the scrutiny of a formal claims tribunal reinforces the commitment of the parties to the international rule of law.

The more that international legal institutions show themselves capable of handling mass claims, the stronger the pressure is on other states to follow such procedures as well. And the more frequently states are seen to accept (and to comply with) awards that go against their interests, the less disgraceful a loss in an international tribunal will be perceived to be and the more likely that states will take the risk of adjudicating their future disputes.

The international community's interest in peace

It cannot be denied that the international community as a whole has interests in the peaceful resolution of disputes. Conflict disrupts alliances that are important for political stability, creates refugee flows and generally distracts from economic development. It leaves civilians in a position of complete uncertainty, unwilling to invest their time and money into productive activity because there is no telling when another episode of violence might recur.

Most claims commissions are established after a period of conflict – outright war or a conflict of a more limited sort. The terms on which commissions are set up are generally arrived at as part of a comprehensive negotiation that is designed to put the parties' overall conflict behind them. A claims commission focuses explicitly on just one aspect of the peace process – monetary compensation for violations of international law – but the positive effects are not so limited. The conflict, and how to bring it to a close, is larger than the individual claims that form the subject matter of the commission's work.

The Iran–US Claims Tribunal adjudicated claims arising in a larger context of the Iranian revolution and hostage crisis; the UNCC was a part of the Iraqi withdrawal after the first Persian Gulf War; and the EECC was created to deal with international law complaints arising in the 1998–2000 Eritrea–Ethiopia border war. The claims that were resolved by these commissions were only part of a larger conflict, each of which had threatened peaceful international relations to a much greater degree than the disputes over individual compensation. The claims are only a part of the overall transition to peace – but where peace is still somewhat fragile, these claims may be an important part.

By bringing the parties into court, a claims commission contributes to the parties' transition to peace. At a minimum, the parties will forge channels of communication, which may become critical if communications are threatened to be cut off. In situations where a resurgence of conflict threatens peace, the commission's existence should help to steer the parties back toward peaceful dispute resolution. The faster the individual claims can be resolved, the less likely it is that dissatisfaction or misunderstanding about the handling of the post-conflict period will spark further hostility. Leaving claims unresolved feeds a continuing atmosphere of distrust and resentment.

In addition, IMCCs are the best way to effect closure. Closure is important because the parties must at some point recognize their grievances as buried. Essential to the dynamic of closure is a party agreement to give the commission exclusive jurisdiction. Agreements setting up commissions often provide that the commission will be the exclusive forum for adjudication of claims.[67] By terminating the possibility of outside litigation, the participants (and claimants) are incentivized to direct their resources into the commission process. A grant of exclusive jurisdiction also puts the parties on notice that, in exchange for being provided with a forum for their claims that would otherwise not exist, the victims are expected to bring their claims to the tribunal in a timely way.

The pacifying effect of moving a dispute from a battlefield into a courtroom, however, cannot be taken for granted. In fact, in some contexts adjudication may serve only to prolong bitterness and animosity. Claims commissions create expectations that would not otherwise exist, because claimants believe that they will have their day in court and will then be given compensation. If these expectations are dashed, the result may be greater popular dissatisfaction and potential political unrest. If no compensation reaches the hands of the individual claimants, the government may be blamed.

Deterrence and unjust enrichment

Compensation for the innocent victims of international law violations is the most obvious and important reason for establishing a mass claims commission. A claims commission's most important task is to compel the responsible party or parties to provide money damages for legitimate, defined sets of individuals who have suffered harm as a result of violations of international law.[68] A tribunal that does not list compensation as its key objective should not call itself a "claims commission."

---

[67] Article V, Section 8 of the 2000 EECC Agreement made the EECC's jurisdiction exclusive. Article VII, Section 2 of the IUSCT Algiers Accord also provides for the IUSCT's exclusivity. However, not all claims commissions require exclusivity, and some instead allow for dual prosecution of claims. Article 22 of the Report of the Secretary-General on UNCC does just this, while providing mechanisms for coordinating final award amounts among tribunals.

[68] See, for example, UNCC, Decision Taken by the Governing Council of the United Nations Compensation Commission at the 27th Meeting, Sixth Session Held on 26 June 1992 Arts. 17, 35, 26 June 1992, S/AC.26/1992/10.

However, resolution of individual claims is not the only objective that might motivate the state to create a claims commission. Other objectives are near-corollaries of the compensation rationale. The best example of a rationale tightly linked to compensation is deterrence.

Deterrence The possibility of deterring future violations of individual rights is obviously very attractive, if you can get it to work. Some scholars have advocated for international criminal tribunals and claims commissions on these grounds, arguing that punishment – and the threat of punishment – by an international tribunal can deter perpetrators if possible penalties and the likelihood of successful prosecution are both high.[69] Commissioners and judges often share these values, frequently referencing deterrence as an important principle in achieving justice through tribunals.[70]

The close link between compensation and deterrence is a function of the dual effect of the payment of damages. For example, if in an award of damages the defendant state is ordered to pay $5 million, this payment serves as compensatory justice; the award indicates that the commission was convinced that the claimant suffered $5 million worth of damage as a result of the defendant's unlawful conduct. Since the defendant state's actions were unlawful under international law (a necessary requirement for the $5 million award to be given) it makes sense under a compensation rationale to impose the cost on the defendant. But the same transfer of $5 million from the defendant to the successful claimant simultaneously acts as a deterrent. Other states in a situation analogous to the defendant will see that the price of their unlawful conduct is the amount that they may be required to pay to make the claimant whole.

Unjust enrichment A similar argument explains a slightly different objective: the avoidance of unjust enrichment. The principle underlying the prevention of unjust enrichment is that the wrongdoer must not be allowed to retain the benefits of his or her crime. Depending on the type of legal violations involved, the defendant may have been unjustly enriched by the violation. This is particularly the case where claims are related to the seizure of property.

---

[69] *See, e.g.*, M. Cherif Bassiouni, "Combating Impunity for International Crimes" (2000) 71 *University of Colorado Law Review* 409, 410.

[70] Padraig McAuliffe, "Suspended Disbelief? The Curious Endurance of the Deterrence Rationale in International Criminal Law" (2012) 10 *New Zealand Journal of Public and International Law* 227, 229, citing judges from the ICTY and Lubanga case in the ICC.

The unjust enrichment theory is linked to both deterrence and compensation, insofar as both concern a single payment that has more than one function. The value of the property that the perpetrator appropriated, looted or seized is at the same time a payment of compensation to the claimant, a penalty against the defendant for having violated international law, and a return to the original owner of the value unjustifiably taken away.

There is considerable skepticism about whether these objectives of compensation, deterrence and avoidance of unjust enrichment can actually be achieved. International legal scholars argue that just as the principle of deterrence is problematic for domestic cases,[71] it is extremely unlikely to be effective as a guiding principle for international criminal courts.[72] In claims commissions, the possibility of successful deterrence seems even more dubious. Unlike criminal tribunals, wrongdoers are not threatened with physical imprisonment; states, not individuals, are sanctioned; and awards are adjusted to prevent overly severe penalties on states.[73] Unjust enrichment is not present in all violations of international law; some unlawful conduct simply destroys value without allowing the perpetrator to enrich itself. For example, deliberate destruction of an archeological monument triggers a right to compensation and an interest in deterring similar conduct in the future, but the perpetrators were probably not enriched by committing the unlawful act (looting archeological artifacts is a different matter, in this respect). In cases where unjust enrichment does exist, the unlawful gains can be eliminated by specifying damages in the amount that the perpetrator unjustly received. To the extent that this amount is non-trivial, avoidance of unjust enrichment reinforces the general incentive structure of compensation and deterrence.

---

71 Minow, *Breaking the Cycles of Hatred*, 229, citing James Gilligan, *Violence: Our Deadly Epidemic and its Causes* (Putnam, 1996) 94–95.

72 Minow, *Breaking the Cycles of Hatred*, (arguing that the appeal of deterrence arguments may be outweighed by the "sustained and damaging critique" of its effectiveness in the international context); Julian Ku and Jide Niezliebe, "Do International Criminal Tribunals Deter or Exacerbate Humanitarian Atrocities?" (2006) 84 *Washington University Law Review* 777 (calculating the deterrence effect of international criminal prosecution by comparing it to the likelihood of domestic sanctions and finding that deterrence is marginal at best in most prosecutions).

73 EECC, Final Award.

Systemic considerations: interests of the international community

Compensation, obviously, is motivated by concern for the individual whose body or property was taken or destroyed. Deterrence, in contrast, is of value to the entire community; it is a systemic value. Compensation is a benefit to the individual who was wronged and suffered damages. Deterrence is a benefit to all potential victims, whose injury can be avoided if the potential perpetrator's course of action can be discouraged.

It is open to debate whether and to what extent future violators of international law are truly influenced by incentives such as these. Some violators may assume that they will never be apprehended. Others assume that international law is completely corrupt, and they can always buy or bully their way out. Still others don't think at all in the heat of the moment. Depending on what one concludes about such empirical matters, one may attach great importance, or none, to the relationship to compensation. In listing reasons for establishing claims commissions, deterrence and unjust enrichment should figure into the calculations as a theoretical matter, but these two corollaries of compensation should be accompanied by a healthy dose of skepticism.

Skepticism about Claims Commissions

Any discussion of the principles underlying claims commissions should start with the premise that the core role of an IMCC is to effect compensation for violations of international law. That is what makes it a claims commission rather than a maritime delimitation arbitration or a land boundary demarcation. But claims commissions sometimes turn out to be poor at doing the one thing that is expected of them. If an institution bills itself as a "claims commission," should it not be judged on whether or not it is successful at providing that service?

What if, for instance, it were clear from the start of the process that most valid claims would not be paid? Would that count against any proposal to solve things through an IMCC? Or, at a minimum, would that be something that ought to be taken into account in the process of institutional design, so that the probability of full compensation would be as high as possible? There seems to be no justification for simply ignoring it.

Adjudication, generally, is not well designed for resolving very large numbers of very small cases. In the context of IMCCs, the problem is particularly acute. The task can be simplified by entrusting the state parties to collect and systematize the claims of their nationals, to act as official contacts between the tribunal and the individual victims, to present the evidence and to distribute any award money when the case is complete. This way of simplifying the adjudication is a "statist" model – it reflects the classic international law premise that states, and only states, can play a role in international affairs.

The alternative is to invite individuals to approach the tribunal directly, not through a state party with total control over their claims. This "individualist" approach leaves to the tribunal the task of organizing, processing and resolving the many thousands of individual compensation requests. The statist model makes the claims commission's work more manageable, but the individualist model makes its work more consistent with the substantive norms that comprise the claims that the tribunal is charged with deciding. There is no way to do both.

Statism and individualism in international mass claims compensations
An example will illustrate this point. Assume that State Alpha and State Beta each have claims against the other, all based on a war between them in which civilians suffered from unlawful denationalization, confiscation and property damage, looting, physical abuse and other violations of the Geneva Conventions, Hague Rules and international human rights law. Pursuant to the peace agreement that they signed as the conflict was winding down, a mass claims compensation case was initiated. After the presentation of all evidence, the filing of memorials and counter-memorials, the appearances at the oral arguments, the examination of witnesses, and so forth, the commission deliberates. Each of the two states is awarded damages from the other, with about $160 million being the total amount due to Alpha from Beta, and $170 million the total amount due to Beta from Alpha.

This example, obviously, is largely modeled on the Eritrea–Ethiopia Claims Commission.[74] What is striking for present purposes is the bottom line. After all seemed to go according to the procedures laid out in the 2000 Algiers Agreement, both sides were given substantial awards to cover the damage done by the other side during the war. Simple arithmetic reveals that the difference between the two awards was a net gain to Ethiopia of around $10 million. Ethiopia's award was sufficient to cancel out entirely the amount that it owed to Eritrea and, in addition, to entitle it to $10 million of net gain. But no payments were made to the injured parties.

---

[74] One key difference is that the example of Alpha and Beta lacks an important element present in the EECC situation. In the actual EECC case, Ethiopia was in violation of the earlier holding of the Eritrea Ethiopia Boundary Commission. It was thus not inclined to argue about what Eritrea might or might not be obligated to do after the EECC's final ruling.

The logical thing to do might be for Alpha to pay Beta the $10 million difference and for the two states to treat the $160 million that each owes the other as cancelled out.[75] Ten million dollars seems to be enough to satisfy the damages award if Beta is at the same time excused from paying Alpha the $160 million that it was awarded, and Alpha is excused from paying Beta the $160 million that it was awarded.[76] Thus, it appears that Alpha should distribute the $10 million to its claimants, probably *pro rata*, and then declare the whole matter finished.

But what about the $160 million? Do Alpha and Beta have a good argument for treating their obligations as canceled out? Assume that Beta does receives the $10 million from Alpha, and distributes the money *pro rata* to all of its nationals who were held to have good claims. The result will be that all worthy claimants get 1/17 of his or her proven claim for compensation. Is that all that they should be entitled to?

In dividing the $10 million *pro rata*, rather than dividing up the $170 million that the Commission decided Beta was entitled to, Beta's claimants have in effect taken on, involuntarily, the task of paying their state's debt of $160 million to Alpha. Of the total amount of recovery, they get only $10 million because their state wants to use the other $160 million to set off the damages it caused to Alpha. Although (as we shall see) there are good arguments indicating that it is wrong for the states to treat the $160 million that way, no existing principle of international law explicitly declares this sort of "set-off" as being illegal. To the contrary, international law recognizes Beta as having the right to divide up the proceeds according to its domestic policies and interests.

But the consequence is that none of Alpha's claimants receive any compensation, and Beta's claimants receive at most about five cents on the dollar. All of the claims from both sides are foreclosed by the commission's "final and binding" decision, and the claimants have no opportunity to try again in some alternative forum. In this respect, the claimants are actually worse off than if there had been no commission at all.

---

[75] Of course, there is also a possibility that Beta might appropriate some of the $10 million owing to its individual claimants, which would not be just and fair but not illegal under international law as it is currently understood. A state has the authority to distribute (or presumably, to confiscate) portions of the Award that in all fairness belonged to individual claimants.

[76] This is assuming that neither Alpha nor Beta was entitled to any of the $160 million as a claimant. The calculations would require separately taking into account any claims that the state had of a property nature (for example, destruction of public facilities such as schools or hospitals, roads or bridges.)

It seems that the only entity to be "compensated" by such a result is the two states themselves. Each did $160 million of damage, illegally, to the other state, and then managed to get the individual claimants to pay for it. And yet, this result has not been denounced by the international community as contrary to the central mission of a claims commission – namely, compensation.

Some historical context

How and why does this happen? It seems as though both groups of claimants (Alpha's and Beta's) lose, and for no good reason. The explanation lies in some foundational assumptions made about a state's right to represent its nationals in international courts. Many of the problems facing IMCCs are connected to the changing perspectives on international human rights over the course of the twentieth century.

The beginning of that century found international law firmly grounded in classic assumptions on the subject, particularly the assumption that only states had any involvement in international affairs. Under this classical theory, the phrase "international" law was meant to be taken literally. "Inter-national" law concerned the law in effect "between nations"; it made no provision for individuals or for other non-state actors. Under this view, a person's legal rights against his or her state were absolutely within that state's domestic jurisdiction and not a matter of international law. This position required rejecting strong notions of human rights, for state sovereignty could always trump human rights limitations on what states could do to their own people.

This view is entirely out of step with the modern human rights paradigm that gained ground throughout the last half of the last century and is now the conventional wisdom. Remnants of the earlier view still remain rooted in international law, but to a much lesser degree than previously. It is no longer considered adequate to answer charges about human rights violations with the defense that such disputes are within the domestic affairs of the state and not subject to international interference. International human rights are understood as being the universal rights of human beings and they are, for the most part, the rights of individuals against the state.[77] There even now exist a limited number of situations in

---

[77] The qualification here is motivated by the awareness that people can also have rights against international organizations and perhaps some quasi-sovereign body. Whether they can have rights against other people is, of course, debated.

which individuals can bring a complaint against the state in an international human rights court.[78]

This profound alteration in the fundamental building blocks of international law dates to around the middle of the twentieth century: the human rights paradigm did not really take root until the end of World War II.[79] The war highlighted the phenomenon of truly *mass* atrocities. Shortly after the war's close, *ad hoc* international criminal courts were set up in Nuremberg and Tokyo to assess the responsibility under international criminal law for the atrocities that had occurred. It was around this time that the Geneva Conventions went into effect, and the United Nations Charter was drafted and adopted. International universal human rights began to be recognized, and the classical view that only states had a place in international law fell increasingly out of favor.

At stake in this transition were both substantive rights and procedural principles. The new substantive rights appeared in legal instruments such as the UN Charter, the Geneva Conventions, the Universal Declaration on Human Rights, and various other agreements prohibiting discrimination on the basis of gender, race, disability, religion and so forth. The new perspective on procedure mainly had to do with standing: whether individuals and not just states could be holders of international legal rights. The modern answer is "yes."

Conflicts of interest and representation by the state

This new substantive and procedural understanding of the nature of human rights and humanitarian law has now raised important questions about representation. In classical international law, the state represents its nationals. It is the state that frames their complaints, collects evidence and presents the claim before the tribunal, and it is the state that receives the financial benefits of the award and distributes them to the claimants as it sees fit.

The difficulty is that while the substantive right to compensation for the harm that was done is now generally understood to inhere in the individual, the transition from statist process to individualist process is not complete. Most claims commissions operating under the assumption

---

[78] See p.41 (Procedural Unsuitability) above.

[79] This is not to say that there were no mass atrocities at earlier points in time; the Armenian genocide would be an obvious counterexample. The point, rather, is simply that it was around the time of the Second World War that the intellectual grounding of the human rights movement came together with the "facts on the ground" of mass atrocities. The Holocaust became the paradigm mass violation by which all future mass atrocities were to be judged.

of individual substantive human rights still, in many respects, operate under statist procedural assumptions. Our hypothetical example of Alpha and Beta falls into this category; while the rights at stake are individualist, the procedural approach seems to be statist (because the relevant transactions seem to all be between the two states).

The reasons for a statist procedure are easy to appreciate. Putting the state in charge of soliciting claims, compiling the evidence, integrating the evidence with arguments about the proper legal standard and other related tasks, has the natural effect of aggregating the thousands of claims that the tribunal must deal with. The most expeditious way to handle such claims is by making the state the representative of all claims; it can consolidate the presentation, negotiate a settlement (or not, as it sees fit) and distribute any award.

Individualist approaches, by contrast, increase the burden on the tribunal. Removing the state from its position of control over the presentation of the claims opens the door for claimants to approach the commission directly. If there is no intermediary between the individual claimants and the tribunal, the tribunal itself must organize the thousands of written submissions and their accompanying evidence, coordinating oral presentations and other procedures, rather than leaving this all to the states. The tribunal, moreover, will have to decide how best to divide up any damages compensation that is awarded. Even assuming a large and experienced support staff, the administrative burden would be quite substantial.

IMCCs that have undertaken some or all of this additional burden – such as the IUSCT and the UNCC – have faced some difficult challenges. The workability of such individualist or mixed statist/individualist models is discussed in Chapters 4 and 7, which deal with the different party structures that have been utilized and how different tribunals have dealt with the respective roles of the state parties and the individual claimants. All we need to say about party structure for present purposes is that a purely statist procedural structure is the easiest for the commission, the claimants and the state parties to deal with, but a purely statist structure is the least satisfactory from the perspective of ensuring that actual compensation will reach the hands of the individual victims.

The choice of whether to employ a statist approach to compensation cannot simply be a matter of which is the easiest procedure to apply from the point of view of the tribunal and the parties. Although statism does have that advantage, more is at stake than pure administrative convenience. Really, the choice between statism and individualism is whether the state, acting as a representative of the claims of its nationals, has the authority to make decisions on their behalf, including some decisions that might terminate, settle or compromise those claims. A statist approach jeopardizes full compensation of the individual claimants, because of the conflict of interests between the individual claimant and the state that claims to represent him or her.

This conflict of interest is more complex than it first appears. It is not merely a question of how to allocate the eventual award among the different individual claimants, although that is itself quite difficult. That question raises the likelihood of conflict between claimants with the same sort of claim, who are competing for the same limited resources. In such circumstances, every dollar that goes to claimant number one is thereby less available to settle the complaints of claimant number two. This is the relevant model where the state has claims of its own that are comparable to the claims of private individuals and institutions. For example, Beta may have wrongfully destroyed property belonging to Alpha, such as a school or administrative building. Such a claim would be the equivalent (in terms of damages) of a private person claiming that Beta destroyed his house or factory.

But sometimes the state's interests do not resemble the interests of the individual claimants. For example, the state has interests peculiar to itself. The obvious example here is Alpha's need to satisfy Beta's judgment. In this scenario, the state asserts priority for all of its claims, on the grounds that they all happen to be *more important* than the claims the private party can make. The assertion that Beta's claim should receive priority over the available assets depends on an argument that the two kinds of claims are different in ways that make the state's claims entitled to higher priority. In the present case, the claim is that a state's payment of a judgment should have higher priority than any responsibility for assuring that its nationals get the compensation that the commission declares them entitled to.

This second argument pits ordinary property claimants seeking compensation for their lost property against Beta's claim that it should receive priority so it can buy off the amount that it owes Alpha. The result of the award would be that each of the state parties would get a credit of $160 million to use as a set-off. The individual claimants that are nationals of Beta would then get some portion of the remaining $10 million, as allocated by Beta. If this approach is adopted, the property rights of the claimants are subordinated to the state's desire to pay off its obligation to the other state. The state would benefit greatly from having a share of the eventual award, because it could use that share (as did the two state parties at the EECC) as a set-off against the award that it would otherwise have to pay to its opponents out of its own money.

Can this really be the right way to proceed? Ironically, the state's use of the award money to buy off a judgment against it gives priority to those who need money because they violated international law. Each state gets a large amount of money – not because it was the *victim* of an international law violation (which it wasn't) but because it was the *violator*. This really turns deterrence on its head, the theory being that because the state has been held to have committed $160 million worth of violations of international law, it should be given that amount to retire the liability, which it would otherwise have to pay as damages. A state's interest in not having to pay the $160 million damages award from its own pocket is taken as a justification for helping itself to the $160 million at the expense of its nationals.

This approach is more convenient for the states than a complicated arrangement involving shuttling around large amounts of cash. If the two state parties can simply agree that the two debts cancel one another out, then there is little or nothing that the tribunal can do to discourage this settlement.

Treating the $160 million as cancelled out also has another advantage from the commission's point of view: it does not require that any money damages actually be paid. This is valuable if one or both of the state parties is impoverished and unlikely to have the resources to pay a large judgment. To the extent that the damages are symmetric and cancel each other out, the commission need not worry about the embarrassment of recalcitrant or impoverished states refusing to go along with paying the damages ordered in the final awards. The opportunity to avoid going head-to-head with one or both of the parties can be very convenient, because such a challenge to the authority of the commission could end up with the commission on the losing side.

However, if that is the approach taken then there is something a bit misleading in the title "compensation commission." At the end of the day, the individual claimants are not entitled to compensation, but only a *pro rata* share of the amount remaining after the set-off. For nationals of the state with the higher liability, there is no recovery at all, even though they or their property were wrongfully looted or destroyed, and even though they are in no way responsible for their state's unlawful activity. Indeed, the claimants are actually *worse off* than they would have been if no IMCC had ever been established. For if there is no IMCC, they would at least have preserved their right to approach another forum, should one become available.

The picture, all around, is rather pessimistic. We are not just referring to the relatively common but unfortunate situation in which the recovery is consumed by attorney fees and arbitration costs (compensation to the arbitrators, registrar's expenses, etc.). Nor is the point simply that worthy claims may erroneously be denied, or that the losing party may not be willing or able to pay the award that is issued against it. All of these problems can occur, and can be serious impediments to compliance with a damages award.

What is more important here about how the dispute works itself out, however, is that worthy claimants have to go uncompensated despite the fact that everything went according to the book, and the tribunal held the claimant entitled to the amount named in the award. The states of which the claimants are nationals have been allowed privileged access to the proceeds, on the (implicit) grounds that it is a higher priority to pay the state's liability than to compensate the claimants. This seems mistaken.

The very establishment of a compensation commission represents a commitment to the idea that compensation for the losses of the victim whose legal rights were violated is more significant morally than the financial health of the government that committed the violations. The whole point of deterrence, moreover, is that paying damages is *supposed to be* painful. If, at the end of the day, the compensation award is not paid because it would be too great a burden to impose on the perpetrator state, it might be better to say so at the outset rather than delay the inevitable day of reckoning. Better not to drag the claimants, the parties, their attorneys, the tribunal and its staff, and the remaining members of the public through years of unpleasantness, unrealistic expectations, wasted money and wasted time.

Reciprocity and the offset of claims

The resolution just described – the $10 million difference is paid to Beta, and the remaining portions of both awards cancel each other out – seems perfectly acceptable from one point of view, but deeply paradoxical from another. Under the statist paradigm, the relevant participants are the states; they can agree to settle claims against one another and are free to drop monetary claims resulting from an arbitration award on a reciprocal basis.

But a good argument can be made that the individualist paradigm should be applied in these circumstances. Alpha should transfer $170 million to a reliable representative of the victims of Beta nationality – not the state itself – and Beta should transfer $160 million to the representative of the victims who are nationals of Alpha. The reliable representatives would then administer some plan for getting the money into the right hands. This would, for obvious reasons, not be popular with the states in question, and it is not clear to what degree the states would permit it.

We will return in Chapter 7 to some general issues about remedies and compliance with the award. Some of the questions posed will be closely related to the discussion about offsets here. The issues that will be addressed in greater detail in that chapter include:

- Should the parties insert into the agreement that established the commission their agreed position on whether to allow set-offs? If the parties agree to such a clause, should it be enforceable?
- Do the two states have the legal authority to cancel out one another's obligations to pay damages for human rights violations?
- How do asymmetric commissions like the UNCC and Iran–US Claims Tribunal operate without running aground on the problem of set-offs?
- Are there any limits on the states trading off their responsibility to pay damages?
- Are there any doctrinal limitations in international law that would deny states the right to set off their awards?

Chapter 7 will also explore what measures can be taken to minimize the likelihood that it will be easy to refuse to pay an award. For example, a mechanism might be designed whereby a reliable third party such as a United Nations agency would act as a neutral agent to help resolve some of these issues. The UNCC reflected somewhat similar assumptions; can its experience be generalized? The answers to such questions lead to more questions, and to more difficult ones. This chapter is only the beginning.

3. The legal and operating structure

In this chapter we set aside thorny questions of legitimacy and turn to the practical challenges of establishing and running an IMCC. We approach the topic from two perspectives: legal structure and operating structure. We begin with a discussion of legal structure, including how the scalability and flexibility of the model allow parties to craft a vehicle that will effect the greatest good for the greatest number in the shortest time. In the second section, we discuss how decisions about legal structure affect how an IMCC will be set up and operated. The focus in this second section is on the human element – empaneling a tribunal and then creating the support structure that will best assist it. In a later chapter we will discuss how the enterprise might be financed, within the strictures established by the arbitration agreement.

THE LEGAL STRUCTURE

This section concerns the distinctive legal structure of international mass claims commissions. It identifies the legal characteristics shared by all or most IMCCs and shows how these connect with the values that public law arbitration is designed to further. It assesses how the IMCC model is superior to a judicial model in several respects, and how it fits better with the long-range goal of IMCC adjudication: compensation for as many victims as possible of a state's unlawful treatment. The arbitral model leads to choices about legal structure, which then informs the operating structure of an IMCC.

A few initial definitions might be helpful, as the language of international mass claims commissions has not been standardized. We propose the following vocabulary:

- The phrases "international mass claims commission," "IMCC" and "international mass compensation commission" will be used interchangeably to refer to the overall dispute-resolution mechanism.
- We will also refer to proceedings as "arbitrations." Our usage of the word is inclusive – it covers not only IMCCs and commercial arbitrations, but also state-to-state arbitrations over public law

issues such as boundary or maritime delimitation disputes. IMCCs (in our view) are a type of arbitration.
- The initial agreement that commits the parties to establishing a claims commission is an "arbitration agreement." Even though it may take another form, such as a paragraph included in a peace treaty, its function is to set out the IMCC's basic terms.
- "Rules of procedure" refer to a legal instrument drafted by the commissioners after the commission has been constituted. Rules of procedure are generally much more detailed than an arbitration agreement.
- "Commission" and "tribunal" both refer to a third-party decision-making body, composed of an odd number of individuals nominated by the parties (or by the other commissioners) to watch over the course of the litigation and ultimately decide the dispute on the merits.
- By "party" we mean the entity or individual that is legally recognized as the owner of the claim or the defense. Under the traditional statist model, this meant the state of which the victim was a national. Today it might mean the victim himself or herself. This usage contrasts with the terms "participant" and "victim." A participant is anyone who may have some more diffuse involvement, while a victim is the entity or individual who suffered the injury as a factual matter.

This harmonizing terminology helps to bring into clearer focus some of the features that IMCCs share.

The Distinctive Features of IMCCs

It seems relatively uncontroversial to say that mass litigation can be a suitable remedy for large-scale violations of international law.[1] There may be doubts about that solution's practicality – and experience with some IMCC litigation arguably supports this pessimism. But no one, so far, has come up with a better idea. There seems, in short, to be no basis for objecting to the establishment of arbitral commissions to aggregate large numbers of closely related claims for efficient claims processing.

Understanding why an IMCC might be preferable to more traditional international legal processes begins by identifying some of the important differences between the two. We identify the important features that

---

[1] Although the question is not free from doubt, Chapter 2 discusses the reasons that an IMCC might be the superior format.

characterize modern mass-claims litigation: size of the claimant pool, party structure and historical context. We see how the concept of party autonomy and the flexibility of the arbitral model generally – and IMCCs in particular – accommodate these characteristics in a way that traditional litigation cannot.

As will become clear, these characteristics are important because how they are addressed in an IMCC tends to offer opportunities to the parties for procedural or substantive advantage. The parties are the ones that shape their arbitral agreement, and they have no reason to include provisions they dislike or to exclude provisions they favor. Over time, experience with this form of arbitration leads to the retention of provisions that work well and the abandonment of those that are ineffective or harmful. This Darwinian process should lead, over time, to procedural devices that benefit both parties.

This matters because there is no compulsory jurisdiction for IMCC disputes. The parties must agree to arbitration, which they are unlikely to do absent some perceived advantage. There is something paradoxical about this: It is not arithmetically possible for both sides to gain. One party's gain is another's loss; the "game" is zero-sum. How, then, can each party see an advantage where it doesn't exist? First, both sides may believe – one of them, mistakenly – that they stand to gain by the result. It is commonplace for litigants to overstate their chance of winning. Second, defining the "game" in broader terms shows that there are aspects of the proceedings that are not zero-sum; for example, both sides gain if the process can be made cheaper and fairer. Finally, the ultimate advantage of the litigation – settling the dispute – inheres to both parties. This "peace dividend" may by itself be enough to induce the parties to arbitrate.[2]

Size of the dispute

The first and most obvious common characteristic of IMCCs is the large *size* of the disputes that these tribunals are responsible for adjudicating. Conventional international-law cases typically involve only two parties – both of which are either states or a state and a large international corporation, intergovernmental organization or other public entity.[3] In

[2] Indeed, as we discuss in Chapters 7 and 8, the combination of diplomatic representation and set-offs may allow state parties to extinguish their liability by pressing the claims of their nationals without paying them compensation.

[3] For instance, the 2015 docket of the Permanent Court of Arbitration consisted of: eight inter-state arbitrations, 76 investor-state arbitrations arising under bilateral/multilateral investment treaties and national investment laws; 44

contrast, the cases we have taken as our three main illustrations – the IUSCT, the UNCC and the EECC – aggregate individual claims by the thousands (if not tens, or even hundreds, of thousands).

It would be difficult to dispute the central importance of size to modern mass-claims litigation. For example, the December 2000 Algiers Agreement,[4] authorizing establishment of the EECC, reflects the assumption that the claims will be large and/or numerous:

> 10. In order to facilitate the expeditious resolution of these disputes, the Commission shall be authorized to adopt such methods of efficient case management and mass claims processing as it deems appropriate, such as expedited procedures for processing claims and checking claims on a sample basis for further verification only if circumstances warrant.
>
> 11. Upon application of either of the parties, the Commission may decide to consider specific claims, or categories of claims, on a priority basis.[5]

Importantly, this provision is simply a delegation of power to the commission to "adopt … methods of efficient case management." As is common with arbitration agreements that create IMCCs, no particular method of efficient case management is required; that is left for the commission to determine. Such methods might include any reasonable procedure that improves manageability (reducing cost, time, available personnel etc.) and might make use of evidentiary devices such as we discuss in Chapter 6: presumptions, placement of the burden of proof and so forth.

The legal structure of the UNCC emerged gradually, initially through a structure created by the Secretary-General at the behest of the Security Council and then through a governing council. But the anticipated scale

---

arbitrations arising under contracts involving a state, intergovernmental organization or other public entity; one arbitration between private parties arising under a contract submitted to arbitration in accordance with the PCA Optional Rules for Arbitration of Disputes Relating to Natural Resources and/or the Environment; one conciliation between a private party and an inter-governmental organization arising under a contract submitted to conciliation in accordance with the UNCITRAL Conciliation Rules (1980); and five other disputes. Permanent Court of Arbitration, *Annual Report* (2015), 20.

[4] Agreement between the Government of the State of Eritrea and the Government of the Federal Democratic Republic of Ethiopia of 12 December 2000, (Algiers Agreement), available at: http://peacemaker.un.org/sites/peacemaker.un.org/files/ER%20ET_001212_AgreementEritreaEthiopia.pdf.

[5] Algiers Agreement, at Article 5, ¶ 10 and 11.

of the enterprise always featured in the design. Security Council Resolution 687 laid out the scope of liability:

> Reaffirms that Iraq ... is liable under international law for any direct loss, damage, including environmental damage and the depletion of natural resources, or injury to foreign Governments, nationals and corporations, as a result of Iraq's unlawful invasion and occupation of Kuwait.[6]

Resolution 687 then went on to order the creation of a "fund to pay compensation for [those] claims ... and to establish a Commission that will administer that fund."[7] The Secretary-General quickly issued a report suggesting how a newly constituted governing council might manage the "tens of thousands" of individual claims that might be expected (an estimate that considerably understated the eventual number of submissions).[8] This first report, and the subsequent work of the governing council, was devoted to thoughtfully working through the best way to efficiently manage the deluge of claims that could be expected to result from this extremely broad mandate.[9]

Both the UNCC and the EECC had the benefit of the earlier experience of the IUSCT, which implicitly anticipated a heavy workload, even if it did not provide for the mass claims processing techniques that would feature in the later IMCCs. The IUSCT established a tribunal:

> for the purpose of deciding claims of nationals of the United States against Iran and claims of nationals of Iran against the United States, and any counterclaim which arises out of the same contract, transaction or occurrence that constitutes the subject matter of that national's claim, if such claims and

---

6 UNSC Res 687, ¶ 16 (3 April 1991).

7 UNSC Res 687, ¶ 18 (3 April 1991).

8 UN Secretary-General, Report Pursuant to Paragraph 19 of Security Council Resolution 687 (1991), ¶ 21, UN Doc S/2255.

9 UN Secretary-General, Report Pursuant to Paragraph 19 of Security Council Resolution 687 (1991), UN Doc S/2255. The Secretary-General recommended several mechanisms to more efficiently process these claims, including: consolidated filings by governments of affected nationals, categorization by injury suffered, differentiation between small-, medium- and large-sized claims, distinguishing between losses incurred by nationals and corporations, and individual consideration of claims ill-suited to mass claims processing. Public international arbitrations outside the mass claims context contain no such provision. *See also* UN Compensation Commission Governing Council, Decision taken by the Governing Council of the United Nations Compensation Commission at the 27th meeting, Sixth session (26 June 1992), UN Doc S/AC.26/1992/10.

> counterclaims are outstanding on the date of this agreement, *whether or not filed with any court*, and arise out of debts, contracts (including transactions which are the subject of letters of creditor bank guarantees), expropriations or other measures affecting property rights.[10]

The parties would have had some idea of the potential scale already, since an inducement for Iran to commit to the program was the US agreement to transfer lawsuits that were then pending in US courts to the IUSCT. The size of the Tribunal – originally made up of nine judges – and the mechanism to increase it by multiples of three and/or break it into three-member panels to facilitate quicker processing signaled that the anticipated volume was expected to be large.[11]

Language that implicitly or expressly contemplates a large volume of claims does not appear in the more common types of public-law arbitrations. Its inclusion reveals the parties' assumption that the individual claims for relief would be numerous and would require specialized processing.[12]

While obviously relevant to the issue of suitability for mass claims treatment, the "size" criterion requires an additional clarification: There are different ways in which a case might be said to be large, not all of which are pertinent to international mass claims. A dispute could be called "large" because there is a great deal of money at stake or because the issue is of great political importance, but this concept of size has little direct bearing on whether an IMCC is an optimal vehicle for resolving the dispute. It may be true, as with the IUSCT and UNCC, that large sums are also at stake, but, for present purposes, this is incidental. Cases like our three contemporary illustrations are "large" because of the number of different individual claims represented, not whether any or all of those individual claims is for a substantial sum.

Party structure: individual claimants or their states?

The second legal characteristic that IMCCs share is that the parties choose whether they will prosecute these many claims on behalf of their

---

[10] Algiers Accords, United States and Iran, 19 January 1981 (Algiers Accords), Article II, ¶ 1. Emphasis added.

[11] Article 3, ¶ 1. Article III of the Algiers Accords also created a special category of smaller claims under $250,000. As of May 2016, the IUSCT's workload totaled 3,936 claims filed. IUSCT Communiqué 16/1 (9 May 2016).

[12] The subject matter of an arbitration will typically reveal whether or not mass claims are contemplated. Commercial arbitrations, even when filed against a state, generally involve private interests. Even when large in dollar figures, the claim is not "mass" as we mean for the present context.

nationals, function as a conduit for those claims or create a framework for individuals to prosecute their own claims. Under conventional, historically grounded international law, the states were the parties to the case, not the victims. The states had an irrefutable right to represent their nationals, and the injured national had no basis in international law for refusing to recognize that representation. When an award was paid, it went to the state party, which could then use the money to pay the individual claims – or not – as it pleased.

IMCC litigation quietly challenges standard statist assumptions. In order to determine the existence or non-existence of a claim for compensation, the focus shifts to injured individuals and their claims. The state is still, of course, an important participant, and technically is still in most respects the party.[13] It is, after all, the states that negotiate these agreements, and one would not expect them to draft themselves right out of the control room.

At the same time, the state's role is implicitly redrawn as representing the claims of the victims, as opposed to presenting claims of its own. Such litigation takes on the appearance of a collection of claims of individuals, rather than a single claim filed for the benefit of the state. This is particularly so when the substance of a compensation case is based on contemporary international human rights or humanitarian law. From the modern point of view, it seems anomalous to assign legal ownership of a complaint for violation of human rights to a state, rather than to the individual whose human rights are at stake. The traditional concept of litigation as decisively state-centered is not explicitly rejected but is simply permitted to fade into the background.

The IMCC's implied repudiation of the conventional statist model leaves unclear exactly who the "parties" to a lawsuit are. However, regardless of the technical legal role of individual claimants, the claims of the real victims cannot easily be dismissed. The size of the case is measured by the number of individual claims that must be resolved, with less emphasis on dollar value or political importance.

In our three IMCCs, this issue played out in three different ways.[14] For the most part, the IUSCT dealt directly with individual claimants and their claims. Although we don't know precisely why this structure was chosen, it may have been dictated at least in part by the inducement previously discussed: the agreement by the United States to dismiss lawsuits pending in US courts, submit them to the IUSCT and confer

---

13 *Dames and Moore v. Regan*, 453 US 654 (1981).

14 Chapter 4 offers a detailed analysis of claimants in the three main IMCCs.

exclusive jurisdiction over the subject matter to the IUSCT. It may have been politically unpalatable to Washington to require individual litigants with pending lawsuits to substitute the United States as the party. Once the choice was made to allow those claimants to continue to "own" the claim, it would have been anomalous to create a subsequent group of claimants represented instead by the United States. The treatment was harmonized in favor of claimants, and each was allowed to bring its own claims, whenever filed.[15] To the extent that Iran or the United States was a party to a claim, it was either as a party to a so-called B case (official claims of one government against the other) or as a defendant in an individual claim.

The exception was a separate category of small claims of less than $250,000, which could, though need not, be brought by one of the governments. In the event, these claims proliferated and became a troublesome bottleneck. The US government eventually negotiated a comprehensive settlement on behalf of the claimants and paid compensation directly to the claimants through the US Foreign Claims Settlement Commission.[16]

The UNCC elected to use governments as intermediaries in processing each of the five categories of claims affecting individuals and corporations.[17] Nearly 100 governments collected claims from their nationals (and, if they chose, from their residents) for each of the relevant categories and consolidated them into a single claim per government. Once the compensation was approved, it was paid to the government for distribution to the claimants. Thirteen offices of three international organizations stepped into the government role for claimants who could not have their claims filed by their own governments (*e.g.*, refugees).

---

15 Algiers Accords, Article III, ¶ 3.

16 In addition to the unresolved small claims for less than $250,000, the agreement covered a block of small claims that the claimants had withdrawn from the IUSCT, a second block that the IUSCT had dismissed for lack of jurisdiction, and a third block that had been filed with the Department of State too late to meet the filing deadline. Also included were certain claims of the United States based on loans from the US Agency for International Development (USAID) to the former government of Iran. Under the terms of the agreement, Iran transferred $105 million to the United States in *en bloc* settlement of all of these categories of claims. Of the 3,066 claims filed, 1,066 received compensation. *See* Foreign Claims Settlement Commission of the US, Completed Programs: Iran, available at: https://www.justice.gov/fcsc/completed-programs-iran.

17 See also Chapter 4 for a detailed analysis of claimants and claims at the UNCC.

Governments also filed their own claims, including Kuwait's claim for environmental damages, which is the sole remaining unpaid claim.

The EECC framework agreement left open the possibility that claimants might file individual claims with the tribunal. This program never materialized, and the EECC relied on a purely diplomatic-representation model. Governments collected and submitted representative evidence to document general patterns of violations. Neither attempted to present this evidence as documenting the claims of a class in its entirety. In other instances, where a government had suffered direct harm (*e.g.*, the destruction of a power plant by bombing), the government was the claimant. The eventual damages award exposed one of the major flaws of the diplomatic representation model: The use of set-offs will ensure that neither government will receive an award that would fully compensate its nationals for the harm suffered, if the government did choose to pay the compensation rather than pocketing the award.

These and other consequences of adopting this model are discussed in Chapter 4 and Chapter 7.

Party autonomy and historical context

A third characteristic of the typical IMCC legal structure is that it draws on party autonomy to accommodate a particular historical context. In traditional judicial proceedings, the parties submit a dispute to a standing tribunal; its rules are fixed at some point in the past, through previous court decisions or by legislation. The body of applicable substantive law is likewise fixed. An arbitration, on the other hand, submits a dispute to an *ad hoc* tribunal; the decision makers are chosen, and the rules are drafted *after* the dispute arises.

The increased freedom of choice can induce parties to accept the perceived risk of submitting a claim to an undefined, unknown process. Allowing the parties some latitude in delimiting the substantive law that will apply, and leaving the procedural particulars open to negotiation, allows them to craft the most mutually advantageous arrangement, consistent with whatever exogenous constraints may apply.

Historical context can be very important in understanding the claims that IMCCs are tasked to deal with – claims relating to genocide, war, revolution or other mass disaster. Imagine in practical terms the variety of claims that could arise out of adjudicating one of these sorts of disputes, and how they might require different procedural norms. One IMCC might oversee the resolution of many small commercial claims established by documentary evidence, while a different one focuses on conduct causing personal injury but leaving no documentary trail. Still a third commission might address state-owned claims for deliberate destruction of public infrastructure, while a fourth relies on illiterate local residents to testify about looting or rape. In some cases, damages may be standardized and provable; in others, damages may reflect intangible harm for which no monetary value can accurately be assigned.

The commissioners will thus have full knowledge of the essence of the parties' versions of the dispute. This knowledge can be key because drafting applicable procedural rules and later interpreting them is the tribunal's job. This allows a tribunal to avoid some pitfalls of the "one-size-fits-all" structure of standing tribunals. In addition, the commissioners will have some appreciation of the parties' incentives to participate in the process and their objectives. A tribunal may need to be sensitive to a long and disputed history between two nation-states that predates the events giving rise to the IMCC. Parties may share few values or objectives, resulting in an atmosphere of pervasive mistrust and acrimony. Regardless of how they choose to accommodate these issues, the commissioners are nonetheless required to respect the terms of the arbitration agreement. In this respect, the parties (who drafted the agreement) retain some additional authority as well.

On a more practical level, the parties need not wholly reinvent the wheel. Where time is short or the parties wish to have some certainty on the general contours of the program, there are advantages to incorporating an established body of procedural or substantive rules into their agreement. In particular, the incorporation of procedural rules will allow the parties to defer agreement on important, but largely ancillary, technical details at what might be a delicate time in the negotiations. The agreement that established the IUSCT took this approach:

> Members of the Tribunal shall be appointed and the Tribunal shall conduct its business in accordance with the arbitration rules of the United Nations Commission on International Trade Law (UNCITRAL) except to the extent modified by the parties or by the Tribunal to ensure that this agreement can be carried out. The UNCITRAL rules for appointing members of three-member Tribunals shall apply *mutatis mutandis* to the appointment of the Tribunal.[18]

The arbitration agreement that led to the establishment of the EECC was similar:

> The Commission shall adopt its own rules of procedure based upon the 1992 Permanent Court of Arbitration Optional Rules for Arbitrating Disputes

[18] Algiers Accord, Article III, ¶ 2.

> Between Two States. All decisions of the Commission shall be made by a majority of the commissioners.[19]

Including these general provisions at the framework stage does more than merely save time and defer disagreement. As will be seen below, the incorporation of the UNCITRAL rules allowed the IUSCT to continue operating when the parties deadlocked on filling commissioner vacancies.

The parties also enjoy some – albeit perhaps more limited – freedom to delineate the substantive law that will apply to resolving their dispute. How they exercise this autonomy varies, but the implications can be profound.[20] They might indicate their choice by formulating a substantive standard, or they might indicate it by specifying the law of some

---

[19] Algiers Agreement, Article 5, ¶ 7. See also Article 4, ¶ 11 (dealing with the Boundary Commissions):

> 11. The Commission shall adopt its own rules of procedure based upon the 1992 Permanent Court of Arbitration Optional Rules for Arbitrating Disputes Between Two States. Filing deadlines for the parties' written submissions shall be simultaneous rather than consecutive. All decisions of the Commission shall be made by a majority of the commissioners.

[20] The effect of the parties' right to designate the applicable legal standard is further illustrated by the Algiers Agreement. In addition to the claims commission that we have been studying, the Algiers Agreement set up a boundary commission (the EEBC). The boundary was to be determined "on the basis of pertinent colonial treaties and applicable international law" and should reflect "the colonial treaty border" and "the borders existing at independence" as provided in the 1964 Cairo Declaration.

It is arguable that inclusion of the specified tests mandated a boundary different from the one that would be drawn in accordance simply with international law. Arguably, the "colonial treaty border" standard would have required the Boundary Commission to decide on the basis of treaties entered into in the first decade of the twentieth century, while the formulation "borders existing at independence" would have attached more importance to events and assumptions in the early 1960s. Most importantly, why would it have been necessary to preface the reference to "applicable international law" with the additional verbiage about "pertinent colonial treaties" unless that additional verbiage somehow made a difference? The language of Article 4 strongly suggests a departure from standard territorial principles.

In the final analysis, the EEBC's decision did not rely on any arguable differences between "colonial treaty boundary," "borders existing at independence" or delimitation according to "pertinent colonial treaties." The importance of the phrasing of the EEBC's mandate lies elsewhere. By incorporating these additional descriptors the Algiers Agreement implicitly confirmed that the parties have the right to reframe the international legal standard if they find another standard more substantively to their taste.

particular jurisdiction (or international law).[21] Whether that specific law might otherwise apply to a state actor is not relevant for these purposes; it is brought in to supply an agreed standard for resolving the dispute. For instance, in the Hanish Islands case (*Eritrea v. Yemen*), the parties agreed to application of the UNCLOS for purposes of delimiting their maritime boundary, even though only one of the parties (Yemen) was a member of UNCLOS.[22]

On other occasions, choice-of-law implications follow from the arbitration agreement's definition of the tribunal's mandate. The agreement that ended the Eritrea–Ethiopia border war described the tribunal's mandate in terms of international humanitarian law, including the 1949 Geneva Conventions, or other violations of international law.[23]

> (1) … The mandate of the Commission is to decide through binding arbitration all claims … (a) related to the conflict that was the subject of the Framework Agreement, the Modalities for its Implementation and the Cessation of Hostilities Agreement, and (b) *result from violations of international*

---

[21] International law is not the only source of substantive law that might be introduced to support recovery at an international mass claims commission. For certain IMCCs, domestic law may be the most important element necessary to establish the cause of action. Consider for example the Commission for Real Property Claims of Displaced Persons and Refugees (CRPC), dealing with the aftermath of the war in the former Yugoslavia. There were international law elements to the conflict, of course; all manner of violations of the laws of war and international humanitarian law took place, including genocide and ethnic cleansing, rape, murder of innocent civilians and others. But the violation that led to the establishment of this commission involved wrongful deprivation of real property. The CRPC was mandated with remedying (if only through a registry of deeds) the loss of homes occurring during the war through unlawful destruction or ethnic cleansing – and real property is undoubtedly a creature of domestic law.

[22] Arbitration Agreement dated 3 October 1996, between the Government of the State of Eritrea and the Government of the Republic of Yemen, at Article 2. ("The second stage shall result in an award delimiting maritime boundaries. The Tribunal shall decide taking into account the opinion that it will have formed on questions of territorial sovereignty, the United Nations Convention on the Law of the Sea, and any other pertinent factor.)

Yemen acceded to UNCLOS in July 1987; Eritrea has not become a party to the Convention. *See Chronological Lists of Ratifications of, Accessions and succession to the Convention and the Related Agreements*, United Nations, Division for Ocean Affairs and the Law of the Sea (accessed 25 November 2016), available at: http://www.un.org/Depts/los/reference_files/chronological_lists_of_ratifications.htm. This was, of course, not a mass claims case, but is brought in here for purposes of illustration.

[23] For an introduction to the EECC, see Chapter 1.

> *humanitarian law, including the 1949 Geneva Conventions, or other violations of international law.*[24]

The IUSCT seemingly recognized that it would be resolving commercial disputes with contractual choice-of-law provisions. Accordingly, the tribunal was given latitude to apply more general legal principles to the unusual factual circumstances that created the claims in the first instance:

> The Tribunal shall decide all cases on the basis of respect for law, applying such choice of law rules and principles of commercial and international law as the Tribunal determines to be applicable, taking into account relevant usages of the trade, contract provisions and changed circumstances.[25]

Where the parties specify the applicable law or provide a mutually agreed-upon substantive standard, their preference should ordinarily be binding. In unusual circumstances a tribunal might decline to enforce the parties' choice, but such situations are rare, probably at least in part because the parties are unlikely to agree upon a choice of law that is profoundly objectionable.[26] The arbitration agreement might instruct the commission to decide a case *ex aequo et bono*, that is, in accordance with equitable rather than strictly legal principles. A provision mandating decision according to "international law" does not authorize the application of equitable norms, unless the parties specify that this is their intention. A decision *ex aequo et bono* is more difficult to predict than a decision on strictly legal grounds because the commissioners are permitted to take a much wider range of considerations into account, including their moral (rather than legal) opinions. The added risk would probably deter most states from agreeing to have their case decided this way and the arbitration agreement may expressly prohibit it.[27] A mutual preference for equitable resolution, expressed in the agreement, ought to be honored, but if unexpressed it should not be inferred.

---

[24] The EECC was further mandated to apply "relevant rules of international law." Emphasis added.

[25] Algiers Accord, Article 5.

[26] If they, in fact, did agree on objectionable principles, the doctrine of *jus cogens* might arguably apply to invalidate that choice.

[27] For instance, the EECC, which did "not have the power to make decisions *ex aequo et bono*."

Autonomy and Adjudication

There are obvious advantages to having available a dispute-resolution mechanism that contributes to geopolitical stability by addressing the harm caused by an armed or diplomatic conflict between nation-states.[28] If, however, that mechanism is perceived (correctly or not) as unfair, unwieldy or ineffective, nation-states may elect to pursue their conflict to its conclusion. Fortunately, party autonomy, which remains the central advantage of an IMCC, is a powerful inducement to choose third-party adjudication over continued conflict. It allows state-parties to eliminate many of the shortcomings of rigid legal structures that might cause a more traditional judicial proceeding to collapse under its own weight. They may adopt whatever rules of processing are suitable for the scale of the program; they may elect to represent their nationals or simply to create the mechanism and allow it to operate.

The parties may therefore incorporate the substantive legal norms and principles of decision-making that are helpful and exclude those that are not. They may borrow what has worked in a predecessor program and reject what has not. They can be creative or they can be conservative. Importantly for our next section, states may prescribe a detailed legal and operational structure in advance, or they may establish a more general framework that they trust to discharge the mandate efficiently and fairly.

THE OPERATING STRUCTURE

As we have shown above, parties that have settled on an IMCC to address a particular political, legal and factual context will have done so in part due to the exceptional flexibility the mechanism allows. In this section, we cover some of the issues that arise in translating that legal and operational flexibility into a functioning program that retains the trust and participation of the state parties. We will also discuss a fourth IMCC to more fully flesh out the basic discussion. The Commission for Real Property Claims of Displaced Persons and Refugees (CRPC), which restored real property to owners who had been dispossessed during ethnic cleansing in the Balkan conflict, left a helpful record of how to structure an IMCC in an area where the conflict occurred. The CRPC offers useful insight on the challenges faced by an IMCC that was a small and

---

[28] Whether the vehicle has broader application to different sorts of mass harms, such as those due to changes in climate, is explored more fully in Chapter 8.

underfunded piece of a comprehensive solution to address a large and complex problem.

The IUSCT, EECC and CRPC were created by or with state parties in order to fully air and resolve the claims of governments, individuals and corporations harmed by a diplomatic or military conflict. The state parties negotiated the fundamental aspects of how each program was to be constituted and conducted, but they delegated the majority of the details to the commissioners themselves. The UNCC, on the other hand, is "not a court or an arbitral tribunal before which the parties appear; it is a political organ."[29] The program operates under the auspices of the UN Security Council and is structured accordingly. Its mandate is to determine whether each claim falls within the scope of Iraq's deemed liability and, if so, how much is owed. Iraq was a spectator when the commission was created, with no direct say in how it was set up or in how it was to be run.[30]

The Basic Structure

The IMCCs discussed here were established, variously, by a standalone arbitration agreement, a comprehensive peace treaty and a United Nations resolution. Despite these differing origins, the commissions' framework documents are similar in one key respect: They do not address the particulars of the commission's structure in any detail.[31] This omission may reflect the time pressure under which negotiations were finalized; a strategic agreement to defer controversial issues that would derail negotiations; or a desire to preserve party autonomy until more is known about the contours of the program.[32]

[29] UN Secretary-General, Report Pursuant to Paragraph 19 of Security Council Resolution 687 (1991), ¶ 20, UN Doc S/2255.

[30] It was, however, given a non-voting seat in the governing council and an opportunity to respond to submissions on behalf of claimants, which allowed it to indirectly influence some of the findings.

[31] For instance, the section of the Algiers Accords that created the Iran–US Claims Tribunal, finalized in the waning hours of the Carter Administration, is just over three pages long. For the text, *see* http://www.parstimes.com/history/algiers_accords.pdf.

[32] This ambiguity can bite in unexpected ways. For instance, Eritrea and Ethiopia sharply disagreed on whether the EECC would be properly seized of *jus ad bellum* claims that had been delegated to another commission. The EECC eventually assumed jurisdiction over the claims, although the decision has not been uncontroversial. *See, e.g.,* Christine Gray, "The Eritrea/Ethiopia Claims

At some point, the parties to any IMCC will need to begin the process of eliminating ambiguity and fleshing out the structure. Much of this work will fall to the small group of lawyers tasked with getting the program underway – typically, the parties' representatives and the appointed commissioners. The threshold step is creating an entity to make operational, administrative and financial decisions, with the legal capacity to implement them. This process begins with the appointment of commissioners, who may then set up a Secretariat to provide administrative, operational and legal support to the commissioners in the formation stage and beyond. We discuss each of these functions in turn.

The Commissioners

Who they are

The primary role of the commissioners is judicial: They apply the governing law to a factual record in order to resolve claims. In all but the largest programs (*e.g.*, the UNCC), the commissioners will also be responsible for some degree of operational oversight – similar to the board of directors of a corporation. Because a program's success depends on the IMCC being constituted and operated in a way that the parties see as balanced and unbiased, the arbitration agreement will generally include some guidance about composition, appointment and leadership of the commissioners, as well as some guidance as to how they will make decisions.

How they are selected

Normal practice is to avoid deadlock by creating a commission composed of an odd number of commissioners. Of these seats, an even number is typically allocated to the state parties to select the commissioners they desire, with the remaining commissioners appointed either by consensus or by a neutral third party. The EECC illustrates the basic model: Each state party had the right to appoint two commissioners, and those four commissioners appointed a President. The IUSCT agreement set up a similar framework, but with some additional flexibility.[33] The original tribunal consisted of nine members, with each state party allotted three

---

Commission Oversteps its Boundaries: A Partial Award?" (2006) 17 *European Journal of International Law* 699.

[33] The IUSCT eventually did most of its work in three three-person panels and met in plenary session when required to by the Algiers Accords (*i.e.*, Christopher Pinto, "Institutional Aspects of the Tribunal," in David D. Caron and John R. Crook (eds), *The Iran–United States Claims Tribunal and the Process of*

commissioners, and these six commissioners selecting the remaining three. The state parties could by agreement increase the tribunal by multiples of three. In order to process claims more quickly, the President could partition the tribunal into three-commissioner chambers, which could operate simultaneously and thereby triple the overall claims-processing capacity. Any enlargement of the tribunal or partition into panels was required to maintain the original 1:1:1 ratio between party-appointed and "neutral" commissioners.[34]

The mechanism used by the CRPC provided for equal representation but also borrowed the corporate-law construct of staggered terms. Of the nine-member commission, the Federation of Bosnia and Herzegovina appointed four members – two to a three-year term and two to a four-year term. The Republika Srbska had the right to appoint two members – one to a three-year term and one to a four-year term. This allocation facilitated ethnic balance: two Serbs, two Bosnians and two Croats,[35] who could be, but were not required to be, replaced at the end of their terms. Perhaps given the fragile relationship among the state parties, the CRPC did not rely on party agreement for the appointment of the remaining three members. These commissioners were instead appointed to full five-year terms by the President of the European Court of Human Rights (who also had the power to appoint one of them as President).

It is generally prudent to include in the arbitration agreement a backstop appointment mechanism to appoint commissioners or fill vacancies when the state parties disagree. The only drawback to consider is whether the mechanism removes an incentive for commissioners and state parties to work together. The IUSCT, for instance, began its work in the immediate aftermath of a protracted crisis that had resulted in a complete diplomatic break between the two state parties. There was no independent diplomatic or political channel to rebuild a working relationship between Iran and the United States. Mistrust persisted, and conflict

International Claims Resolution: A Study by the Panel on State Responsibility of the American Society of International Law (ASIL, 2000), 101.

[34] IMCCs use different terms to refer to commissioners who are either appointed by state-party consensus or by a non-party. We use the terms "international commissioner," "neutral commissioners" and "non-party commissioner" interchangeably.

[35] *See* Commission for Real Property Claims of Displaced Persons and Refugees (CRPC): End of Mandate Report: Executive Summary (1996–2003), 2.

occasionally threatened to derail the program.[36] Each party was initially able to appoint commissioners who were able to agree on the remaining three,[37] but keeping the panel at full strength was to prove a continual challenge. Party-appointed arbitrators at the IUSCT often found that agreement was elusive unless there were two open seats and some sort of *quid pro quo* available.[38] The decision to apply the appointing authority mechanism from the UNCITRAL Model Law[39] to the IUSCT has been cited as indispensable to the ability of the tribunal to function, particularly given the misaligned incentives of the state parties to ensure that the tribunal functioned smoothly.[40]

The mechanism may not ever be needed. The EECC, for instance, specified that the UN Secretary-General would step in to make any appointment (*i.e.*, commissioner or President) that had not been made by

---

[36] The nadir was the 1984 assault on Judge Mångard by two Iranian arbitrators, but one US commissioner has also written about "the pervasive Iranian tactics of verbal and psychological abuse to which most, if not all, of the presiding arbitrators have been subject." George Aldrich, "The Selection of Arbitrators," in Caron and Crook (eds), *The Iran–United States Claims Tribunal and the Process of International Claims Resolution*, 65. Or, as Caron and Crook succinctly observed: "The tribunal has not dealt effectively with conflict." "Tribunals as Institutions," in *The Iran–United States Claims Tribunal*, 6.

[37] This process was not without some strategic behavior by the arbitrators themselves. Each side came up with a slate of names, few of whom appeared on both lists. The US arbitrators were concerned that agreement to any Iranian suggestion would not be reciprocated and therefore felt that some sort of "linkage" was required. Aldrich, "The Selection of Arbitrators," 69.

[38] Aldrich, "The Selection of Arbitrators," 71.

[39] The United Nations Commission on International Trade Law (UNCITRAL) Model Law on International Commercial Arbitration (1985), with amendments as adopted in 2010, is a set of model rules that the parties can agree will govern the conduct of an arbitration. The appointing authority is a mechanism that steps in to delegate the appointment of an arbitrator to a third party when the parties cannot agree. The parties may either agree an appointing authority or, if none has been agreed, either party may ask the Secretary-General of the Permanent Court of Arbitration in The Hague to make the appointment. *See* UNICTRAL Model Law, at Article 6 (designation of appointing authority), and at Articles 8–10 and 14 (appointment of arbitrators).

[40] "Had there been no such institution, resignations would have imperiled the very existing of the Tribunal. Moreover, as the Americans generally saw more need for a continually functioning Tribunal than did the Iranians, we would have been under intense pressure to agree to Iranian candidates about whom we entertained serious reservations." Aldrich, "The Selection of Arbitrators," 71.

the applicable deadline.[41] The state parties quickly appointed a panel, which proceeded to take up and complete its work over a six-year period with no vacancies. The CRPC did not include a mechanism to fill party-appointed vacancies. It might have been more prudent to have included the mechanism, but only one vacancy (which went unfilled for the final two years of the CRPC) occurred during the seven years the program operated, and that single vacancy does not appear to have impeded the CRPC from fulfilling its mandate.[42]

The UNCC – which was not the product of a bilateral negotiation between state parties – eventually modeled itself on existing allocations of power within the United Nations. The resolution creating the UNCC contained nothing beyond the fact of the commission and a broad statement of its jurisdiction. It was up to the Secretary-General to draft a report to flesh out the working structure of this mammoth enterprise, which ultimately processed 2.7 million claims for an asserted value of $352.2 billion. The Secretary-General set up a tiered governance structure, consisting of a "policy-making level" and a "functional level."[43] The UNCC, which is now in its final phase, is overseen by the policy-making entity, known as the Governing Council. The Governing Council is a 15-member body that mirrors the composition of the 15-member UN Security Council. China, France, the Russian Federation, the United Kingdom and the United States are permanent members, with 10 non-permanent members selected by the UN General Assembly for two-year terms. The terms of the non-permanent members are staggered so that five are replaced each year. The members are nominated from a register of presumptively qualified candidates maintained by the Secretary-General.[44]

The governing council, in turn, is assisted by three-member panels of expert commissioners who focus on the "functional" work of verifying and evaluating claims and preparing recommendations for governing

---

[41] Algiers Agreement, Article 4; *see also*, Eritrea–Ethiopia Claims Commission, Rules of Procedure, Article 7.

[42] Commission for Real Property Claims of Displaced Persons and Refugees (CRPC): End of Mandate Report: Executive Summary (1996–2003), 9.

[43] UN Secretary-General, Report Pursuant to Paragraph 19 of Security Council Resolution 687 (1991), ¶ 4, UN Doc S/2255.

[44] UN Secretary-General, Report Pursuant to Paragraph 19.

council approval.[45] Commissioners are appointed pursuant to nominations made by the Secretary-General on an *ad hoc*, as-needed basis and confirmed by the Governing Council.[46] There were 19 total panels of "functional" commissioners appointed to review the claims. Candidates were chosen by the Secretariat, usually from a registry it maintained for that purpose, and then confirmed by the Governing Council.[47]

Qualities – necessary and preferred

The expectation of an IMCC is that providing some measure of justice to a large group of claimants can help create long-term political stability and peace. This process requires a collegial group of open-minded, consensus-seeking individuals who have the time and expertise to ensure a fair hearing and equitable outcome. Identifying and appointing commissioners who have the necessary qualities is an important undertaking.

The starting point for creating a list of candidates will be the arbitration agreement, which may, but frequently does not, contain guidance about the minimum required qualities.[48] Whatever statement is included at such a preliminary phase of the program is often obvious or too general to be useful.[49] The agreement might also set out some disqualifications, which tend to constrain commissioner nationality in

---

45 UN Compensation Commission Governing Council, Decision taken by the Governing Council of the United Nations Compensation Commission at the 27th meeting, Sixth session (26 June 1992), Article 18, UN Doc S/AC.26/1992/10.

46 UN Compensation Commission Governing Council, Decision taken by the Governing Council of the United Nations Compensation Commission at the 27th meeting, Sixth session (26 June 1992), Article 20, UN Doc S/AC.26/1992/10.

47 UN Compensation Commission Governing Council, Decision taken by the Governing Council of the United Nations Compensation Commission at the 27th meeting, Sixth session (26 June 1992), Article 20, UN Doc S/AC.26/1992/10.

48 The UNCC, which would need a deep bench of candidates to draw on over a long period, eventually set out a list of characteristics to be considered. These included geographical representation, professional qualifications, relevant expertise and experience in the particular subject matter of a claim, and experience and integrity. UN Compensation Commission Governing Council, Decision taken by the Governing Council of the United Nations Compensation Commission at the 27th meeting, Sixth session (26 June 1992), Article 19, UN Doc S/AC.26/1992/10.

49 For instance, the agreement establishing the CRPC stated that commissioners should be of "high moral standing." General Framework Agreement for Peace in Bosnia and Herzegovina Dayton, The Republic of Bosnia and Herzegovina, the Republic of Croatia and the Federal Republic of Yugoslavia (Dayton Accords), Annex 7, at Article IX, ¶ 2, 14 December 1995.

order to give effect to the parties' agreement on geographical representation. For instance, the EECC arbitration agreement prohibited the participation of nationals or permanent residents of a state party.[50] The IUSCT and CRPC agreements were silent on nationality, but each was structured to allow but not require the state parties to appoint their own nationals (which they did), and to result in the selection of non-state-party nationals for the remaining positions. The UNCC took no position other than that each member of a panel should have a different nationality from the others.[51] As a result, the 59 panel commissioners appointed represented 40 different nationalities (with the Governing Council constituted to mirror the UN Security Council).[52]

Professional qualifications Arbitration agreements establishing international claims commissions are usually silent on professional qualifications, including whether a commissioner must be a qualified lawyer.[53] The arbitration agreements discussed in this chapter are no exception. Nevertheless, with the exception of the UNCC (discussed below), there is no obvious advantage in appointing a layperson to an essentially legal role, and these positions are almost always filled by trained lawyers.[54] Beyond the basic legal qualification, however, no credential exists to certify a candidate as presumptively qualified. Consequently, the vetting process will generally be thorough and painstaking. Even in a professional community as small as public international arbitration, it can take some effort to identify a pool of candidates who are capable and, equally important, willing to consider the appointment.

We can only speculate about what intangible qualities a state party seeks in its commissioners. There is no obvious incentive to make these deliberations public; in fact, there is some risk of contributing to

---

[50] Algiers Agreement, at Article 5, ¶ 2.

[51] UN Compensation Commission Governing Council, Decision taken by the Governing Council of the United Nations Compensation Commission at the 27th meeting, Sixth session (26 June 1992), Article 28, UN Doc S/AC.26/1992/10.

[52] UN Secretary-General, Report Pursuant to Paragraph 19.

[53] In domestic arbitration, non-lawyers may be appointed as arbitrators to ensure that a panel has the relevant expertise to deal with a particular dispute. For example, a claim arising out of misstatement of a financial statement in a securities law claim might be best handled by a panel that includes at least one accountant.

[54] To the extent that some sort of non-legal expertise might be required, the panel will typically rely on the parties to adduce evidence from experts, and the arbitration agreement might allow the commissioners to also engage third-party experts. The role of experts is discussed below.

sensitivities that appointments are based more on the sympathies of a prospective commissioner than on legal acumen. However, the IUSCT can offer insight into how party-appointed commissioners might go about nominating neutral commissioners.

The United States appointed its commissioners to the IUSCT relatively quickly. These US commissioners then compiled a consolidated list of candidates for consideration as third-party commissioners. They consulted law professors, judges, experienced arbitrators and the US government in order to produce a comprehensive list. They next created a short list of potential third-party commissioners who possessed the relevant expertise and whose reputations both state parties might find acceptable. Vetting consisted of exhaustive reviews of each individual's public record, as well as interviews with colleagues and with the candidate himself or herself. At the same time, the Iranian commissioners were going through their own process of compiling a list of acceptable neutral commissioners. After lists were exchanged, there was a process of bargaining that eventually led to three neutral appointments – two Swedish and one French.[55]

The world has moved only slightly since the 1980s. Some of the preliminary work of identifying and eliminating candidates can now be done through online searches of public information. Nevertheless, the strategic task of identifying and interviewing candidates to determine those with a reasonable chance of being acceptable to the other party will always require a hands-on approach. There is no way to conduct this exercise without a series of personal interviews and a degree of political savvy in anticipating the other state party's preferences.

The UNCC came at the task of assessing minimum qualifications differently. Neither the governing council nor the panels of commissioners required the appointment of lawyers. The governing council drew on a larger and more diverse talent pool because it was a policy-making entity: It decided political, administrative and financial matters (*e.g.*, the mechanism for determining the level of Iraq's contribution to the compensation fund). Decisions that had a legal dimension were generally limited to *pro forma* approvals of recommendations made by a "functional" panel of commissioners. Legal training was not required for appointment as a panel commissioner. As will be seen below, the UNCC appointed commissioners who were experts in "fields such as finance,

---

55 Aldrich, "The Selection of Arbitrators," 68–69.

law, accountancy, insurance, [and] environmental damage assessment,"[56] depending upon the requirements of any particular claim.

Relevant expertise and experience An IMCC routinely deals with specialized, arcane and complex issues concerning how international law applies to state actors. Panels should comprise practitioners or academics with backgrounds in international law, preferably with practical experience in state-to-state proceedings. Relevant experience might include representing a party before, or acting as an arbitrator at, the Permanent Court of Arbitration, the International Court of Justice or the International Criminal Court.

An additional criterion to consider is whether a candidate comes from the civil or the common-law tradition. These traditions have different ideas about certain relevant issues, such as whether one party is to assist the other in establishing an evidentiary record. International arbitrations generally require one or more neutral commissioners on a panel, which – given the relative dearth of common-law jurisdictions[57] – will tend to result in a mix of common- and civil-law-trained commissioners. The flexibility inherent in most IMCCs will allow commissioners to work through the different approaches when they conflict, but the state parties who created the program might prefer one approach over the other. Commissioners with some experience in international arbitration will have been exposed to the practical and theoretical aspects of navigating these differences.

Additional areas of expertise that might be necessary or useful can be gleaned by looking to the substantive law specified by the parties and the expected nature of the claims. This may involve some educated guesswork until the point at which claims come in and details emerge. At the more straightforward end of the spectrum, the CRPC commissioners were asked to ratify findings made under Bosnian law regarding the ownership of real property. This required expertise in local law, which came from the party-appointed ("national") commissioners. The CRPC noted in its final report that the national commissioners were indispensable to the process.[58]

---

[56] UN Secretary-General, Report Pursuant to Paragraph 19.

[57] They are Australia, Barbados, Brunei, Canada, England and Wales, Hong Kong, India, Malaysia, New Zealand, Northern Ireland, Pakistan, Republic of Ireland, Scotland, Singapore, South Africa, Sri Lanka and the United States.

[58] *See* Commission for Real Property Claims of Displaced Persons and Refugees (CRPC): End of Mandate Report: Executive Summary (1996–2003), 9:

The EECC represents a more complex example. The commission was asked to apply international humanitarian law to claims arising out of an armed conflict. While international humanitarian law is certainly a recognized area of expertise, the claims that materialized ranged from the expected (treatment of POWs) to the attenuated (indirect damage to the economy of a state party) to the genuinely novel (denationalization of a generation of native-born citizens who were declared enemy aliens and expelled). The commissioners relied on the parties to develop legal arguments and an evidentiary record to complement their considerable and varied experience.

The IUSCT was largely a commercial dispute-resolution mechanism. The law was generally that of the relevant contract, augmented by conflicts of law analysis to resolve inconsistencies and fill gaps. Nevertheless, the sweep of the claims and parties was sufficiently broad that the tribunal dealt with significant issues of international law and sovereignty, including a line of cases analysing the concept of dominant and effective nationality;[59] a dispute about whether the United States had honored its commitment to ensure that matters decided by the IUSCT were not re-litigated in US courts;[60] and the question of whether the United States had issued Treasury regulations inconsistent with its obligations under the arbitration agreement.[61]

Of the four IMCCs discussed in this chapter, the UNCC processed the largest and most complex set of claims. At the same time, it played the narrowest legal role. The UNCC was charged with compensating "under international law … any direct loss, damage, including environmental damage and the depletion of natural resources, or injury to foreign governments, nationals and corporations, as a result of Iraq's unlawful invasion and occupation of Kuwait."[62] Other than a cluster of issues surrounding causation, the panel commissioners were relieved of addressing issues surrounding jurisdiction and liability that other commissions dealt with regularly. Accordingly, the UNCC appointed international

---

"One of CRPC's strengths was its National Commissioners. Extensive employment of national staff and national legal experts engenders cooperative efforts among disparate groups of claimants, and serves as local buy-in for decisions taken."

[59] *Islamic Republic of Iran v. United States*, Decision 6 April 1984, 5 Iran–US CTR 251.

[60] *Islamic Republic of Iran v. United States*, Cases Nos. A15 and A24, Award No. 602-A15 (2014).

[61] *Esphahanian v. Bank Tejarat*, 2 Iran–US CTR 157 (1983).

[62] SC Res 687, ¶ 16 (3 April 1991).

lawyers, but also international professionals with the relevant expertise for the particular category of claim that was allocated to a particular panel.[63]

The UNCC is the exception among IMCCs in including non-legal expertise on the panel itself. In most cases, IMCCs that must decide non-legal issues requiring specialized knowledge must look outside the commission for expert input. Typically, IMCCs rely primarily on the participants to adduce whatever expert evidence proves a particular assertion, and on the adversarial process to tease out the relevant issues. The IUSCT was required to use this approach exclusively; it made its awards on evidence adduced by claimants without engaging third-party experts.

Where the adversarial process comes up short, IMCCs may have the option of engaging third-party experts to provide whatever evidence or analysis is lacking. In practice, this avenue is rarely invoked, but it appears wise to have it available. The EECC, for example, was authorized in the framework document to "retain consultants and experts to facilitate the expeditious completion of its work."[64] The EECC procedural rules fleshed out a process for engaging experts and affording the state parties an opportunity to be heard, but, like the IUSCT, the EECC ultimately relied on the record created by the state parties. The CRPC had the authority to "receive assistance from international and nongovernmental organizations, in their areas of special expertise falling within the mandate of the [CRPC]."[65] In the event, the "expertise" of the CRPC was in-house. It successfully created a local staff that "maximized usage of national experts who brought invaluable knowledge of the national languages, structures, legal systems and laws."[66]

Temperament and character Expertise alone has little value without the ability to function in a difficult, uncertain and high-stakes environment. IMCCs do not deal with discrete controversies brought by private

---

[63] In particular, the UNCC was looking for commissioners with expertise "in fields such as finance, law, accounting, insurance, environmental damage assessment, oil, trade and engineering." UN Compensation Commission Governing Council, Decision taken by the Governing Council of the United Nations Compensation Commission at the 27th meeting, Sixth session (26 June 1992), Article 28, UN Doc S/AC.26/1992/10.

[64] Algiers Agreement, at Article 5, ¶ 6.

[65] Dayton Accords, Annex 7, Chapter 2, Article X, ¶ 4.

[66] Commission for Real Property Claims of Displaced Persons and Refugees (CRPC): End of Mandate Report: Executive Summary (1996–2003), 2.

parties before a standing institution designed to provide due process. They are *ad hoc* structures designed by the parties to the dispute, and, importantly, they are voluntary. The participation of state parties depends on their continual subjective determination that the IMCC is functioning consistently with their *ex ante* expectations.

Commissioners routinely confront unique legal issues that can have implications for large groups of claimants, for political stability and for the conduct of nations. There may be no obvious correct answer to a problem, and it will be up to the commissioners to arrive at the best solution. The relationship between the parties may be so acrimonious that professional decorum is abandoned. The post requires, as Judge George Aldrich noted when discussing the IUSCT, "good judgment, a judicial temperament (by which I mean instinctive fairness, patience, and objectivity), experience in both commercial and international law, reasonable attention to detail, and psychological toughness to ensure that threats and bullying tactics are ineffective."[67]

An IMCC that allows the state parties a say in appointing commissioners will need to balance the political or ideological preferences of those state parties with an appointment process that eliminates undue bias. Concerns about bias are ameliorated somewhat by the battery of rules and norms applicable to a lawyer participating in a public international arbitration.[68] Attorneys appearing in any proceeding or transaction are ethically required to identify and eliminate conflicts of interest before agreeing to the representation. Because these norms are not enforceable by third parties, tribunals may choose to go a step further and incorporate ethical guidelines regarding conflicts of interest into their rules of procedure, together with a mechanism to allow limited challenges of arbitrators for bias.[69]

---

67 Aldrich, "The Selection of Arbitrators," 72.

68 The array of rules and norms applicable to a lawyer participating in a public international arbitration is a large topic. They may include the lawyer's home jurisdiction, the seat of the arbitration, the place where the hearing takes place, and the location of the controversy being arbitrated. *See Guidelines on Party Representation in International Arbitration*, International Bar Association, Preamble.

69 *See, e.g.,* the EECC procedural rules, which required a prospective arbitrator to disclose "any circumstances likely to give rise to justifiable doubts as to his/her impartiality or independence" and allowed a state party to challenge an arbitrator if those circumstances have not been disclosed before the appointment is made. Rules of Procedure, Eritrea–Ethiopia Claims Commission, at Articles 4 and 5. *See also*, Rules of Procedure, Iran–US Claims Tribunal, at Article 9–12, which also provided that an arbitrator could abstain from hearing

The President or Chair

Arbitration agreements generally say little about the president (a term we will use interchangeably with chair), other than to establish the position and remove the state parties from direct participation in the appointment.[70] Despite the lack of detail, the position is important: In addition to acting in a legal capacity as a full commissioner, the president will be responsible for ensuring that a claims commission runs smoothly and fairly. The president will need the legal expertise to operate as a commissioner, the managerial ability to oversee senior staff, and the diplomatic skill to command the respect of all participants.

Selection

The selection of a president may be either a consensus appointment of a mutually agreeable candidate by party-appointed commissioners, as was done in the EECC and the IUSCT, or a designation by a non-party institution or individual, as in the CRPC. In each case, whatever conflict-of-interest norms and challenge mechanisms ensure the impartiality and objectivity of a commissioner will apply equally to the appointment of the president. The UNCC, as ever, operates by different rules. The Governing Council elects its own President and two Vice-Presidents, each for two-year terms. These positions have historically been held by non-permanent members of the UN Security Council.

As with commissioners generally, and for the same reasons, little is known about the deliberations of IMCC participants in selecting a

individual cases for the same reason. The UNCC specified that a prospective commissioner could not have a financial interest in any claim submitted to that commissioner or a panel on which that commissioner sat. UN Compensation Commission Governing Council, Decision taken by the Governing Council of the United Nations Compensation Commission at the 27th meeting, Sixth session (26 June 1992), Article 21, UN Doc S/AC.26/1992/10. Article 22 created an express obligation of disclosure of any fact that could give rise to "justifiable doubts about impartiality or independence."

[70] EECC: "The president of the Commission shall be selected by the party-appointed arbitrators … [and] shall be neither a national nor permanent resident of either party."), *Rules of Procedure*, Eritrea–Ethiopia Claims Commission, at Article 5, ¶ 3. IUSCT: ("[T]he [party-appointed] members shall by mutual agreement select the remaining third of the members and appoint one of the remaining third President."), *Rules of Procedure*, Iran–US Claims Tribunal, at Article III, ¶ 1. CRPC: "The President of the European Court of Human Rights shall appoint the remaining members … and shall designate one such member as the Chairman." Dayton Accords, Annex 7, at Article IX, ¶ 1.

President. What little we know comes from the IUSCT, where the US-appointed commissioners identified candidate-neutral commissioners with an eye toward eventually having to agree with their Iran-appointed counterparts on a President:

> In the background [of the process of selecting three neutral commissioners] there also lurked the question of the President, in particular, whether that should be part of the initial deal on appointments or whether it should be negotiated only after agreement had been reached on the three appointments. While the powers of the President were limited … [they] seemed important enough to make the decision one of substance.[71]

The President as manager

As will be seen below under "The Secretariat/Registry," an IMCC can choose the degree to which the tribunal will directly oversee the IMCC's operations. Unless the operations are entirely outsourced to a standing body, there will be some oversight, which typically falls to the president. Administrative tasks generally include working with the Secretariat on the management of claims, scheduling and conduct of filings and hearings, the composition of smaller chambers, the assignment of cases, preparation and notification of awards to parties and payment agents, and whatever other powers the commissioners might conclude are "inherent in the office."[72] Operational oversight will usually entail interaction with staff on dozens of matters related to making sure the commission has the appropriate financial arrangements, staff, office space, supplies, equipment and technology to conduct its business.

---

71 Aldrich, "The Selection of Arbitrators," 69.

72 *See e.g.,* Pinto, "Institutional Aspects of the Tribunal," 101–102.

Acting pursuant to Article III of the Claims Settlement Declaration, and exceptionally, in the exercise of powers inherent in the office, the President makes provision for the orderly performance of the Tribunal's functions through "Presidential Orders" and other forms of directives. Presidential Orders have made provision for, *inter alia*, rules applicable to reallocation of work among chambers, or between a chamber and the Full Tribunal; designation of a chamber that is not in recess to deal with, in addition to its own work, any requests for interim measures and any other urgent matters that might arise in cases before the Full Tribunal or another chamber; substitution of a Party-Appointed Member of a chamber temporarily absent or indisposed by a Member of another chamber appointed by the same party, or in similar circumstances, for suspension of proceedings, for the constitutional of a Special Chamber to deal with certain issues, and for dissolution of that Chamber.

The President as diplomat

In addition to the management role, a president's ability to function as a leader and a diplomat will be key. The president will ideally manage the process of arriving at decisions that all commissioners support. Decisions to be made will range from *ad hoc* decisions on points of procedure during a hearing, to the outcome of a multi-million-dollar claim, to approval of a periodic budget, to large capital expenditures.

Although IMCCs are generally structured to make legal and operational decisions by majority vote, the preference is for consensus in order to avoid the appearance of divided or seemingly politicized decisions.[73] The EECC, for instance, went beyond its arbitration agreement to include in its procedural rules a non-binding statement that it would strive for unanimity.[74] Ironically, the only decision that departed from consensus was a dissent by President van Houtte in a claim involving the bombing of a civilian power plant by the Ethiopian Air Force.[75] The CRPC adopted decisions by majority, with the party-appointed commissioners meeting periodically between plenary sessions "to review draft decision proposals, discuss particular claims if necessary and exchange views on other matters of importance."[76] The IUSCT, on the other hand, was too complex and the workload too large to function by consensus. The full chamber met only to deal with cases or issues arising under paragraph 3 of Article II (regarding assets of the former Shah in the United States) and paragraph 4 of Article VI of the Claims Settlement Declaration (concerning the interpretation of the agreement). Three-person chambers heard and decided individual cases.[77] All of these entities made decisions by majority vote.

---

[73] Paradoxically, consistent unanimity can give the appearance that cases are not necessarily being decided solely on the merits but on some sort of "horse trading" of individual claims in order to ensure an artificially balanced overall result.

[74] *Rules of Procedure*, Eritrea–Ethiopia Claims Commission, Article 18, ¶ 2. The President was authorized to make procedural determinations when there was no majority view or when authorized by the panel. *Rules of Procedure*, Article 18, ¶ 3.

[75] Eritrea–Ethiopia Claims Commission, Separate Opinion of the President Relating to Eritrea's Claim 25, Aerial Bombardment of Hirgigo Power Station (19 December 2005), 3.

[76] Commission for Real Property Claims of Displaced Persons and Refugees (CRPC): End of Mandate Report: Executive Summary (1996–2003), 9. During plenary sessions, the party-appointed commissioners presented a report to the full commission.

[77] Pinto, "Institutional Aspects of the Tribunal," 97.

The 15-member UNCC governing council rules provide for decisions by a nine-person majority, except with regard to ensuring that payments are made to the compensation fund, which must be either decided by consensus or referred to the Security Council.[78] The right of veto, which is held by the five permanent members of the Security Council, is expressly denied to the Governing Council. In the event, the Governing Council has operated entirely by consensus. The guidelines also allow the Governing Council to invite nations that have "a particular interest in its work to participate with a vote in its discussions."[79] The governing council invoked this provision to allow Iraq to participate in nearly all of its meetings.

The president also maintains the working relationship with and, to the extent possible, between the parties. Procedural rules, which help manage expectations and ensure smooth workflow, can usually be varied by party agreement. A party may request a change that will be mutually advantageous (*e.g.*, a relaxation of an unrealistic deadline), but it is equally likely that one state party might seek a unilateral accommodation that is substantively trivial (*e.g.*, the waiver of a notice formality that has been overlooked), but requires a generosity that might not be reciprocated if positions were reversed. While the easy legal answer might be to simply reject the request, the president may attempt to broker an agreement that the parties find fair and reasonable.

The Secretariat/Registry

Regardless of how much care goes into vetting and appointing commissioners, they will generally have neither the time nor the appetite required to create or micromanage a large bureaucracy. Quickly appointing competent, experienced administrators to establish a Secretariat and delegating to them the appropriate operational and legal authority to begin work will free the commissioners to focus on legal issues. The process of creating an administrative infrastructure begins with establishing a Secretariat, which will be responsible for quickly getting the equivalent of a small business up and running.

The Secretariat takes responsibility for the operational aspects – finding and furnishing suitable premises, hiring adequate staff with the

[78] Although the governing council was set up to mirror the UN Security Council in many respects, this does not include the unilateral veto power enjoyed by the UN Security Council's permanent members.

[79] UN Secretary-General, Report Pursuant to Paragraph 19 of Security Council Resolution 687 (1991), ¶ 10, UN Doc S/2255.

required expertise, and putting into place the financial systems that will ensure that the IMCC can incur and pay expenses. The Secretariat may also directly manage the registry, which supports the core mission of receiving, vetting, tracking and processing claims, as well as issuing and paying awards. Some IMCCs split the Secretariat and registry into separately managed departments. The choice depends largely on the scale of the operation, as well as on whether the commissioners seek more hierarchy and fewer direct reports, or whether they prefer direct oversight over each function. The IMCC cannot begin to operate in any meaningful way until it is an established legal entity with the appropriate regulatory approvals (*e.g.*, operating permits and tax identification numbers) and the capacity to contract. The Secretariat must have the power to open bank and investment accounts, enter into leases, purchase and insure real and movable property, hire and terminate staff and consultants, establish relationships with vendors and service providers, and make regulatory and tax filings.

Smaller IMCCs with simpler needs that have some flexibility in their location and operations can outsource these functions to a standing institution, such as the Permanent Court of Arbitration in The Hague. The PCA has physical premises and permanent staff and the ability to establish all core functions contemplated by an arbitration agreement. It can, with little notice, set up a dedicated Secretariat and registry, which will provide legal and administrative support, serve as the official channel of communication between state parties and tribunals, and ensure safe custody of documents. It can also manage financial administration, logistical and technical support for meetings and hearings, and travel arrangements.[80] An additional advantage is that, absent some exceptional request or circumstance, commissioners need not manage the operation.

The EECC used the PCA to meet its relatively simple needs. The EECC did not need a formal physical headquarters nor a large support team. It was a state-to-state proceeding that dealt directly with the two state parties instead of with individual claimants. The PCA was easily able to handle filings, schedule and hold infrequent hearings, and provide a central point of contact for the commissioners and state parties.[81] Nor did the EECC administer a compensation fund. The required financial

---

[80] In 2015, the PCA's docket consisted of 138 cases, eight of which were public international arbitrations between states. Permanent Court of Arbitration, *Annual Report* (2015), 12.

[81] The EECC worked intermittently in short, intense bursts around filings and hearings. The filings were voluminous but nowhere near what might be seen in a mass claims setting.

expertise was limited to establishing a bank account to receive operating funding from the state parties, making timely disbursements and providing routine accounting. To the extent necessary, the PCA also facilitated the commissioners' deliberations and preparation of awards. The commissioners worked mostly telephonically, met in person when hearings were scheduled, and drew on their own professional resources for legal research.

A larger commission that expects to operate a more complex program over a longer period of time will generally find it more cost-efficient to create a customized infrastructure, as did the IUSCT. With a quasi-judicial mandate to resolve a large number of claims for substantial damages, the commissioners created a formal institutional apparatus designed for the long term. The IUSCT started in the PCA, but only as a temporary accommodation until it could set up its own Secretariat and registry. Until the Dutch government confirmed that the IUSCT had the necessary capacity to contract, the PCA acted as the intermediary institution to facilitate the immediate hiring of a secretary-general, the tribunal's chief administrative officer.[82] The secretary-general was responsible for "ensuring that the staff and facilities were maintained as directed by the tribunal, and were available as required … and would be called upon to advise the President on a range of non-judicial matters connected with the composition and functioning of the IUSCT as well as the conduct of its external relations."[83]

Once the IUSCT's legal personality was established, it swiftly rented a headquarters, purchased equipment and began to recruit staff.[84] At its peak, the staff numbered approximately 90. The IUSCT elected to create a separate operational unit by appointing a registrar, which had independent responsibility for the receipt, processing and safekeeping of documents, including the initial review of claims for compliance with IUSCT rules.[85] The IUSCT had no responsibility for the compensation fund, which was held at the Dutch Central Bank – N.V. Settlement Bank – and was governed by a separate escrow arrangement. The IUSCT Secretariat did, however, have financing arrangements to pay operating expenses, including a separate account for the cost of expert advice.[86]

---

[82] Pinto, "Institutional Aspects of the Tribunal," 97.

[83] Pinto, "Institutional Aspects of the Tribunal," 97.

[84] Pinto, "Institutional Aspects of the Tribunal," 98.

[85] This included the use of the IUSCT's two official languages, the number of copies, and the authentications. Pinto, "Institutional Aspects of the Tribunal," 103.

[86] Pinto, "Institutional Aspects of the Tribunal," 108.

From the outset, the IUSCT consciously confronted its approach to making decisions regarding oversight of the administrative staff. Unlike the UNCC, discussed below, the IUSCT decided against establishing a strong Secretariat that would operate under general policy guidance from the commissioners. It decided instead to have the arbitrators "run the show" through a special Committee on Administrative and Financial Questions (CAFQ). The CAFQ consisted of an Iranian-appointed commissioner, a US-appointed commissioner and a neutral commissioner. The agents for the state parties, the secretary-general and the registrar were also invited to participate. The CAFQ took a direct role in proposing administrative, financial and human resources policies; advising on those policies as implementation questions arose; and recommending regulations concerning the registration and service of documents.[87] The CAFQ also worked with the secretary-general to create an annual budget that it delivered to the full tribunal for approval.

The CRPC shows how a commission that begins under less-than-ideal circumstances might still build a formidable operation that is tailored to its very specific objectives:

> In 1996, equipped with only the nucleus of ten staff and the text [of the framework document], the substantive challenges facing the Commission were great. There were over two million [potential claimants], many without documents proving their property rights. Official property books were in disarray, destroyed, altered or had vanished, and many property books were relocated within or between the hostile entities during the war. In some cases, these property records were outside of [Bosnia and Herzegovina]. There was widespread political obstruction to accessing property records, and war-time discriminatory laws relating to abandoned property were still in effect.[88]

Despite this, the commissioners quickly met in Sarajevo and appointed a Secretariat, which created a large and sophisticated operation that went well beyond setting up a headquarters and hiring administrative staff. Before the CRPC even began to receive claims, it first had to create and then populate a standardized evidentiary database using dissimilar records from diverse sources. Once it had devised a claim form to facilitate decision-making, it then created a registry to collect, process and match claims received from internally displaced persons and exiled refugees.[89] The CRPC augmented this administrative nerve center in

87 Pinto, "Institutional Aspects of the Tribunal," 97.
88 CRPC, End of Mandate Report: Executive Summary (1996–2003), 5.
89 CRPC, End of Mandate Report: Executive Summary (1996–2003), 7.

Sarajevo with an operational network of 23 field offices to reach the large population of potential claimants who lived in rural areas and outside the country.

At its peak, the CRPC was a large bureaucracy, headed by an executive officer who oversaw a legal department, an IT department, an Executive Finance Unit, an Executive Office Management Unit, an Executive Monitoring Unit, a Department of Legal Policy and Affairs, and an Executive Public Information Unit. The commissioners did not appear to have a particularly hands-on role in supervision. They met in plenary session eight to twelve times a year in Sarajevo, but they also communicated through telephone conferences and correspondence.[90] The party-appointed commissioners were on-site and met more frequently to "exchange views on other matters of importance," but there was no formal oversight committee.

The UNCC is the largest and most complex of these entities and was able to quickly build a large operation by having the entire UN apparatus at its disposal. It operated as a mass claims program with an urgent humanitarian mission to quickly compensate individuals who had been forced to flee Kuwait,[91] had suffered personal injury or death as a consequence of the Iraqi invasion[92] or had suffered pecuniary loss under $100,000.[93] It then segued into a more traditional dispute-resolution program with individual review of larger claims. To service such a large operation, the UNCC Secretariat provides administrative, financial management, technical and legal support to the "policy-making" governing council and to the panels of commissioners. It also operates the registry.[94] Unlike the other IMCCs discussed in this chapter, the UNCC has responsibility for maintaining its compensation fund, which requires not only the capacity to establish bank accounts and move funds, but the financial savvy to manage and invest idle money and the internal controls

---

90 CRPC, End of Mandate Report: Executive Summary (1996–2003), 9.

91 These were the Category A claims, which resulted in an aggregate of US$3.1 billion in compensation being paid to approximately 850,000 successful claimants.

92 These were the Category B claims, which resulted in an aggregate of $13.4 million in compensation being paid to approximately 3,900 successful claimants.

93 These were the Category C claims, which resulted in an aggregate of $5.1 billion in compensation being paid to approximately 659,000 successful claimants.

94 UN Compensation Commission Governing Council, Decision taken by the Governing Council of the United Nations Compensation Commission at the 27th meeting, Sixth session (26 June 1992), Article 11, UN Doc S/AC.26/1992/10.

to prevent even the appearance of impropriety as to how the money is handled and paid.[95]

As mentioned, the Secretariat was granted a great deal of operational independence. It is headed by an executive secretary who is appointed by the UN Secretary-General after consultation with the policy-making Governing Council. The Governing Council established a committee on administrative matters, but its oversight role was fairly limited. It reviewed and provided guidance on major administrative and budgetary matters and approved a biannual budget.

At the height of claims processing, the Secretariat was made up of approximately 300 lawyers, accountants, loss adjusters and information technology specialists. It is now a small staff of approximately 15 people in Geneva, which primarily maintains the compensation fund and keeps track of the several billion dollars that flow in and out of the various accounts.[96]

CONCLUSION

This chapter has examined how state parties that have agreed to seek a peaceful resolution of their dispute might begin to build a viable structure. We saw in the first section how the central advantage of an IMCC is the degree of latitude it grants the parties in crafting the optimal legal environment to resolve their dispute. The parties are able to overcome issues of scale, standing and historical context and to compensate, however imperfectly, claimants that might otherwise be left without a remedy.

Decisions made about legal structure must then be translated into an effective, functioning program that retains the voluntary participation of its participants. This daunting responsibility rests on a panel of commissioners whose selection must be structured to yield geographic balance, impartiality, expertise, character and – for lack of a better word –

---

95 The handling of the compensation fund was periodically audited by the UN Office of Internal Oversight Services. The final audit report, with a rating of "satisfactory" was released in 2015. See Audit of the United Nations Compensation Commissions Claims Payments, UN OIOS, Assignment No. AE2014/820/02 (12 March 2015).

96 Even in the waning days of the program, significant amounts of money move through its accounts. During the period from 1 November 2013 through 31 October 2014, the UNCC disbursed four quarterly payments totaling $4.27 billion. Audit of the United Nations Compensation Commissions Claims Payments, UN OIOS, Assignment No. AE2014/820/02, ¶14 (12 March 2015).

chemistry. Before building out an administrative and operational support structure, the commissioners must grapple with and decide what degree of oversight feels optimal for the particular program. The overarching lesson of this chapter is that none of these questions can be reduced to a "best" answer; each must be examined and decided by the commissioners and the parties without whom the program would not exist and will not continue.

4. Who are the claimants and what are the claims?

This chapter examines the kinds of claimants to whom an international claim process is open and the types of claims that those selected claimants can bring for resolution and compensation in front of a claims commission.

The choice of the kinds of claimants and types of claims is paramount to the success of any IMCC. It is fundamental for its credibility as a dispute resolution mechanism, its feasibility as a compensation project and its ability to provide satisfactory justice and closure. Indeed, although each IMCC is necessarily unique and has a narrow mandate to hear specific claims from defined claimants, certain common trends are evident. In this chapter we will analyse the choices made by policy makers when establishing an IMCC and will extrapolate general conclusions that could guide the establishment of future IMCCs.

All IMCCs recognize states as claimants, either – as we will see below – on their own behalf, or on behalf of their nationals. Certain claims commissions, including the Iran–US Claims Tribunal, accepted claims filed directly by both natural persons and corporations. International organizations generally cannot submit claims, though the UNCC provided that they could submit claims on behalf of certain individuals.

In parallel to the kinds of claimants, the choice of the types of claims that will be heard by the IMCC is also key to its success. Certainly, the kind of claims is strictly linked to the events that resulted in the creation of the IMCC and to the types of losses and injury suffered. Thus, claims heard by the Iran–US Claims Tribunal mostly related to contracts, while claims submitted to the EECC predominately relate to breaches of humanitarian law.

Other important start-up policy decisions are how to categorize and group claims in easily decipherable categories and how to ensure payments of any awarded sum. Indeed, because claims commissions will hear numerous claims, it is important to group them in a way that will allow for easier and more expedited proceedings. The issue of how to approach and secure payments of any awarded amount is also important. Chapter 5 deals with cost and Chapter 7 with available remedies. This chapter will analyse how this specific issue was approached as a policy decision related to the payment of claims and claimants.

As a snapshot: The Iran–US Claims Tribunal was established to decide claims (and counterclaims) of US nationals against Iran, claims (and counterclaims) of Iranian nationals against the United States, and claims (and counter-claims) of the United States and Iran against each other arising out of contractual arrangements between them for the purchase and sale of goods and services. Overall, 3,936 claims were filed. An Award on Agreed Terms terminated 2,388 claims for less than $250,000 in 1990.[1] Iran filed 53 claims against the United States, and the US filed 24 claims against Iran. As of May 2016, the total amount awarded to US parties is $2,166,998,515.43 and the US Dollar equivalent of £303,196.00, DM 297,051.00 and Rls. 97,132,598 (excluding any interest to be calculated by the Escrow Agent). Iran and Iranian parties have been awarded $1,014,553,515.03 and the US Dollar equivalent of Rls. 7,977,343 (excluding any interest to be calculated).[2]

The UNCC was a much bigger operation. It received approximately 2.69 million claims seeking a total of approximately $352.5 billion in compensation. The UNCC awarded compensation of a total of $52.4 billion to about 1.5 million claims. Claims were filed by nearly 100 governments on their behalf, on behalf of their nationals or on behalf of corporations. The United Nations Development Programme (UNDP), the United Nations High Commissioner for Refugees (UNHCR) and the United Nations Relief and Works Agency for Palestine Refugees in the Near East (UNRWA) also filed claims for individuals who could not have their claims filed by a government.[3]

Conversely, the more recent EECC was more contained. Under the Algiers Agreement, Eritrea and Ethiopia could submit claims on their own behalf and on the behalf of their nationals, both natural and juridical persons.[4] Eritrea received awards in 32 numbered claims and Ethiopia in 16 numbered claims. However, the final numbers do not tell the whole

---

[1] Iran–US Claims Tribunal, Award on Agreed Terms No. 483-CLTDs/86/B38/B76/B77-FT (filed 20 June 1990).

[2] *See generally* Iran–US Claims Tribunal, Communiqué (9 May 2016), available at: http://www.iusct.net/General%20Documents/Communique%2016.1%20(9%20May%202016).pdf.

[3] *See generally* United Nations Compensation Commission, What We Do – The Claims, available at: http://www.uncc.ch/claims.

[4] Agreement between the Governments of the State of Eritrea and the Federal Democratic Republic of Ethiopia art. 5(8), 12 December 2000, signed in Algiers.

story, as several claims involved multiple claimants and many involved events that occurred over large areas.[5] The final total awarded monetary compensation was $174,036,520 to Ethiopia, $161,455,000 to Eritrea in respect of its own claims, and $2,065,865 in respect of claims presented on behalf of individuals.[6]

The next sections unpack this information and assess and analyse it in useful and digestible bits.

KINDS OF CLAIMANTS

A fundamental decision that has to be taken when establishing any international claims commission is which claimants will be allowed to submit compensation claims. This is paramount because the class of claimants has to be large enough to cover all entities that suffered a loss, injury or any compensable damage, yet limited enough to make the compensation exercise credible, meaningful and possible.

Claimants' access to claims commissions mirrors the evolution of personal jurisdiction in public international law. Thus, while traditionally only states could (on their own behalf or on behalf of their nationals) bring claims for compensation in front of an international claims commission, more recently a more diverse and open category of claimants has been given direct access to compensation from claims commissions.[7]

All past claims commissions, including those examined in this book, allow states to bring claims. Under certain rules individuals could also bring claims directly, or the state of nationality or residency could bring a claim on behalf of their nationals. More rarely, international organizations and corporations have been granted direct access also. Non-governmental organizations (NGOs) have not been allowed to directly

---

[5] Arthur W. Rovine (ed.), *Contemporary Issues in International Arbitration and Mediation* (Brill–Nijhoff, 2012), 82.

[6] Eritrea–Ethiopia Claims Commission, Final Award: Eritrea's Damages Claim (17 August 2009), available at: http://www.pca-cpa.org/upload/#les/ER%20Final%20Damages%20Award%20complete.pdf; Eritrea–Ethiopia Claims Commission, Final Award: Ethiopia's Damages Claim (17 August 2009), available at: http://www.pca-cpa.org/upload/#les/ET%20Final%20Damages%20Award%20complete.pdf.

[7] *See generally* Rudolf Dolzer, "Mixed Claims Commissions," in *Max Planck Encyclopedia of Public International Law* (Oxford University Press, 2011). *See also* Chapter 2.

present claims, which is also in line with their present standing in most international human rights tribunals.[8]

States as Claimants

The Iran–US Claims Tribunal, the UNCC and the EECC all allow states to file claims on their own behalf for losses and injuries that they suffered. And indeed, claims from states, either on their own behalf or on behalf of their nationals, are the traditional form in which compensation is awarded in international law.[9]

The Iran–US Claims Tribunal

Article II(2) of the Claims Settlement Declaration specifies that the Tribunal has jurisdiction over official claims that the United States and Iran had against each other based on contractual arrangements between Iran and the United States for purchase and sale of goods and services.[10] The jurisdiction of the Tribunal also includes all related counterclaims.[11]

Usefully, and to avoid any doubt, the Claims Settlement Declaration defines the meaning of both Iran and the United States. Iran is defined as "the Government of Iran, any political subdivision of Iran, and any agency, instrumentality, or entity controlled by the Government of Iran or

---

[8] *See generally* Christiane Bourloyannis-Vrailas, "The European Court of Human Rights," in Giorgetti, *Rules and Practice*; Christina Cerna, "The Inter-American Commission on Human Rights and the Inter-American Court of Human Rights," in Giorgetti, *Rules and Practice*.

[9] *See* Dolzer, "Mixed Claims Commissions," para. 17 (stating "Although in most instances the claims dealt with had arisen out of damages incurred by individuals, only States were enabled to file claims with the commissions in the 19th century in accordance with the traditional rules on the status of individuals in international law; it was even rare for individuals to be allowed to be represented by counsel, to present memorials to the commission, to participate in oral proceedings, or to appear as witnesses. This practice changed after World War I when individuals were granted direct access to commissions under some agreements. No uniform practice developed. Under the terms of the Agreement between the United States and Mexico (1923), for instance, a valid claim had to be signed by the affected individual, but otherwise, the proceedings were conducted by agents of the States concerned").

[10] Claims Settlement Declaration, art. II(2), 19 January 1981 (stating that "[t]he Tribunal shall also have jurisdiction over official claims of the United States and Iran against each other arising out of contractual arrangements between them for the purchase and sale of goods and services").

[11] Claims Settlement Declaration, art. II(1).

any political subdivision thereof."[12] Similarly, the United States is defined as "the Government of the United States, any political subdivision of the United States, and any agency, instrumentality or entity controlled by the Government of the United States or any political subdivision thereof."[13]

Initially, all inter-state claims were assigned to the Full Tribunal. By Presidential Order 1, though, state claims were then generally assigned to individual chambers.[14]

The number of total claims filed was not large, yet the total claimed sum was considerable, totalling tens of billions of dollars.[15] The United States filed 24 claims and Iran 53, for a total of 77 claims. As of May 2016, 72 of these claims had been finalized by award, decision or order.[16] All claims by the United States have been decided. The remaining claims were brought by Iran against the United States. A significant claim, related to a $400 million Trust Fund used by Iran to purchase military equipment from the United States prior to the Islamic Revolution, was settled in 2016 when the United States returned the entire sum to Iran as well as about $1.3 billion as a compromise on the interest due.[17]

The United Nations Claims Commission

The mandate of the UNCC similarly provided that governments could submit claims to the commission.[18] Note that the framework of the UNCC was somewhat atypical because it was not based on a bilateral agreement signed in the aftermath of a bilateral war. The UNCC was created as a subsidiary organ of the Security Council to process claims and pay compensation for losses and damages suffered as a direct result of Iraq's unlawful invasion and occupation of Kuwait. A series of UN Security Council resolutions, particularly Resolutions 687(1991), 692(1991), 986(1995) and 1483(2003), created the framework for the UNCC and established the responsibility and liability of Iraq for losses

---

12 Claims Settlement Declaration, art. VII(3).

13 Claims Settlement Declaration, art. VII (4).

14 *See generally* Jeremy K. Sharpe, "The Iran/United States Claims Tribunal," in Giorgetti, *Rules and Practice*, 552–555. *See also* George A. Aldrich, *The Jurisprudence of the Iran/United States Claims Tribunal* (Clarendon, 1996).

15 Sharpe, "The Iran/United States Claims Tribunal," 545.

16 Iran–US Claims Tribunal, Communiqué.

17 Press Release, John Kerry, Hague Claims Tribunal Settlement (17 January 2016), available at: http://www.state.gov/secretary/remarks/2016/01/251338.htm.

18 *See generally* Timothy J. Feighery, "The United Nations Compensation Commission," in Giorgetti, *Rules and Procedures*.

and damages. Specifically, Res. 687(1991) provides that Iraq was "liable under international law for any direct loss, damage, including environmental damage and the depletion of natural resources, or injury to foreign Governments, nationals and corporations."[19] Iraq's responsibility was already established, and the UNCC acted in many cases as a claims resolution body. The Commission adopted a more traditional adversarial process only for large and complex claims.

Under Decision 10 of the UNCC Governing Council, governments were entitled to submit claims directly and on behalf of their nationals or residents.[20] As will be further explored below, claims at the UNCC were divided into different categories. Category "F" was reserved for claims by governments, and claims were submitted directly by 43 governments (and six international organizations) for a total requested amount of over $236 billion.[21] More than 400 claims were submitted in this category, including those by Australia, Germany, India, Iran, Israel, Jordan, Kuwait, Pakistan, Turkey, Saudi Arabia, Syria, the United Kingdom and the United States.[22] Claims were filed for losses that included damages to diplomatic premises and government premises, losses due to evacuation cost and the provision of relief to citizens. Several claimants also filed claims for environmental damages and depletion of natural resources. Overall, the total awarded sum was of $14.76 billion.

Governments and international organizations also submitted claims on behalf of specific individuals. These claims will be examined below.

The Eritrea–Ethiopia Claims Commission

Under the Framework Agreement negotiated by Eritrea and Ethiopia in Algiers in December 2000 (the Algiers Agreement), the EECC was part of the effort of the two governments to address the negative socio-economic impact of the war on civilian populations, especially those who were deported.[23]

---

[19] UNSC Res 687, ¶ 16 (1991).

[20] UN Security Council, Decision taken by the Governing Council of the United Nations Compensation Commission at the 27th meeting, Sixth Session held on 26 June 1992, Doc No. S/AC.26/1992/10 [hereinafter Decision 10, UNCC].

[21] *See generally* United Nations Compensation Commission, "What We Do – The Claims – Category F," available at: http://www.uncc.ch/category-f.

[22] UNCC, "What We Do."

[23] Agreement Between The Government of The Federal Democratic Republic of Ethiopia and The Government of The State of Eritrea (Algiers Agreement), art. 5, 12 December 2000 (providing that "1. Consistent with the Framework

Under Article 5 of the Algiers Agreement more specifically, the mandate of the Commission was to decide, through binding arbitration, claims for loss, damage or injury by one government against the other government or entities owned and controlled by the other party.[24] Unlike the Iran–US Claims Tribunal, neither the Agreement nor further decisions by the EECC provided any further definition as to what entities should be considered as being "Eritrea" and "Ethiopia" or entities controlled or owned by them. This is understandable, given the jurisdiction of the EECC, which is focused on violations of international humanitarian law, including the 1949 Geneva Conventions, and does not – like the Iran–US Claims Tribunal – include contractual claims where a contract can be signed by different entities whose public nature needs to be verified.

The work of the EECC focused on damages caused by war activities. These included injury to the civilian populations, including physical and mental abuses; looting and destruction of private and public property; destruction of cultural property; displacement of people; and injury suffered by prisoners of war. The cost of military operations, preparing for military operations and the use of force could not form part of a claim under the framework Agreement.

Eritrea filed a total of 32 claims, and Ethiopia filed a total of eight claims. Each head of claims contained several sub-claims, so that eventually the claims filed by Ethiopia and Eritrea were largely of similar types. All claims filed by Ethiopia were filed both "by and on behalf of

---

Agreement, in which the parties commit themselves to addressing the negative socio-economic impact of the crisis on the civilian population, including the impact on those persons who have been deported, a neutral Claims Commission shall be established. The mandate of the Commission is to decide through binding arbitration all claims for loss, damage or injury by one Government against the other, and by nationals (including both natural and juridical persons) of one party against the Government of the other party or entities owned or controlled by the other party that are (a) related to the conflict that was the subject of the Framework Agreement, the Modalities for its Implementation and the Cessation of Hostilities Agreement, and (b) result from violations of international humanitarian law, including the 1949 Geneva Conventions, or other violations of international law. The Commission shall not hear claims arising from the cost of military operations, preparing for military operations, or the use of force, except to the extent that such claims involve violations of international humanitarian law").

[24] Algiers Agreement.

the Ethiopian government," while Eritrea filed 26 claims "by and on behalf" of Eritrea and six claims on behalf of Eritrean nationals.[25]

Both Eritrea and Ethiopia also submitted claims for damages and losses to large sections of the population as their own claims.[26] These were not the typical individual claims which are espoused by a state, but actual state claims submitted on its own behalf.

These claims included claims related to the treatment of prisoners of war (POWs) by both Eritrea and Ethiopia. Indeed, in looking at Eritrea's claim, the Commission noted that the POWs' claim had been brought to the Commission by Eritrea pursuant to Article 5 of the Agreement seeking a finding of liability against Ethiopia "for loss, damages and injury suffered by the Claimant as a result of the Respondent's alleged unlawful treatment of its prisoners of war who were nationals of the Claimant."[27] In two parallel cases, the EECC found both parties liable. For example, Eritrea was found liable for failure to provide adequate medical care to Ethiopian POWs; Ethiopia was found liable for failure to release and repatriate Eritrean POWs.[28] Other similar claims filed by the state and related to losses and damages to entire sections of the population concerned the accusation of widespread rape that both parties made against the other. In these cases, both Eritrea and Ethiopia were found liable for failure to prevent acts committed by their troops, rather than for advancing a government policy.[29] Eritrea also submitted a claim against Ethiopia for the deprivation of Ethiopian nationality for several classes of Eritrean and other nationals.[30]

---

25 See Sean Murphy, Won Kidane and Thomas R. Snider, *Litigating War: Arbitration of Civil Injury by the Eritrea–Ethiopia Claims Commission* (Oxford University Press, 2013), 61.

26 Murphy, Kidane and Snider, *Litigating War.*

27 Eritrea–Ethiopia Claims Commission, Partial Award, Eritrea's Claim 17: Prisoners of War ¶ 1, 1 July 2003. *See also* Partial Award, Ethiopia's Claim 4, 1 July 2003.

28 *Id.*

29 Eritrea–Ethiopia Claims Commission, Ethiopia's Western/Eastern Front Claims, Partial Award, ¶ 68; Eritrea's Western Front/Aerial Bombardment Claims, Partial Award.

30 Interestingly, the EECC rejected one such claim exactly because it was filed on behalf of Eritrea and not on behalf of the nationals who had been deprived of Ethiopian nationality. *See* EECC, Damages Award, ¶ 254 (stating: "Eritrea cannot claim compensation for its own account for the first of the liability findings listed above (for "erroneously depriving at least some Ethiopians who were not dual nationals of their Ethiopian nationality." At the liability phase, the Commission found that Eritrea's claims predicated upon injuries

Claims by states are the most common form of claims submitted to a claims commission and probably the easiest to administer procedurally in terms of the threshold of required evidence.[31] Issues to take into consideration when establishing a claims commission include whether and how to provide a definition of what entities will be considered a part of the state. In a multilateral conflict, it will also be important to secure access to all the necessary parties involved.

Claims from the state can take multiple forms. The Iran–US Claims Tribunal allowed the two parties to file claims only on their own behalf. In contrast to the traditional espousal of claims by states, claims by individuals were only private claims. Importantly, Iran and the United States agreed to litigate small claims (valued at less than $250,000) on behalf of the individual claimants. In both the UNCC and the EECC, states could bring cases on their own behalf and also on behalf of individuals. There was one major difference between the two commissions: under the UNCC, claims filed on behalf of individuals remained claims of the individuals and required specific claimants to be named, but under the EECC, Eritrea and Ethiopia filed claims relating to large sections of the population on their behalf. The issue of compensating individuals for their injury and losses remained an internal question to be resolved domestically, at a later stage.

Specifying what kind of claims a state can submit is fundamental when establishing a claims commission. The issue of individuals as claimants is discussed next.

Individuals as Claimants

A second important category of claimants often able to recover for losses and damages through an IMCC mechanism is represented by individuals. Individuals are the ones who most likely suffered the most extensive injury and loss during the upheavals that resulted in the establishment of the claims commission, so it is significant to ensure that they are also the ones who are compensated for loss and injury.

A fundamental policy choice to be made is whether individuals will be allowed to submit claims directly or whether they must do so through their state of nationality or residence. This choice has immediate repercussions in terms of number of cases, their complexity, the procedures to

inflicted upon persons holding only Ethiopian nationality did not conform to the jurisdictional requirements of the December 2000 Agreement, and could not be the basis for compensation accruing directly to the State of Eritrea.").

[31] *See* Chapter 6.

be applied (including mass proceedings and discovery) and the methodologies for payments of awards.

The claims commissions analysed below offer the full spectrum of choices.

The Iran–US Claims Tribunal

In the Iran–US Claims Tribunal, individuals, both natural and legal, had immediate access to the Tribunal and could submit a claim directly. Under the Claims Settlement Declaration, the Iran–US Claims Tribunal was established to decide "claims of nationals of the United States against Iran and claims of nationals of Iran against the United States."[32] The Tribunal was also open to counterclaims arising from the same contract, transaction or occurrence that constituted the subject matter of the claims of the national, provided that the claims and counterclaims were outstanding on the date of the Agreement "whether or not filed with any court, and aris[ing] out of debts, contracts … expropriations or other measures affecting property rights." Under the same provision, a national could be both a natural person with a US or an Iranian nationality, or a corporation or other legal entity organized under the laws of Iran or the United States.[33]

Claims by nationals of Iran or the United States are defined as:

> claims owned continuously, from the date on which the claim arose to the date on which this Agreement enters into force, by nationals of that state, including claims that are owned indirectly by such nationals through ownership of capital stock or other proprietary interests in juridical persons, provided that the ownership interests of such nationals, collectively, were sufficient at the time the claim arose to control the corporation or other entity, and provided, further, that the corporation or other entity is not itself entitled to bring a claim under the terms of this Agreement.[34]

Under the Iran–US Claims Tribunal rules, private claimants were not required to exhaust local remedies, and once claims were submitted to the Tribunal they were excluded from Iranian, US or any other local court.[35] Under Article III of the Settlement Declaration, claims valued at more than $250,000 were considered large claims and claimants were

32 Claim Settlement Declaration art. II(1).
33 Claim Settlement Declaration art. II(1).
34 Claim Settlement Declaration art. VIII(2).
35 Claim Settlement Declaration art. VIII(2).

responsible for litigating them.[36] Iran and the United States were instead responsible for presenting small claims, that is those valued at less than $250,000.

The Iran–US Claims Tribunal received about 1,000 large claims and 3,000 small claims, mostly from US parties against Iran. The great majority of the small claims (about 2,500 – of which 2,400 were from the United States and 100 were from Iran) were settled by a lump-sum payment by Iran to the United States of $105 million and then allocated by the Foreign Claims Settlement Commission.[37]

The United Nations Claims Commission

Under the framework created by the UNCC, only governments and international organizations were entitled to submit claims.[38] Thus, individual claims had to be submitted by their states of nationality or residency.[39] Governments were also responsible for submitting claims on behalf of corporations or other entities incorporated or organized under the law of the state at the time the claim arose. Predictably, and to avoid duplication, only one government could submit a claim on behalf of an individual or a corporation.

Allowing only governments to submit claims on behalf of nationals may have been necessary for several reasons. The UNCC, for example, was established after a complex multilateral conflict. In that context, moreover, prior to Iraq's invasion, the economy of Kuwait relied heavily on millions of low-skilled workers, especially from Asia. They were the ones who suffered the first and immediate impact of the invasion. When they had to flee, they did so in a hurry, bringing little or no documentation with them. The UNCC was then confronted with the prospect of hearing millions of separate claims or allowing states to organize, present and provide claimants with initial support.

To make sure that individuals were properly compensated, the Governing Council of the UNCC adopted several major decisions: first, it granted priority to small individual claims; then it adopted mass claims

---

[36] Claim Settlement Declaration art. III(3). ("Claims of nationals of the United States and Iran that are within the scope of this Agreement shall be presented to the Tribunal either by claimants themselves or, in the case of claims of less than $250,000, by the government of such national.")

[37] *See* Sharpe, "The Iran/United States Claims Tribunal," 552–553.

[38] Decision 10, UNCC, art. 5(1) (approving the Provisional Rules for Claims Procedure).

[39] Decision 10, UNCC.

methodologies that allowed expeditious review of the claims; and finally, it established specific payment processes for individual claimants.[40]

First, in an important and groundbreaking decision, the Governing Council decided to prioritize the processing and payment of certain individual claimants (called category "A," "B" and "C").[41] Thus, it decided to process on an urgent basis the claims of individuals who were forced to leave Iraq or Kuwait because of Iraq's invasion; the claims of individuals who suffered serious personal injuries or of individuals whose spouse, child or parent died because of the invasion; and the claims of individuals who suffered personal losses of up to $100,000. This humanitarian decision indicated an important shift of the traditional practice of previous IMCCs – including, as seen above, the IUSTC – that focused first on losses suffered by governments.[42] It also set the tone for the work of the UNCC.

Small and urgent individual claims made up a substantial number of cases. Claims, however, were for small amounts and were capped at $2,500 per person or $10,000 per family.[43] The UNCC thus decided that a detailed individual review was neither warranted nor feasible – also because, as seen above, the legal responsibility of Iraq for damages had already been established. Small urgent claims were therefore reviewed using mass claims processing and computerized methodologies.[44]

Certain individual claims could also be submitted by international organizations. This was particularly the case for Palestinians' claims, which were submitted by UNRWA and UNHCR.

---

40 First Session of the Governing Council of the United Nations Compensation Commission, Criteria for Expedited Processing of Urgent Claims, S/AC.26/1991/1 (2 August 1991). *See also generally* United Nations Compensation Commission, "What We Do–Claims Processing," available at: http://www.uncc.ch/claims-processing.

41 United Nations Compensation Commission, Decision 17, "Priority of Payment and Payment Mechanism: Guiding Principles, S/AC.26/1994/1 17 December (1994) (24 March 1994) [hereinafter UNCC Decision 17].

42 Carlos Alzamora, "Reflections on the UN Compensation Commission" (1993) 9 *Arbitration International* 349, 351 ("[F]or the first time in the history of international compensation institutions and procedures, interest of the individual prevails over that of business or even Governments.").

43 First Session of the Governing Council of the United Nations Compensation Commission, Criteria for Expedited Processing of Urgent Claims, S/AC.26/1991/1 ¶¶ 10–16 (2 August 1991).

44 *See* Chapter 6.

A final precedent-setting decision by the UNCC related to the way compensation was paid to the successful individual claimant.[45] The methodology employed by the UNCC ensured – through several steps – that the state actually delivered the payment to the named individual to whom it had been awarded. Thus, once awarded, the Commission sent funds to the government or international organization who had submitted the original claims.[46] These entities were then responsible for distributing the funds to the successful claimants within six months of receiving the payment and for reporting back to the Governing Council on all payments made within three months.[47] The Governing Council also required governments to provide an audit certificate, at least annually. Governments and international organizations were allowed to deduct a maximum of 1.5 percent of the sum paid to offset the cost of processing the payments. The periodic payment reports also had to include all deductions made. Failure by governments and international organizations to report on the distribution of funds resulted in the suspension of any further payments.[48] Monies for payment not distributed within 12 months – for example, because claimants could not be located – had to be returned to the Commission, under penalty of suspension of further funds.[49] Should claimants be subsequently located or the payment become possible, the Commission would return the amount to the government or international organization for distribution. All payments were suspended on 30 September 2006.[50]

This unique payment process was certainly cumbersome for both the UNCC and governments. However, it was also necessary not only to

---

[45] UNCC Decision 17.

[46] United Nations Compensation Commission Governing Council, Decision 18, Distribution of Payments and Transparency (1994) [hereinafter UNCC Decision 18]. *See generally* UNCC, Distribution of Compensation Awards by Submitting Entities, available at: http://www.uncc.ch/distribution-compensation-awards-submitting-entities.

[47] UNCC Governing Council Decisions taken to enhance transparency and avoid double recovery include: Decision 13 (1992), Further Measures to Avoid Multiple Recovery of Compensation by Claimants; UNCC Decision 18.

[48] United Nations Compensation Commission Governing Council Decision 48, Return of Undistributed Funds (1998).

[49] UNCC Decision 48.

[50] United Nations Compensation Commission, Distribution of Compensation Awards by Submitting Entities, available at: http://www.uncc.ch/distribution-compensation-awards-submitting-entities.

ensure the proper distribution of all final payments, but also to guarantee transparency of the process and ultimately the credibility of the claims process.

The Eritrea–Ethiopia Claims Commission

The rules of procedure of the EECC provided for the possibility of submitting two kinds of claims: individual claims and mass claims, which would require a lower standard of evidence and would result in a fixed amount of compensation. The parties, however, decided not to pursue mass claims and only filed individual claims. Chapter 2 of the Rules of Procedure of the EECC identified three categories of individual claims: claims filed by one government against the other on its own behalf; claims valued at more than $100,000 filed on behalf of identified individuals; and specific claims that the Rules of Procedure identified as requiring individual attention.[51]

Essentially all claims submitted to the Commission were filed by the parties as individual claims of the governments themselves, and not (as was the case in the UNCC) as claims filed on behalf of nationals and transmitted to the Commission by the individual's government. So, parties filed most claims alleging harm and injury to unnamed individuals and property, rather than providing the names of specific claimants. Ethiopia filed all of its claims as government claims. Eritrea filed most of its claims as government claims, but filed six claims on behalf of named nationals. The EECC ultimately awarded compensation to four named Eritrean individuals.[52] Specifically:

1. Hiwot Nemariam and Belay Redda (who were husband and wife when the claim was filed – the husband then passed away) received together $319,615 for failure to provide humane and safe treatment in transport from Ethiopia, lack of access to bank accounts, and unlawful deprivation of property;

---

[51] *Eritrea–Ethiopia Claims Commission, Rules of Procedure*, Chapter Two (Oct. 2001) ("This Chapter applies to all claims that are to be individually arbitrated. These claims include all claims by the government of one party on its own behalf against the government of the other party, all claims for compensation in excess of $100,000 on behalf of persons, and any other claims for which individual treatment is required by Chapter Three [Mass claims].") [hereinafter EECC Rules].

[52] Final Award, Eritrea's Damages Claims, § VIII – Individual Claims (17 August 2009).

2. Sertzu Gebre Meskel was awarded $1.5 million for unlawful deprivation of property;
3. Mebrahtu Gebremedhin received $21,250 for lack of access to bank accounts and unlawful deprivation of property; and
4. Mebrat Gebreamlak received $225,000 for lack of access to bank accounts and unlawful deprivation of property.[53]

When assessing claims submitted by Eritrea and Ethiopia on their behalf, but relating to claims of sections of the population, the EECC noted that the awards were made in respect of an unknown number of claimants. For example, in its award of damages in favor of Eritrea dealing with claims for denationalization, it stated that:

> given the severe limitations of the record, the Commission awards compensation in the amount of $50,000 *in respect of the unknown, but apparently small, number* of dual nationals who were arbitrarily deprived of their Ethiopian nationality while present in third countries.[54]

Similarly, when reviewing a claim submitted by Ethiopia, the EECC found Eritrea liable, *inter alia*, for "permitting intentional and indiscriminate killings" and "beatings" of civilians in Dalul and Elidar Weredas by its military personnel or by other officials of the State of Eritrea, without further specifying the names or numbers of the individuals involved.[55]

This method of presenting and submitting claims by Eritrea and Ethiopia might have been necessary because of the exceptional circumstances surrounding the creation of the EECC and the difficulties in collecting evidence and locating individuals after the war. Indeed, had they chosen to submit individually named claims, Eritrea and Ethiopia

---

53 The claim filed by Fekadu Andremeskal was dismissed.

54 Final Award, Eritrea's Damages Claims ¶ 267 (17 August 2009) (emphasis added). Similarly, it stated, "In light of these unusual circumstances – a highly disputed record regarding the extent of wrongful expulsion, imperfect evidence, the unusual character of the delict, and the serious character of the event for many of those affected – the Commission awards compensation in the total amount of $15,000,000 in respect of the wrongful expulsion of an unknown, but considerable, number of dual nationals by local Ethiopian authorities." ¶ 302.

55 Eritrea–Ethiopia Claims Commission, Partial Award Western and Eastern Fronts Ethiopia's Claims 1 & 3, VII. Eastern Front (Ethiopia's Claim 3), Award, F (2) (19 December 2005).

would have been required by the rules to submit specific names, places of residency and nationality information for all claims by persons.[56]

This situation, however, also created an unusually delicate situation for the Commission. On one side, the EECC could not award compensation directly to individuals because Eritrea and Ethiopia had exercised their sovereign right to submit claims on their own behalf only; on the other side, the EECC tried to ensure that sums awarded to the two litigants for claims for injuries suffered by people were used for the benefit of those injured or distributed directly to them. Thus, when awarding compensation to both Eritrea and Ethiopia to compensate the other party's failure to prevent rape in specific areas, the EECC expressed "the hope that Eritrea (and Ethiopia) will use the funds awarded to develop and support health programs for women and girls in the affected areas."[57]

Further, in a 2006 letter addressed to the parties, the EECC requested that Parties inform the Commission in their first filing of how they intended to ensure the "distribution of damages received to civilian victims, including presently available information on existing or anticipated structures and procedures for this purpose."[58] In a subsequent Decision, the EECC recognized that the Parties had chosen to pursue inter-state claims and that they each had the authority to decide how to distribute damages awarded to them, yet the Commission also reiterated its confidence that the Parties would be mindful of their respective

---

56 EECC *Rules* art. 24(3) ("Statements of Claim shall include a precise statement of the following particulars: (a) The names and addresses of the parties; (b) If the claimant is the government of a Party or an agency of such government, whether the claim is solely of that government or agency or whether it includes the claims of persons, and, if the latter, the identification of such persons, including their names, places of residence and nationalities; (c) A statement of the facts supporting the claim or claims; (d) The violation or violations of international law on the basis of which the claim or claims are alleged to have arisen; (e) Any other points at issue; (f) The relief or remedy sought; (g) The Commission's jurisdiction over the claim or claims; (h) Whether the claim or claims have been filed in any other forum.").

57 Final Award, Eritrea's Damages Claims ¶ 239 (17 August 2009) (stating "Accordingly, the Commission awards Eritrea (as it does Ethiopia in its parallel Award) $2,000,000 in damages for failing to prevent the rape of known and unknown victims in the towns of Senafe, Barentu and Teseney. In so doing, the Commission expresses the hope that Eritrea (and Ethiopia) will use the funds awarded to develop and support health programs for women and girls in the affected areas.").

58 Eritrea–Ethiopia Claims Commission Letter to the Parties of 13 April 2006, cited in Eritrea–Ethiopia Claims Commission, Decision Number 8 (27 July 2007) [hereafter EECC Decision 8].

responsibilities to ensure that effective measures were taken so that their nationals who were victims of armed conflict received relief.[59] In the same decision, the EECC also specifically acknowledged that in relation to many claims for which it had found liability, it would have probably been "impossible, and certainly inordinately expensive, to attempt to identify the specific individuals who suffered injuries as a result of various illegal acts committed against them,"[60] for example for "victims of rape, physical abuse and intentional killings."[61] Therefore, in light of the humanitarian objectives of the EECC, it invited the Parties to specifically consider the means in which relief could be best achieved, including by "different kinds of relief programs for categories of victims, for example to provide health, agricultural and other services."

Alas, neither Eritrea nor Ethiopia ever paid the amount awarded to the other party, and thus neither received any compensation for the loss and injury suffered by it and by its people.[62] The question of how to distribute the award fairly to the victims remained moot under the circumstances.

The examples examined above show the complexity of recognizing claims of individuals. Each Commission followed a different path: under the Iran–US Claims Tribunal, individual claimants were allowed to submit claims directly to the Tribunal, though Iran and the United States agreed to litigate small claims on behalf of their nationals. For the UNCC, governments submitted millions of claims on behalf of their nationals, each of whom was a named claimant. Governments had a responsibility to deliver any awarded sum to their nationals, and this responsibility included a duty of reporting and returning any non-deliverable amounts. Under the EECC, the two litigants could submit claims on behalf of their nationals, but chose to submit most claims on their own behalf. Only Eritrea filed claims on behalf of named individuals, and even then filed only six such claims. When these claims pertained to injuries and losses suffered by the population, the Commission tried to ensure that programs would be instituted to directly benefit victims.

Several reasons explain the different choices made in addressing individual claims. First, the kind of injuries and losses played a fundamental role. Contractual claims are easily resolved in a classic individual–state arbitration, while the same setting could be too cumbersome to litigate individual injuries for violations of humanitarian law.

59 EECC Decision 8.
60 EECC Decision 8.
61 EECC Decision 8.
62 *See* discussion in Chapter 7.

Second, the complexity of the situation and the number of expected claims certainly affect the choice of the procedure to be adopted to litigate individual claims. Thus, if a substantial number of claims is expected – as it was for the UNCC – grouping them and allowing state representation is more efficient, especially in a situation of finite temporal and financial resources. Third, the cost and time needed to collect evidence for certain injury must also be considered. Thus, as noted by the EECC, it would have been essentially impossible – and very expensive – to identify victims of rape, physical abuses and intentional killings under the circumstances that existed after the Eritrea–Ethiopia war.[63] Hence it would make sense to allow states to file claims on their own behalf in respect of a class of victims the existence of which is certain, but the composition of which is not. What is paramount is to ensure that any sum awarded for such claims is used to benefit the victims whose suffering is being compensated by the IMCC process.[64]

Thus, claims by individuals can be presented to a claims commission in a variety of forms, which are deeply related to the factual circumstances from which the IMCC ensued. Regardless of the different procedures adopted, however, what remains fundamental is that any sum awarded is given – or at least used – to compensate the victims of the injury or loss. Only that would truly fulfill the mandate of a compensation commission.

Other Claimants

Under the rules of procedure of certain claims commissions, additional claimants may also be allowed to submit claims either on their behalf or on behalf of some other claimants. This is not very common, yet the UNCC provides a good example of claims submitted by other claimants.

Article 5 of UNCC Decision 10 provides that international organizations may submit claims on their own behalf. Several did so under UNCC Claim Category F. The UNCC also allowed international organizations to submit claims on behalf of individuals whose claims could not be submitted by a government, such as the Palestinians.

Corporations were also allowed to directly file their claims under the UNCC if their government did not submit a claim on their behalf.[65] Their

---

63 EECC, Decision 8.

64 *See also* Chapter 8.

65 United Nations Compensation Commission, Decision 10, art. 5(1)(d): "A corporation or other private entity is required to request the State of its incorporation or organization to submit its claims to the commission." However,

claims were heard under Claim Category "E." Corporations were also allowed to file claims directly as individuals under the Iran–US Claims Tribunal.[66]

Claims by Dual Nationals

Claims of dual nationals deserve special consideration in the context of post-conflict claims commissions. The issue arises from the fact that under classic international law, individuals could not bring an international claim against the state of their nationality. Indeed, most procedural rules would bar that. Further, the right to file an individual claim against a state in an IMCC also derives from the fact that the individual is a foreigner with few options to recover compensation for the injury suffered in the foreign state's domestic setting.[67] What then of individuals who validly hold nationalities from both sides of the conflict? When would they be entitled to file a claim against one of their states of nationality? Would they at all? The three commissions examined here were all confronted with the issue of dual nationals to decide who had the right to submit claims, and against which party.

The Claims Settlement Declaration specifically provided that the Iran–US Claims Tribunal was created to decide claims of US nationals against Iran and claims of Iranian nationals against the United States. The Rules defined who was a national and what were claims of nationality; however, they did not resolve the issue of dual nationals.[68] Yet, because

---

when the State fails to submit within the provided time-limit, the corporation of other private legal entity could submit the claim itself within three months and must also provide an explanation as to why a government is not submitting its claim." UNCC Decision 10, art. (5)(3).

66 Claim Settlement Declaration art. II(1).

67 Gregory Townsend, "The Iraq Claims Process: A Progress Report on the United Nations Compensation Commission & (and) U.S. Remedies," (1995) 17 *Loyola Los Angeles International and Comparative Law Review* 973.

68 Article VII, Claim Settlement Declaration ("For the purpose of this Agreement: 1. A "national" of Iran or of the United States, as the case may be, means (a) a natural person who is a citizen of Iran or the United States; and (b) a corporation or other legal entity which is organized under the laws of Iran or the United States or any of its states or territories, the District of Columbia or the Commonwealth of Puerto Rico, if, collectively, natural persons who are citizens of such country hold, directly or indirectly, an interest in such corporation or entity equivalent to fifty per cent or more of its capital stock. 2. 'Claims of nationals' of Iran or the United States, as the case may be, means claims owned continuously, from the date on which the claim arose to the date on which this

of the strong historic and economic ties between the two countries, the issue of dual nationals soon became a central question to the work of the Iran–US Claims Tribunal. When could a dual Iranian–US national be allowed to file a claim against Iran or the United States? The Iran–US Claims Tribunal followed the International Court of Justice in *Nottebohm*. In a precedent-setting decision, the Tribunal decided that for jurisdictional purposes, a dual US–Iranian national would be considered the national of his or her "dominant and effective nationality" in the period between the formation of the claim and the date of the establishment of the Tribunal.[69] To assess the "effective and dominant nationality" the Tribunal would need to review "all relevant factors, including habitual residence, center of interests, family ties, participation in public life and other evidence of attachment."[70]

The question of dual nationals was also particularly relevant for the work of the UNCC. The question in those circumstances was the exclusion of Iraqi nationals from the process. The Commission took a different and more liberal approach from the one adopted by the Iran–US Claims Tribunal. In its first session, the UNCC Governing Council decided that "[c]laims will not be considered on behalf of Iraqi nationals who do not have bona fide nationality of any other state."[71]

The significance of the decision was elaborated by a Category "B" Panel of Commissioners which related to individual claims for serious

---

Agreement enters into force, by nationals of that state, including claims that are owned indirectly by such nationals through ownership of capital stock or other proprietary interests in juridical persons, provided that the ownership interests of such nationals, collectively, were sufficient at the time the claim arose to control the corporation or other entity, and provided, further, that the corporation or other entity is not itself entitled to bring a claim under the terms of this Agreement. Claims referred to the arbitration Tribunal shall, as of the date of filing of such claims with the Tribunal, be considered excluded from the jurisdiction of the courts of Iran, or of the United States, or of any other court.").

69 *Iran v. United States of America*, Case A18 (Apr. 6, 1984), 5 Iran–US CTR 251 (quoting at 256 *Nottebohm* Case (*Liechtenstein v. Guatemala*), 1955 ICJ 4, 22 (Judgment of Apr. 6)).

70 *Iran v. United States of America*, 265.

71 Governing Council of the United Nations Compensation Commission (S/AC. 26/1991/1), paragraph 17:1, available at: http://www.uncc.ch/sites/default/files/attachments/documents/dec_01.pdf.

personal injury or death.[72] In its first installment of claims relating to the eligibility of certain claimants, the Panel concluded:

> Governing Council Decision 1, para. 17 states that: "Claims will not be considered on behalf of Iraqi nationals who do not have bona fide nationality of any other State." The first installment contained no claim submitted by an Iraqi national. In instances where there was some doubt as to the nationality of the claimant, the Panel checked the identity documents found in the claim, and took into account the affirmations provided by the respective Government.[73]

Therefore, under the UNCC, Iraqi nationals were allowed to file a claim if they possessed a bona fide nationality of any other state, regardless of their dominant and effective nationality.

The situation at the EECC was more complex. Under Article 5(1), the EECC was tasked with deciding claims of nationals of one party against the government of the other party. Still, Article 5(9) provided:

> In appropriate cases, each party may file claims on behalf of persons of Ethiopian or Eritrean origin who may not be its nationals. Such claims shall be considered by the Commission on the same basis as claims submitted on behalf of that party's nationals.[74]

For historical reasons, there were a large number of dual Eritrean and Ethiopian nationals. The wrongful deprivation of nationality was a core claim made by Eritrea against Ethiopia. In an important decision, the EECC recognized:[75]

> the continued force of the rule of dominant and effective nationality in many circumstances. However, it believe[d] that application of the rule must be qualified in situations, such as those presented here, involving claims centered on expulsion or deprivation of nationality by the respondent State. It cannot be that, in such situations, international law allows a State wrongfully to expel persons or deprive them of its own nationality, but then deny State responsibility because of the very social connections or bonds of nationality it wrongfully ended.[76]

---

[72] Category "B" Panel, First Installment, A. 2. Eligible claimants/ a (exclusion of claims by Iraqi nationals), available at: http://www.uncc.ch/sites/default/files/attachments/documents/r1994-01.pdf.

[73] Category "B" Panel, Annex II, 14.

[74] Algiers Agreement, Art. 5(9).

[75] Eritrea–Ethiopia Claims Commission, Final Award – Eritrea's Damages Claims, available at: http://legal.un.org/riaa/cases/vol_XXVI/505-630.pdf.

[76] EECC, Final Award – Eritrea's Damages Claims.

Citing Article 5(9), the EECC then concluded that the provision was a "compelling indication that the Parties did not view the general rules of diplomatic protection as applying in the unusual circumstances that led to that Agreement."[77] Thus, the EECC made awards in favor of Eritrea for "dual Eritrean–Ethiopian nationals who were arbitrarily deprived of their Ethiopian nationality while present in third countries" and for the wrongful expulsion of "dual nationals by local Ethiopian authorities."

Dual-national claims go to the very core of the jurisdiction of an IMCC. Each of the commissions examined here chose a different approach to the issue, also reflecting the deeply different underlying situations. While the Iran–US Claims Tribunal recognized the classic rule of the "effective and dominant" nationality as a way to establish which nationality should prevail, the UNCC and the EECC departed from that approach and adapted the dual nationality to the specific factual situations they confronted. The UNCC allowed claims from bona fide dual nationals, while the EECC allowed Eritrea to file claims on behalf of certain individuals who were deprived of Ethiopian nationality.

TYPES, GROUPING AND NUMBER OF CLAIMS

In parallel to the choice of who can be a claimant, IMCC negotiators must decide which claims should be included and which should be barred. A successful IMCC must be able to resolve a sufficient number of claims to justify its creation. It must resolve those claims that can be finally and fully compensated with the funds that are available. It must also have jurisdiction over the appropriate number of claims to ensure that its decisions create a sense of justice and thus foster the reconciliation process for which it was created. As a general matter, this may also mean that certain costs or damages may be barred from compensation. For example, military costs were not recoverable under any of the commissions examined here.[78]

How to categorize and group them once they are identified is an important consequence related to the choice of the types of claims that will be allowed. This is very important because an expedient and efficient procedure is essential for the success of the IMCC.

---

[77] EECC, Final Award – Eritrea's Damages Claims.

[78] The Algiers Agreement provided that "The Commission shall not hear claims arising from the cost of military operations, preparing for military operations, or the use of force, except to the extent that such claims involve violations of international humanitarian law." Art. 5(1).

The sections below review and discuss the types of claims selected in the constitutive instruments of the Iran–US Claims Tribunal, the UNCC and the EECC. They will also examine how the rules of procedures and subsequent decisions of each commission categorized and grouped different kinds of claims.

Claims in the Iran–US Claims Tribunal

Under the provisions of the Claims Settlement Declaration of 19 January 1981, the Iran–US Claims Tribunal was created to decide two distinct categories of claims: private and public.[79] All claims had to be filed with the Tribunal by 19 January 1982. Private claims were claims defined as:

> [c]laims of nationals of the United States against Iran and claims of nationals of Iran against the United States, and any counterclaim which arises out of the same contract, transaction or occurrence that constitutes the subject matter of that nationals claim, if such claims and counter-claims are outstanding on the date of this Agreement, whether or not filed with any court, and arise out of debts, contracts (including transactions which are the subject of letters of credit or bank guarantees), expropriations or other measures affecting property rights.[80]

Private claims were divided into large and small claims. Large claims were valued at more than $250,000 and small claims for less than $250,000. Approximately 1,000 claims were filed for amounts of $250,000 or more, and approximately 2,800 claims for amounts of less than $250,000. Overall, 960 large claims and 2,884 small claims were

---

[79] Art. II, Claims Settlement Declaration. Note that the same provision also included interpretation claims, which were not limited by temporal jurisdiction. Thirty-seven interpretation claims have been filed, of which 17 were terminated and 20 finalized by award, decision or order. See IUSCT, Communiqué No 16/1, of 9 May 2016, available at: http://www.iusct.net/General%20Documents/Communique%2016.1%20(9%20May%202016).pdf. *See* Art. II(3) ("The Tribunal shall have jurisdiction, as specified in Paragraphs 16–17 of the Declaration of the Government of Algeria of January 19, 1981, over any dispute as to the interpretation or performance of any provision of that Declaration.").

[80] Art. II(1), Claims Settlement Declaration. The provision excluded certain particular claims, namely "claims described in Paragraph 11 of the Declaration of the Government of Algeria of January 19, 1981, and claims arising out of the actions of the United States in response to the conduct described in such paragraph, and excluding claims arising under a binding contract between the parties specifically providing that any disputes thereunder shall be within the sole jurisdiction of the competent Iranian courts, in response to the Majlis position."

finalized by award, decision or order. A 1991 award on Agreed Terms terminated 2,388 claims valued at less than $250,000. These claims were finally resolved in the United States by the Foreign Claims Settlement Commission.[81] As of May 2016, 516 large claims and 330 small claims were terminated by an order or a decision.[82]

Official claims, called "B" claims, related to official claims of one government against the other and were based on Article II(2) of the Claims Settlement Declaration. Official claims are defined simply as "claims of the United States and Iran against each other arising out of contractual arrangements between them for the purchase and sale of goods and services."[83] Seventy-two "B" claims were finalized by award, decision or order, while 18 such claims were terminated by order or decision.[84]

Overall, the total amount awarded to all US claimants has been $2,166,998,515.43 and the US Dollar equivalent of £303,196.00, DM 297,051.00 and Rls. 97,132,598, excluding interest. Iranian claimants have so far been awarded $1,014,553,515.03 and the US Dollar equivalent of Rls. 7,977,343.[85]

Claims at the United Nations Claims Commission

The kinds of claims and their grouping was more complex at the UNCC, which is by itself a more complex operation. The Governing Council identified the types of claims, which were later organized by the Commission into six categories: A, B, C, D, E and F.[86]

Category "A" claims were claims submitted by individuals who had to flee from Iraq or Kuwait during the period of 2 August 1990 to 2 March

[81] Award on Agreed Terms No. 483-CLTDs/86/B38/B76/B77-FT, filed 22 June 1990.

[82] Communiqué No 16/1 of 9 May 2016, available at http://www.iusct.net/General%20Documents/Communique%2016.1%20(9%20May%202016).pdf.

[83] Art. II(2), Claims Settlement Declaration.

[84] Communiqué No 16/1, of 9 May 2016, available at http://www.iusct.net/General%20Documents/Communique%2016.1%20(9%20May%202016).pdf.

[85] Communiqué No 16/1, of 9 May 2016, available at http://www.iusct.net/General%20Documents/Communique%2016.1%20(9%20May%202016).pdf.

[86] By June 1992, the Governing Council adopted Decision 10 approving the Provisional Rules For Claims Procedure ("the Rules") annexed to the decision, governing all aspects of the processing of claims as well as the selection and appointment of Commissioners. Further elaborations of the Rules were made subsequently, as the need arose, for instance in Governing Council Decisions 35 and 114.

1991.[87] These claims were for a fixed amount of $2,500 for individuals and $5,000 for families. For those claimants that only filed an "A" claim, the maximum eligible payment was of $4,000 for individuals and $8,000 for families. The Commission received over 90,000 claims in this category, from 77 governments and 13 offices of international organizations. The Commission awarded compensation to over 850,000 successful claimants for a total of more that $3.1 billion. The highest number of claims was awarded to Egyptian nationals (298,668 successful claimants). Other successful claimants were from India (101,257), Sri Lanka (80,547), Bangladesh (61,769), Kuwait (60,669), Jordan (50,263), Pakistan (32,841), Philippines (30,256), Sudan (20,994), Iran (19,242), Syria (16,544) Vietnam (15,989), Yemen (12,170) and China (10,179).

Category "B" claims were individual claims for serious personal injury to the person or for the death of a spouse, child or parent as a consequence of Iraq's invasion and occupation of Kuwait.[88] Similar to Category "A" claims, Category "B" claims were also for a fixed amount, in this case of $2,500 for individuals and $10,000 per family. About 6,000 "B" claims were filed by 47 governments as well as seven offices of three international organizations. About 3,900 claims were successful for a total of $13,450,000 awarded to claimants. Successful claimants originated from Kuwait (2,117), Jordan (446), Egypt (331), India (189), the United Kingdom (148), Israel (96), Sudan (80), Bangladesh (79), Yemen (53), the United States (50), Pakistan (50), Syria (48), France (47), Philippines (45) and Sri Lanka (40).

Category "C" claims were also for individual claims, and they included claims for damages of up to $100,000 each.[89] Category "C" claims included "twenty-one different types of losses, including those relating to departure from Kuwait or Iraq; personal injury; mental pain and anguish; loss of personal property; loss of bank accounts, stocks and other securities; loss of income; loss of real property; and individual business losses."[90] Eighty-five governments and eight offices of three international organizations filed a total of 1.7 million claims seeking compensation for a total of about $11.5 billion. Claims submitted under this category also included a consolidated claim submitted by the Central Bank of the

---

[87] See UNCC, "What We Do – The Claims – Category A," available at: http://www.uncc.ch/category.

[88] *See* UNCC, "What We Do – The Claims – Category B," available at: http://www.uncc.ch/category-b.

[89] *See* UNCC, "What We Do – The Claims – Category C," available at: http://www.uncc.ch/category-c.

[90] UNCC, "What We Do – The Claims – Category C."

Government of Egypt on behalf of 800,000 workers whose remittances were not deposited, as well as about 3,000 late Palestinian claims.[91] Successful claimants were awarded more than $5.1 billion in compensation. Category "C" claims originated from Egypt (311,601), Kuwait (193,989), Jordan (40,374), India (38,891), Syria (20,167), Pakistan (11,683), Bangladesh (8,669), Palestine (7,281), Philippines (5,769), Sudan (5,304) and others (28,791).

Category "D" claims were the final category of individual claims and covered claims in excess of $100,000.[92] The types of losses were similar to Category "C" but the sum requested was higher. Claims in the "D" category included departure costs, loss of real property and income, and business-related losses. Approximately 12,000 claimants requested approximately $16.5 billion. The more than 10,000 successful claimants were awarded $3.3 billion. Claims were filed by 50 governments and eight offices of three international organizations. Successful claimants came mostly from Kuwait (5,986), Jordan (1,558), India (849), Yemen (352), Palestine (308), the United Kingdom (307), the United States (274), Syria (155), Pakistan (155) and Canada (153), with the remaining 576 awarded claims coming from the other 40 governments and the international organizations.

Category "E" claims covered claims by corporations, other private legal entities and public sector enterprises.[93] The Commission further organized claims into four separate categories:

- "E1" Claims were related to claims from the oil sector, also known as Well Blowout Control (WBC). The Commission received 105 claims for losses related to petroleum activities from corporations that had operations in the Persian Gulf;[94]
- "E2" Claims were made up of 2,500 claims from non-Kuwaiti corporations for contract and financial losses, increased business costs, loss of goods and loss of or damage to property, excluding the oil sector and construction and engineering claims;[95]

---

91 See UNCC, "What We Do – The Claims – Category C- Relevant Decision of the Governing Council – Category C," available at: http://www.uncc.ch/relevant-decisions-governing-council-category-c.

92 See UNCC, "What We Do – The Claims – Category D," available at http://www.uncc.ch/category-d.

93 See UNCC, "What We Do – The Claims – Category E," available at: http://www.uncc.ch/category-e.

94 UNCC, "What We Do – The Claims – Category E."

95 UNCC, "What We Do – The Claims – Category E."

- "E3" Claims involved 400 claims from non-Kuwaiti corporations related to construction and engineering, excluding the oil sector, and including projects in Iraq, Kuwait and other Persian Gulf countries;
- "E4" Claims were claims of Kuwaiti corporations, for a total of 3,600 claims for loss of and damage to property, and claims for loss of profits and increased costs of both performance and cost of performance. "E4" claims excluded oil sector claims.

Under the category "E" claims, the commission awarded a total of $26.3 billion in compensation to about 4,000 claims coming from Kuwait (2,451), the United Kingdom (260), Germany (110), the United States (95), Israel (88), Egypt (66), India (55), Turkey (55) Saudi Arabia (45), the Netherlands (44), Italy (37), France (36) and others (361). This category includes the largest claims awarded by the UNCC: $14.7 billion for losses of oil production and sales that resulted from the damages inflicted on Kuwait's oil fields.

Category "F" claims were submitted by 43 governments and six international organizations for losses including costs for evacuation and for providing relief to citizens, damages to diplomatic premises and to other government property.[96] One important type of claim was for environmental damages, which included claims for damages caused to air, soil and water because of the invasion of Kuwait. Claimants submitted about 400 claims for over $236 billion.

These claims were also divided into four categories:

- "F1" Claims were claims for departure and evacuation costs and for damages to physical property that belonged to either government or international organizations. The Commission received 100 claims under this sub-category.
- "F2" Claims encompassed 63 claims from Jordan and Saudi Arabia seeking $18.4 billion and which excluded all environmental damages claims.
- "F3" claims included 62 claims filed by Kuwait for $114 billion and excluded claims for environmental damages.
- "F4" claims were claims for environmental damages. These 170 claims comprised claims for environmental damage and depletion of natural resources, including for oil-well fires and discharge of oil into the sea, as well as assistance costs from outside governments.

---

[96] UNCC, "What We Do – The Claims – Category F," available at: http://www.uncc.ch/category-e.http://www.uncc.ch/category-f.

Finally, a mixed Category of "E/F" comprised 123 claims for export guarantee and insurance seeking about $6.1 billion.

The Commission awarded compensation for a total of $14.4 billion. The most successful claimant was Kuwait (86 claims awarded for a total of $12 billion), followed by Saudi Arabia (61 claims awarded for a total of $1.438 billion) and Jordan (21 claims awarded for a total of $241 million).

Table 4.1 summarizes the number of claims submitted and awarded, the compensation sought and awarded, and the compensation paid and left to pay.

Claims in the Eritrea–Ethiopia Claims Commission

Claims heard by the EECC represent a distinct variety of post-conflict injury, and they uniquely include specific violations of international humanitarian law. The categories, forms and procedure of claims were decided by EECC Decision Number 2.[97] It described six categories in which claims could be filed:

Category 1: Claims of natural persons for unlawful expulsion from the country of their residence;

Category 2: Claims of natural persons for unlawful displacement from their residence;

Category 3: Claims of prisoners of war for injuries suffered from unlawful treatment;

Category 4: Claims of civilians for unlawful detention and for injuries suffered from unlawful treatment during detention;

Category 5: Claims of persons for loss, damage or injury other than those covered by the other categories;

Category 6: Claims of Governments for loss, damage or injury.

Mass-claims procedures could also be used for Categories 1 to 5.

Eritrea and Ethiopia decided to file their claims under Category 6, and no mass claims procedure was used. Each party chose a specific methodology to submit the claims, yet they largely covered the same issues and types of claims. Once received, the EECC grouped the claims according to issues and geographical areas covered by the claim. This allowed the EECC to cover the same issues, even if presented differently by the two parties, in a common and comparable way.

---

[97] Eritrea–Ethiopia Claims Commission, Decision Number 2, August 2001.

Table 4.1 Current status of payment

Sub-category	No. of claims submitted	Compensation sought ($)	No. of claims awarded compensation	Compensation awarded ($)	Percentage of awarded amount against claimed amount	Net compensation paid ($)	Outstanding award amounts ($)
A	923,158	3,455,092,500	852,499	3,149,692,000	91.16	3,116,924,873	0
B	5,734	20,100,000	3,935	13,435,000	66.84	13,377,388	0
C	1,738,237	11,503,877,999	672,452	5,185,716,912	45.08	5,178,317,570	0
D	11,915	16,539,501,201	10,343	3,348,902,861	20.25	3,347,980,604	0
E1	105	44,740,422,417	67	21,522,047,546	48.1	16,885,022,476	4,629,324,488
E2	2,445	13,661,076,541	954	916,054,517	6.71	915,480,192	0
E3	398	8,538,543,367	159	402,562,327	4.71	402,563,804	0
E4	3,623	11,796,336,671	2,868	3,456,889,662	29.3	3,458,491,969	0
E/F	123	6,148,493,927	57	311,282,668	5.06	311,282,668	0
F1	100	18,902,591,737	70	291,171,423	1.54	291,171,423	0
F2	63	18,417,163,597	46	264,422,123	1.44	264,099,732	0
F3	62	113,905,394,877	60	8,259,433,226	7.25	8,259,433,226	0
F4	168	84,904,244,069	109	5,261,746,450	6.2	5,260,112,735	0
Tot.	2,686,131	352,532,838,903	1,543,619	52,383,356,715	14.86%	47,704,258,660	4,629,324,488

Note: This is an only slightly modified version of a table available on the UNCC website, UNCC, Current status of payment, available at: http://www.uncc.ch/summary-awards-and-current-status-payments.

Between 2003 and 2005, the Commission issued four groups of partial and final awards which reviewed the liability of both parties. Specifically, it issued the following awards on Eritrea's claims:

- Prisoners of War (Eritrea's Claim 17) (Partial Award, 1 July 2003);
- Central Front (Eritrea's Claims 2, 4, 6, 7, 8 & 22) (Partial Award, 28 April 2004);
- Civilians' Claims (Eritrea's Claims 15, 16, 23 & 27–32) (Partial Award, 17 December 2004);
- Western Front, Aerial Bombardment and Related Claims (Eritrea's Claims 1, 3, 5, 9–13, 14, 21, 25 & 26) (Partial Award, 19 December 2005);
- Pensions (Eritrea's Claims 15, 19 & 23) (Final Award, 19 December 2005);
- Loss of Property in Ethiopia Owned by Non-Residents (Eritrea's Claim 24) (Partial Award, 19 December 2005);
- Diplomatic Claim (Eritrea's Claim 20) (Partial Award, 19 December 2005).[98]

It also issued the following partial or final awards on liability on Ethiopia's claims:

- Prisoners of War (Ethiopia's Claim 4) (Partial Award, 1 July 2003);
- Central Front (Ethiopia's Claim 2) (Partial Award, 28 April 2004);
- Civilians' Claims (Ethiopia's Claim 5) (Partial Award, 17 December 2004);
- *Jus Ad Bellum* (Ethiopia's Claims 1–8) (Partial Award, 19 December 2005);
- Western and Eastern Fronts (Ethiopia's Claims 1 & 3) (Partial Award, 19 December 2005);
- Ports (Ethiopia's Claim 6) (Final Award, December 19, 2005);
- Economic Loss Throughout Ethiopia (Ethiopia's Claim 7) (Partial Award, 19 December 2005);
- Diplomatic Claim (Ethiopia's Claim 8) (Partial Award, 19 December 2005).[99]

---

98 http://www.haguejusticeportal.net/Docs/Court%20Documents/PCA/ER%20Final%20Damages_Award_complete.pdf.

99 http://www.haguejusticeportal.net/Docs/Court%20Documents/PCA/ET_Final_Damages_Award_complete.pdf.

In terms of compensation, the EECC awarded Eritrea $161,455,000 in respect of its own claims for *jus in bello* violations and $2,065,865 to individual claimants.[100] Specifically, the EECC awarded Eritrea:

- $13.5 million for losses of residential and business property on the Central and Western Fronts;
- $35,965,000 for damage to and destruction of buildings on the Central and Western Fronts;
- $1.5 million in respect of injuries to civilians due to loss of access to health care on account of damage to or destruction of Eritrean hospitals and other medical facilities and loss of medical supplies;
- $100,000 for damage to cultural property, specifically $50,000 for damage to the Stela of Matara and $50,000 for damage to the Tserona Patriots Cemetery;
- $4 million for mistreatment of prisoners of war;
- $2 million for failing to prevent the rape of known and unknown victims in the towns of Senafe, Barentu and Teseney;
- $1,550,000 for forcible expulsion of the population of Awgaro;
- $50,000 in respect of the unknown, but apparently small, number of dual Eritrean–Ethiopian nationals who were arbitrarily deprived of their Ethiopian nationality while present in third countries;
- $15 million in respect of the wrongful expulsion of an unknown, but considerable, number of dual nationals by local Ethiopian authorities;
- $11 million for receiving, caring for and resettling rural Ethiopian nationals wrongfully expelled from Ethiopia;
- $2 million for failure to provide humane and safe treatment for persons being expelled from Ethiopia;
- $46 million for expellees' losses of property on account of Ethiopia's wrongful actions;
- $24,525,000 for Ethiopia's failure to return or provide compensation after the war for vehicles it requisitioned from non-resident Eritreans;
- $1.5 million for other property losses of non-resident Eritreans;
- $2.6 million for imprisoning Eritrean civilians on security charges or detaining them for unknown reasons, under harsh and unacceptable conditions;
- $155,000 for violation of Eritrea's diplomatic premises and property.

100 EECC, Eritrea Damages Award, Section IX.

The Commission also awarded compensation to named Eritrean individuals for Ethiopia's failure to provide humane and safe treatment in transport from Ethiopia, lack of access to bank accounts and unlawful deprivation of property.[101]

Similarly, the EECC awarded Ethiopia $174,036,520.[102] Specifically, for violations by Eritrea of *jus in bello*, Ethiopia was awarded:

- $11 million for death, physical injury, disappearance, forced labor and conscription of Ethiopian civilians;
- $2 million for failing to prevent rape of known and unknown victims in Irob, Dalul and Elidar Weredas;
- $13.9 million for looting, and destruction of and damage to houses;
- $20,195,000 for damage, destruction and looting in Zalambessa;
- $2.5 million for death, injury and property damage in Mekele;
- $315,000 for looting of and damage to government buildings and infrastructure;
- $4.5 million for looting, destruction and damage to religious institutions;
- $3,216,000 for seizure and looting of the Saba Dimensional Stones Share Company;
- $7.5 million for mistreatment of Ethiopian prisoners of war;
- $2 million for failure to protect Ethiopian civilians in Eritrea from threats and violence;
- $1.5 million for failure to ensure Ethiopian civilians in Eritrea access to employment;
- $50,000 for failure to ensure that Ethiopian civilians in Eritrea were able to receive medical care to the same extent as Eritrean nationals;
- $2 million for wrongful detention and abusive treatment of Ethiopian civilians in Eritrean custody;
- $1.5 million for harsh treatment of Ethiopian civilians at the Hawshaite detention camp;
- $10 million for detaining significant numbers of Ethiopian civilians under harsh conditions during and after May 2000;
- $500,000 for deaths and injuries suffered by detainees at the Wi'a Camp;
- $2 million for failure to protect the property of Ethiopian detainees expelled from Eritrea;

101 EECC, Eritrea Damages Award, Section IX.
102 EECC, Ethiopia Damages Award, Section XII.

- $1 million for failure to protect the property of other departing Ethiopians;
- $1.1 million for failing to ensure the safe and humane repatriation of departing Ethiopians in transports that were not conducted or supervised by the ICRC.[103]

The Commission also awarded Ethiopia compensation for Eritrea's violation of *jus ad bellum*. Namely, Ethiopia was awarded:

- $45 million for human suffering and lost income associated with internal displacement of persons;
- $8.5 million for Ethiopian civilian deaths and injuries;
- $6 million for damage to civilian property, primarily from shelling;
- $3.5 million for damage to public buildings and infrastructure;
- $2.5 million for looting, destruction and damage to religious institutions;
- $5,605,000 for destruction in Zalambessa;
- $1.5 million for deaths and injuries caused by landmines;
- $250,000 for destruction of Disaster Prevention and Preparedness Bureau facilities in Adigrat;
- $162,500 for damage to other government facilities on the Central Front;
- $75,000 for other government losses on the Central Front;
- $125,000 for looting of property from the Relief Society of Tigray;
- $150,000 for damage in Adi Goshu;
- $625,000 for shelling damage in Sheraro;
- $65,000 for damage caused by the attack on the Mekele airport;
- $4 million for profits lost by Ethiopian Airlines;
- $1,703,020 for failing to provide Ethiopian Airlines access to its bank accounts at the Bank of Eritrea;
- $7.50 million for reconstruction and assistance to internally displaced persons.[104]

The paragraphs above showed the diversity, scale, reach and extent of the claims heard by claims commissions. It also highlights the importance of a well-crafted definition of the subject-matter jurisdiction of a commission.

---

103 EECC, Ethiopia Damages Award, Section XII.
104 EECC, Ethiopia Damages Award, Section XII.

TEMPORAL JURISDICTION

Another important policy choice to be made when creating a claims commission relates to the temporal jurisdiction to be covered. The challenge in this situation is to find the right equilibrium to ensure full coverage of claims directly related to the international upheaval that resulted in the creation of a claims commission, but also to ensure that there is no overreach and that no claims are included that were pre-existing or not directly related to the events. A precise and clear timeframe, with an indisputable starting and finishing time, is essential for the successful work of a claims commission. The IUSCT, the UNCC and the EECC all carefully detailed their temporal jurisdiction in their constitutive instruments.

The "General Declaration" that established the Iran–US Claims Tribunal provided that all existing claims between the two parties would be resolved through binding arbitration.[105] The Claim Settlement Declaration further specified that the Iran–US Claims Tribunal would have jurisdiction over private claims, and counterclaims arising out of the same contract or transaction, if such claims and counterclaims were outstanding as of 19 January 1981 (the date of the agreement), whether they had been filed or not with any court and arising out of debts, contracts, expropriations or other measures affecting property rights.[106] The jurisdiction of the Iran–US Claims Tribunal relating to official claims was limited to contractual arrangements between them for the purchase and sale of goods and services.[107] Because claims related essentially to property rights, the timing of the underlying injury was relatively easy to determine by examining the contract or other official measures.

In terms of filing deadline, the Settlement Declaration provided that claims had to be filed within a year from the entry into force of the Agreement or within six months from the date in which the President of the Tribunal was appointed, whichever of the two occurred later.[108]

---

[105] General Principle B, Declaration of the Government of the Democratic and Popular Republic of Algeria (General Declaration) (19 January 1981), 1 Iran–US Cl. Trib. Rep., p. 4, available at: http://www.iusct.org.

[106] Art. II(1), Claims Settlement Declaration.

[107] Art. II(2), Claims Settlement Declaration.

[108] Art. III(4), Providing that "[n]o claim may be filed with the Tribunal more than one year after the entry into force of this Agreement or six months after the date the President is appointed, whichever is later. These deadlines do not apply to the procedures contemplated by Paragraphs 16 and 17 of the

The temporal jurisdiction of the UNCC reflected the more complex underlying situation. Security Council Resolution 687 provided that "without prejudice to the debts and obligations of Iraq arising prior to" 2 August 1990, Iraq was liable under international law for direct losses, damages and injuries resulting from Iraq's unlawful invasion and occupation of Kuwait.[109] The question of what were claims arising prior to 2 August 1990 – the date of the invasion of Kuwait – was therefore pivotal to correctly limiting the jurisdiction of the UNCC. An "E2" Panel was the first to confront the issue and concluded that:

> when the performance giving rise to the debt had been rendered by a Claimant more than three months before Iraq's invasion and occupation of Kuwait, that is, prior to 2 May 1990, a claim based on payment owed for such performance is to be considered as a debt or obligation arising prior to Iraq's invasion and occupation of Kuwait and is therefore outside the jurisdiction of the Commission.

This interpretation was followed and applied by all subsequent panels and resolved the jurisdictional question.[110]

Under the EECC, the question of temporal jurisdiction was more complex. Indeed, it was initially addressed only tangentially in the Agreement. Article 5 provides that the EECC would decide claims related to the conflict.[111] Hence, one of the first tasks of the EECC was to specify its temporal jurisdiction. It did so in its Decision Number 1, in which it decided that:

> the central reference point for determining the scope of its mandate under Article (5)1 of the Agreement is the conflict between the parties. In the overall context of the relevant documents cited in Article (5)1, the Commission understands this to mean the armed conflict that began in May 1998 and was formally brought to an end by the Agreement on December 12, 2000.

Declaration of the Government of Algeria of January 19, 1981," available at: http://www.iusct.net/General%20Documents/2-Claims%20Settlement%20Declaration.pdf.

[109] UNSC Res 687 (1991) (reaffirming that "that Iraq, without prejudice to the debts and obligations of Iraq arising prior to 2 August 1990 which will be addressed through the normal mechanisms, is liable under international law for any direct loss, damage, including environmental damage and the depletion of natural resources, or injury to foreign Governments, nationals and corporations, as a result of Iraq's unlawful invasion and occupation of Kuwait.").

[110] "Report and Recommendations Made by the Panel of Commissioners Concerning the First Installment of 'E2' Claims" (S/AC.26/1998/7) ¶ 90.

[111] Algiers Agreement, Art. 5.

> There is a presumption that claims arising during this period "relate to" the conflict and are within the Commission's jurisdiction.[112]

In the same decision, the EECC also concluded that certain claims after 12 December 2000, could also "relate to" the conflict if a party could demonstrate that those claims arose as a result of the armed conflict between the parties or occurred in the course of the forces' disengagement. Claims before May 1998 (date of the beginning of the hostilities) did not come within the jurisdiction of the EECC because the conflict that was at the center of the EECC had not yet occurred.

CONCLUSION

This chapter covers the basic jurisdictional provisions in claims commissions. It discusses in detail who are the claimants, what are the claims and when can these claims be brought under the rules of the Iran–US Claims Tribunal, the UNCC and the EECC.

The importance of several issues emerges from this analysis. First and foremost, it is important that subject matter and personal and temporal jurisdiction are all clearly defined and determined at the outset and in the constitutive instruments of each claims commission. That clarity will allow the work of the commission to run smoothly. That said, however, each commission can be empowered to facilitate proceedings by using certain procedural mechanisms, including giving priority to small claims and individual claimants, and ensuring that claims are grouped so as to make proceedings and decision-making more manageable. Finally, the importance of ensuring that sufficient funds exist to compensate claims and that the awards are paid to successful claimants remains paramount. In this vein, the importance of the support of the international community for the activities of claims commissions cannot be overestimated.[113]

---

[112] EECC, Decision Number 1, 1 August 2001, Section B.

[113] *See* generally Chapter 7.

5. The financial structure of claims commissions

Lawyers are not uninterested in money, but they are notoriously indifferent to the mechanics of managing it. The legal profession's antipathy toward the details of finance normally matters little. Lawyers advise on the law and defer to the MBAs on the business. Unfortunately, this division of labor is unavailable in the urgent post-conflict situations that we explore in this book. MBAs are not generally drawn to a closed-end venture that lacks a profit motive, leaving the lawyers in unfamiliar territory.

Mapping this terrain is more art than science, but one thing is certain: absent rational economics, no IMCC will go much beyond a framework document. Even though an IMCC might serve non-pecuniary aims,[1] compensation of some sort will be the primary objective. Without individual justice, lasting peace will prove elusive.

With such high stakes, an important first step is to calibrate the ambitions of an IMCC to its resources. This begins with a clear assessment of the available funding and a budget to estimate and allocate expenses. This chapter explores some of the financial issues that will arise as an IMCC decides how to conducts its affairs.[2] For this discussion we will draw on the experience of the three IMCCs that are the primary subject of this book, the IUSCT, EECC and UNCC, augmented by four additional IMCCs, the German Forced Labor Compensation Program (GFLCP), Claims Resolution Tribunal for Dormant Accounts in Switzerland II (CRT-II) and the Commission for Real Property Claims of Displaced Persons and Refugees (CRPC).

The additional IMCCs assist in building a more rounded understanding of the financial affairs of a typical IMCC. Nothing requires an IMCC to

[1] *See* Chapter 2 and Chapter 7 for a discussion of the various stakeholders and the interests they have in submitting a dispute to an IMCC. Non-pecuniary objectives include creating a meaningful alternative to armed conflict, providing closure of painful incidents, and ultimately serving as a transition to peace.

[2] These expenses also decrease the amount that is available for domestic investment, which can be critical to restarting a post-conflict economy.

make its financial data public, and there is no discernible advantage to an IMCC in voluntarily subjecting itself to a public audit. Consequently, the publicly available financial data rarely goes beyond top-line amounts, are not issued in a standard format, and are not published consistently (*e.g.*, quarterly, semi-annually or annually). These dissimilar datasets offer no basis for a rigorous analytical assessment, but there is enough of a critical mass to piece together a narrative that will necessarily traffic in some degree of informed speculation. We begin with a description on the key issue of funding mechanisms. A final section discusses the various categories of costs that claims commissions will face and how they relate to each other. The IMCCs discussed below have been described in depth in Chapter 1.

In Chapter 8, we recognize that IMCCs fall on something of a spectrum from "thick" to "thin." A large part of this characterization revolves around funding and other practical issues that are important to an IMCC's operation. IMCCs that have an assured funding method (as opposed to requesting periodic contributions from state parties) also tend to have larger budgets, dedicated staff, longer tenures with some method for accumulating precedent, and the other practical accoutrements of domestic courts. These we describe as "thick." "Thin" IMCCs rely more on outsourcing, tend to have shorter time horizons, have no permanent and secure independent funding mechanism, and overall have less of an institutional presence in the generation of international law. To a large degree, the differences between the various IMCCs described in this chapter track differences between where they fall on the spectrum of thick to thin.

One unassailable conclusion is that these IMCCs range from the expensive to the enormously expensive. On the merely expensive end is the CRPC, which received an annual average of $4.8 million over its seven years of operations ($33.5 million total).[3] Total operational expenditure for the GFLCP (another mass claims commission, but with fixed-sum compensation) during the peak year of 2001 was DEM 18.7 million ($8.7 million).[4] On the enormously expensive end is the United Nations Claims Commission (UNCC), which evaluated over 2.7 million claims

[3] Commission for Real Property Claims of Displaced Persons and Refugees (CRPC): End of Mandate Report: Executive Summary (1996–2003), at 14.

[4] The International Organization for Migration (IOM) carried out the mass claims processing. It received 320,000 completed claims forms: 306,000 for Slave and Forced Labor and Personal Injury, and 14,000 for Property Loss. The major portion of the overall endowment, almost DEM 8.7 billion ($4.1 billion) was distributed to surviving forced laborers in the form of individual lump-sum

between 1991 and 2007, at its peak employed as many as 320 staff and has cost an average of $25 million annually.[5]

FUNDING

Our primary topic is examining how to identify, allocate and control costs, but we pause first to consider funding.[6] Funding is obviously tied up with the discussion of compensation as a remedy, which is examined in some depth in Chapters 4 and 7. Our purpose here is not to determine whether compensation is the optimal remedy, but to examine how compensation is related to operational funding and what implications this has for how an IMCC operates.

The funding models used by the IMCCs in this chapter are described briefly below:

UNCC:	a stable source of capital diverted automatically to pay successful claims and operational costs;
CRT-I, CRT-II:	an identified group of unclaimed assets to be distributed to identifiable owners with operational costs paid separately by the holder of those assets;
GFLCP:	an initial pool of funds to be exhausted to pay compensation and operational costs;
IUSCT:	an initial pool of funds to pay awards with a commitment to replenish, and with operational costs paid separately;

payments. *See* German Forced Labor Compensation Program Fact Sheet, International Organization for Migration, available at: http://www.iom.int/files/live/sites/iom/files/What-We-Do/docs/German-Forced-Labour-Compensation-Programme-GFLCP.pdf.

[5] This number has dropped considerably as the UNCC has wound down its operations. For the year ended 31 December 2015, the UNCC's operating expenses of about $1.8 million related primarily to staff costs of approximately $1.2 million and other costs of $0.5 million, mainly for the rental of office space, accounting support services, and conference costs. *See* Report of the Board of Auditors to the Security Council on the financial statements of the United Nations Compensation Commission for the year ended 31 December 2015, S/2016/814 (September 19, 2016), at 9/53.

[6] Funding for payment of compensation – a critical component of an IMCC's success or failure – is explored in Chapter 7.

EECC: a bilateral agreement with state parties agreeing to pay awards to each other and to pay operational costs separately; and

CRPC: an equitable remedy of restoration of title to real property, with an aspirational commitment to provide compensation as an alternative remedy, and with operational costs to be allocated to state parties.[7]

Some structures are more desirable than others, but the funding of an IMCC is more a product of circumstance than design. The commissioners and the Secretariat will be given a mechanism and asked to make it work. In theory, the UNCC model comes closest to ideal: the compensation fund and the operating costs are committed and seemingly secure. In fact, the Holocaust-era programs had the fewest problems, presumably because the commercial parties who held the accounts had ample resources to fund the IMCC, as well as a reputational interest in putting liabilities incurred by a previous generation in the rear-view mirror.

Security of Funds

Where a program involves a return of unclaimed or dispossessed assets, funding issues will be confined to operational costs, which rarely pose a problem. Lapsed funding for compensation, however, can consume time and resources or even potentially derail the program. For instance, the IUSCT has twice heard disputes between the state parties regarding funding. Under the framework document, Iran agreed to replenish to $1 billion the security account, out of which awards are paid, whenever it fell below $500 million. This occurred repeatedly, even as Iran has continued to fund the IUSCT operational costs, albeit with some prodding.[8] The United States prevailed on the merits in both disputes, but the

---

[7] This was an alternative to the primary remedy: restitution of real property to pre-conflict owners. Commission for Real Property Claims of Displaced Persons and Refugees (CRPC): End of Mandate Report: Executive Summary (1996–2003), 1.

[8] A 2003 communication from then-President George W. Bush to Congress gives a sense of ongoing US efforts to compel Iran to honor its financial obligations under the Algiers Accords:

> Iran continues to fail to replenish the Security Account established by the Algiers Accords to ensure payment of awards to successful US claimants. Thus, since November 5, 1992, the Security Account has continuously remained below the $500 million balance required by the Algiers Accords.

resulting awards were largely symbolic. The IUSCT cannot order any remedy beyond telling Iran to do what it agreed to do. Moreover, because there are no outstanding claims against Iran in excess of the $500 million threshold, the breach is largely technical. However, the inability to enforce the award underscores how vulnerable an IMCC can be to state-party recalcitrance.

The UNCC avoided these problems by diverting funds directly from the Iraqi oil industry into accounts to fund compensation and pay operating expenses. The providential coincidence of an acknowledged wrongdoer with a ready cash stream to be confiscated at the source has allowed the UNCC a *de facto* enforcement mechanism to avoid the difficulties experienced by the IUSCT.

The EECC resulted in substantial awards to Ethiopia ($174.0 million) and to Eritrea ($161.4 million).[9] The net result was an award of $12.5 million to Ethiopia. Ethiopia has never demanded payment of the EECC award, perhaps because it had already refused to honor the award of the Eritrea–Ethiopia Boundary Commission.[10] Both Eritrea and Ethiopia complied with their separate obligations to pay operating costs of both the EECC and the EEBC.

> As of March 31, 2003, the total amount in the Security Account was $93,246,103.11, and the total amount in the Interest Account was $53,782,536.99. Because Iran continues to fail to comply, the United States is actively pursuing Case No. A/33 to require Iran to replenish the Security Account now and in the future. … The United States also continues to pursue Case No. A/29 to require Iran to meet its obligation of timely payment of its equal share of advances for Tribunal expenses when directed to do so by the Tribunal.

108th Congress, 1st Session, House Document 108-71, A Report on The National Emergency with Respect to Iran, Message from the President of the United States Transmitting a Six Month Periodic Report on the National Emergency with Respect to Iran That Was Declared in Executive Order 12170 Of November 14, 1979, Pursuant to 50 USC 1641(c) and 50 USC 1703(c) (May 14, 2003).

[9] *See* Final Award, Ethiopia's Damages Claims between The State of Eritrea and The Federal Democratic Republic of Ethiopia, 17 August 2009, 105–106 and Final Award, Eritrea's Damages Claims between The State of Eritrea and The Federal Democratic Republic of Ethiopia, 17 August 2009, 95–96.

[10] The EEBC was a commission created by the Algiers Framework Agreement that created the EECC. The mandate of the EEBC was to "delimit and demarcate the colonial treaty border based on pertinent colonial treaties (1900, 1902 and 1908) and applicable international law." *See* Algiers Agreement, Article

One way to avoid these expected and unexpected difficulties is to pre-fund a compensation pool in an amount adequate to cover awards and costs and then deplete that fund gradually. The GFLCP followed this approach with success. German government and industry established a foundation, which was careful not to represent the program as anything other than nominal lump-sum compensation to claimants or their heirs. By the end of the program, it became clear that the foundation was over-endowed. It paid awards and operating costs and continues to operate as a grant-making entity that funds programs to further human rights, including those that touch on "coming to terms with forced labor" under the Nazi regime.[11]

Unfortunately, most post-conflict scenarios do not come with a liquid asset that can be diverted to escrow or a private benefactor to endow a foundation. A state party facing asymmetrical "victor's justice" is much more likely to have been ravaged by the conflict. Humanitarian concerns will, and (in our view) should, predominate. The question then becomes who will pick up the IMCC's operating expenses. The CRPC experience demonstrates that the international community is an unreliable financial partner. The geopolitical incentives to support the establishment of an IMCC do not necessarily extend to assuming financial responsibility for its success. Where financial responsibility has devolved to state parties who are contesting liability, the obvious incentive is to withhold funding compensation until net liability is determined. The commitment by state parties to fund the operating costs of such an IMCC should be made explicit.

Even with explicit funding commitments, international law has its limits. Ideally, a security interest would be created in some sort of asset (*e.g.*, highly rated sovereign debt) that could be foreclosed in order to secure payment. Practically speaking, setting up this sort of mechanism adds yet another layer of complexity and is likely to prove politically unpalatable to the state parties, whose participation in an IMCC relies heavily on preserving as much autonomy as possible. Practically speaking, few financial enforcement tools are available, short of polite requests, public opprobrium and the entry of symbolic awards.

In some cases, an IMCC might be able to restructure obligations to ensure the program's viability. Most IMCCs will exist for years and

---

4. Although the award "delimited" the border on paper, Ethiopia never permitted "demarcation" – *e.g.*, the placing of boundary markers on the ground.

[11] A list of the programs supported by the Foundation is available at: http://www.stiftung-evz.de/eng/home.html.

ideally should be given some latitude to adjust to subsequent developments. After Saddam Hussein was deposed in 2003 and occupied Iraq descended into sectarian chaos, diverting Iraqi revenue into the UNCC compensation fund took a back seat to rebuilding the economy and infrastructure and restoring political stability.[12] The UNCC has – through the Security Council – adjusted the formula several times, most recently suspending the obligation temporarily. As of early 2017, the only unpaid compensation is owed to Kuwait, which is presumably not prejudiced by delay in the service of regional political stability and peace.

Financial Management

The Algiers Accords that created the IUSCT were negotiated under significant pressure and, with a change of presidential leadership looming, in some haste. Little attention was paid to administrative minutiae (*e.g.*, managing the security account) that the United States, at least, appeared to assume were obvious. A dispute quickly arose over what to do with interest earned by the $1 billion deposited with the Dutch Central Bank – N.V. Settlement Bank. Washington had simply assumed that the interest would be credited to the account and compounded; Iran asserted title to the funds.[13] While the matter was pending, the Dutch central bank deposited the interest in a separate account, which arrangement the IUSCT later endorsed as permanent.[14] The IUSCT ruled that Iran could access the interest account only to replenish the security account and to recoup the balance when the IUSCT disbanded. Finally, the IUSCT ruled that it had no power to order the funds in the interest account to be paid directly to a claimant. This result was not unworkable, but it was anomalous: an award that could not be satisfied out of the balance in the security account could also not be paid out of the interest that had accrued on that account, unless Iran agreed.

If a sizable amount of money is to be held by an IMCC, banks should be brought in early to ensure that proposed financing arrangements cover all reasonably foreseeable contingencies, including cultural differences

---

[12] More detailed background on the protracted process of securing Iraq's contributions to the fund, including the creation of the "Oil for Food" Program can be found in Chapter 1 and Chapter 7.

[13] The original misunderstanding about these arrangements was probably complicated by Islam's views on the payment of interest, which is not consistent with Sharia law except under tightly controlled circumstances.

[14] Iran and United States, Decision No. DEC 12-A1-FT (3 August 1982), 4–5.

about finance. The optimal course is to delegate to the financial institution that holds the funds as much agency as it will agree to take. The state parties should backstop this discretion with a formal, fast-track dispute-resolution process overseen by an expert. Some other issues to be determined in advance include how the funds will be held and disbursed, how they will be invested and with what degree of discretion, whether settlements will be paid out of the fund (another problem for the IUSCT, which was eventually resolved only by Iran consenting to the practice), the mechanics of paying settlements and successful claims, making provision for the timing and standards of audits, and returning any remaining funds when the program wraps up.

COST

Framework agreements generally say little about costs, save a reference to how they will be allocated. It will fall to the commissioners and Secretariat to compile a budget that spells out the details of categories and expected amounts. Because market discipline cannot be relied upon to brake unnecessary or excessive spending, it will be important to ensure that costs are controlled (*e.g.*, outsourced through competitive bidding) and periodically audited, all without creating a sclerotic bureaucracy that consumes even more funding. Oversight is arguably most important when costs are paid out of a fixed fund, since operating expense reduces amounts available to pay compensation and creates conflicts of interest. As discussed above, the GFLCP paid all of its claims with money to spare, but it has not been immune from criticism regarding the opacity surrounding its operations.[15]

When costs are underwritten by a third party or donor, the pressure for oversight will (or should) come from the donor. The larger reputational

---

[15] See Dzeno Association Report, "Compensations to Roma Victims of the Holocaust and the International Organization for Migration" (undated draft) recommendations, 18:

- Consider the possibility that Roma people may not have been properly assisted in this matter.
- Not to support any programs on behalf of Roma if they are administered by IOM.
- To demand and publish all reports and financial records related to IOM programmes.
- Make all information accessible and transparent. IOM should pay special attention to transparency in their usage of money. Thus, they should clearly state not only how much money they received for each programme, but

stakes attached to this sort of funding make it important to cost the enterprise properly. Future donors will hesitate to underwrite commissions if they are mismanaged or are seen as inefficient vehicles designed to generate employment for bureaucrats at the expense of claimants.

When the costs are underwritten by one or more of the state parties, oversight is important, but the main issue to be resolved is the allocation of costs.[16] In an asymmetrical proceeding where liability is uncontested, like the UNCC, costs can be allocated to the party assuming liability. In a symmetrical proceeding, such as the IUSCT or the EECC, the two governments often agree to bear expenses equally. An equal allocation on a pay-as-you-go basis worked surprisingly well in these two programs, considering it relies entirely on good-faith deposit of advance funds on demand by the Secretariat. Despite occasional disharmony, the IUSCT state parties have continued to fund the tribunal without interruption for nearly four decades. The governments of Eritrea and Ethiopia also met their shared underwriting obligations without default, even as the process of implementing the findings of the EEBC disintegrated. This might have something do with an unwillingness to be perceived as the cause of an IMCC's collapse over a comparatively trivial amount.

Drivers of Cost

The factors affecting operating cost can be immutable (*e.g.*, location of the commission), uncertain (*e.g.*, the number of claims to adjudicate; duration) or left to the discretion of the commission (*e.g.*, evidence-gathering procedures), but none of these variables operates in a vacuum. Larger decisions about priorities will ripple through the cost structure. For instance, a decision to privilege speed will require larger staff. Larger

---

also the exact number of people who applied for and received compensation or assistance in each country.

- To publish all reports and financial records related to IOM programmes.

[16] In all of these cases, underwriting the operational cost of a commission will be in addition to the costs the parties pay for their own efforts to prepare and present a case. These include employing counsel, collecting evidence, preparing and submitting pleadings, securing expert opinions, translating documents and attending hearings. The UNCC allowed states filing on behalf of their citizens to net these costs out of the award. *See* Marco Frigessi di Rattalma and Tullio Treves, *The United Nations Compensation Commission: A Handbook* (Springer, 1999), 10. That model is the exception. A 2007 ICC report showed that party costs in international arbitration are 82 percent of the overall cost. *See* "Techniques for Controlling Time and Costs," in *Arbitration Report from the ICC Commission on Arbitration* (ICC Publication 843, 2007).

staff will increase capital costs for putting plant and equipment in place. We discuss first a few of these larger framework issues before discussing the expense line items that account for a majority of operating costs.

Technology

Since the IMCCs discussed in this chapter began (and, in most cases, wound down) operations, technology has undergone a revolution that is only beginning to be tapped by the legal profession. Most of us now carry around a device that has more computing power than NASA used in 1969 to land on the moon, and the internet can harness that power in ever more productive ways. The cost of this technology continues to decrease, so that the upfront development costs of custom applications are easier to justify. The more a pool of potential claims can be standardized, the more technology can step in to produce speedy results at a lower cost. But even in cases where heterogeneous claims will be individually considered, technology has much to offer. New developments in artificial intelligence, cloud computing, imaging and even social media will drive costs down further, freeing humans to do the heavy analytical work, requiring fewer of them to do it and allowing an IMCC to do more with less.

Number and complexity of claims

This is perhaps the most important variable in a commission's budget. The workload of a commission can range from that of the UNCC, which evaluated nearly 169,000 largely standardized claims per year for 16 years, to the IUSCT, which has issued a total of 602 awards to resolve individual claims.[17] Although, in advance, the number of expected claims can only be estimated, the exercise is useful in helping to ensure that the parties shape jurisdiction carefully to avoid an unmanageable or unaffordable workload.[18]

---

17 IUSCT Communiqué No. 16/1, Statistical Report (9 May 2016).

18 A closely related question, with obvious cost ramifications, is whether the categories of harm have been delineated precisely. The experience of IOM attempting to interpret the parameters of the GFLCP is instructive: "In order to avoid raising expectations and eventually being flooded with incompensable claims, early on [the] IOM sought clarification on issues such as 'extremely harsh living conditions' in which forced labourers had to be held to qualify for compensation, or the eligibility of Italian Military Internees. By the time it received clarification – which was in both instances late and restrictive – tens of thousands of internees and Western European claimants had unfortunately

Making cost judgments based solely on expected volume, however, is imprudent. An enormous number of very simple claims can consume fewer resources than a smaller number of extremely complex claims. To manage these different situations, trade-offs are inevitable. Mass-claims processing of standardized categories of claims can drastically reduce the time and cost needed compared to processing claims individually. Adopting relaxed standards of proof and fixed compensation will further reduce time and expense. This approach is more realistic in an asymmetric situation where liability is not an issue. The GFLCP, for example, operated as a purely mass claims program that paid a fixed sum to narrowly defined categories of claimants who provided minimal documentation.[19] The CRPC, CRT-I and CRT-II also processed a considerable volume of homogeneous claims in a reasonably short period. None of them needed to resort to fixed compensation because the relief sought was return of an asset.[20]

The cost savings from adopting this sort of swift, rough justice are considerable, but claimants might pay a price. On the processing side, the awards will be paid more quickly, the claims will require less proof, and fewer humans will be needed to process the claims. Where a lump-sum amount is paid, however, the compensation may fall well short of the actual loss. Where an asset is returned, it may have depreciated or appreciated, and this nuance will be lost when volume is the priority.

If more precise justice is sought, a different set of trade-offs awaits. The individual awards more accurately reflect individual losses, but expenses will mount as humans with specialized training make individual

---

already submitted claims to IOM." German Forced Labor Compensation Programme Holocaust Victim Assets Programme (Swiss Banks), Activity Report July 2000–December 2001, International Organization for Migration, Document No. MC/INF/248 (3 May 2002), 4.

[19] Category A included persons who were exploited as forced laborers in a concentration camp or a closed ghetto. Each received an amount of EUR 7,670. Category B included persons who were deported from their home countries to the German Reich or to German-occupied territories and then subjected to forced labor under detainment, conditions resembling detention, or similar extremely harsh living conditions. Each received payments of EUR 2,560. *See* http://www.stiftung-evz.de/eng/the-foundation/facts-and-figures.html?L=0.

[20] CRT-II did eventually adopt a fixed-compensation category to assist claimants who were able to make a *prima facie* claim but who lacked supporting documentation and could not be located in the account database. Holocaust Victim Assets Litigation Case No. CV 96-4849 Swiss Banks Settlement Fund Distribution Statistics as of 31 December 2015 (Amounts Approved and Paid by the Court).

judgments about value. There may also be indirect costs if the process becomes bogged down: Awards will be delayed, claimants unable to produce evidence of loss will be denied any recovery and other claimants may have died.

The IUSCT, which litigated each claim before a tribunal on a full evidentiary record, took claims for two years (the deadline was January 1982). Eight years later, so many small claims had accumulated that the IUSCT outsourced them to the Foreign Claims Settlement Commission, a standing entity within the U.S. Department of Justice.[21] Forty years and five presidential administrations later, the IUSCT is in the very final stages of winding down. The EECC, which had the flexibility to adopt mass claims processing, chose instead to group together large numbers of factually similar claims as single causes of action brought by the respective governments, took almost ten years to fully litigate.

The UNCC combined mass claims and individual claims into a large program that saved on cost by drawing wherever possible on technology and statistical analysis. It also took express notice of the difficulty experienced by the IUSCT in efficiently processing smaller claims. The UNCC elected to create several categories of individual harms and give those claimants priority. It assigned these categories a lump-sum compensation payable upon satisfying minimal standards of proof.[22] It later took up individual consideration of the more complex cases brought by corporations, international organizations and governments.[23] The UNCC

---

21 If practice makes perfect in claims processing, the FCSC must surely be the gold standard. Since 1948 it has been the conduit to which the United States outsources its mass claims programs and has gained considerable experience in conducting programs of this kind. Of the 3,066 claims for under $250,000 transferred to the FCSC from the IUSCT, 1,066 awards were made totaling $41.5 million. Claimants received actual damages to a limit of $10,000. An additional 578 claims were withdrawn or dismissed for failure to appear, and 1,422 claims were denied. The process took five years. Foreign Claims Settlement Commission of the US, Completed Programs: Iran, available at: https://www.justice.gov/fcsc/completed-programs-iran.

22 *See* Chapter 4 for a full description of the categories of claims and fixed-sum amounts.

23 The structure reflected a realization that the IUSCT had exposed several flaws in the individual arbitral model, militating in favor of an "administrative approach":

> It was the "mass claim dimension" of the case under discussion that constituted an insurmountable hindrance to the adoption of the arbitral approach [used by the IUSCT]. … It seems beyond doubt that the adoption of a case-by-case approach to each particular damage, which is the typical

responded quickly to urgent humanitarian needs (on the positive side), but it is one of the most expensive IMCCs ever created. Like the IUSCT, the UNCC continues to operate and is in the final stages of parceling out payments to satisfy one remaining large claim to Kuwait.

Length of the commission's mandate

A commission with a short-term mandate will need more resources for a shorter time than a similarly situated commission with a less ambitious deadline. Deadlines have the beneficial effects of imparting urgency in cases where humanitarian concerns predominate and of ensuring that a commission does not linger after its objectives have become irrelevant or unattainable. Artificially constraining the duration of a commission, however, can not only impair its ability to make individual determinations or grapple with more complex issues, but also drive up costs without any efficiency gains.

Very few commissions are created with hard and fast limitations on their duration (the CRPC is an exception); most are given implicit authority to operate until all claims have been processed. The context will generally dictate how long that will take, but an IMCC that is not constrained by humanitarian concerns, market discipline or limited funding can take some time to achieve its objectives. The Holocaust-era programs, for instance, were compensating historical wrongs and could take more time. Other IMCCs might be more urgent but have a more complicated task. The UNCC was relieved of determining liability, but it still had to balance the immediate humanitarian needs of tens of thousands of individuals, the complicated commercial claims of corporations and governments, and large claims for environmental damage. The EECC was one of two interrelated commissions. The state parties addressed first the location of their shared border – the aspect of their dispute that triggered the war – and the compensation claims of individuals, businesses and state parties took far longer to resolve.

There is some correlation between the duration of an IMCC and its cost, but it is not exact. For instance, total personnel cost to process a given number of claims will result in engaging a larger staff for a shorter period or a smaller staff for a longer period. The smaller staff for a longer

---

> approach of traditional arbitration, would have brought, under the given circumstances, and particularly with regard to the huge number of urgent claims, to a sort of denial of justice. Thus the choice to adopt the so-called "administrative approach", which envisages various modern techniques … as for example the sampling technique, was legally and *de facto* a necessity.

See di Rattalma and Treves, *The United Nations Compensation Commission*, 10.

period will likely incur more cost for property, plant and equipment over the longer duration, but the larger staff over a shorter period will drive up other costs. More space will be required to house them, more equipment will be needed for them to do their work, and more management personnel will be needed to ensure that the Secretariat functions smoothly. Moreover, a demand for qualified employees might drive salaries for this relatively small talent pool higher. The problem will become particularly noticeable if the decision about location puts the commission in a smaller or remote market, where the entity will find itself importing talent, paying expatriate living expenses and incurring relocation costs.

Speed, on the other hand, sacrifices some of the efficiency that no doubt was the hoped-for consequence of a mass claims proceeding. The commission will have more time to find a suitable space and negotiate a long-term contract on favorable terms. It will be able to attract and retain talented, experienced staff looking for stable, long-term employment, thus reducing turnover and training expense while maintaining productivity. It will also be able to make long-term decisions about the productivity and efficiency gains that might result from using customized technology and mass claims techniques.

Categories of Cost

Headquarters

An IMCC's headquarters location will affect the cost of nearly everything related to operations: salaries, office space, telecommunications, equipment, supplies and utilities. Once a venue has been designated, offices can be built or purchased, rented on an arm's-length basis from unaffiliated parties, or rented or borrowed from existing institutions. An IMCC might also consider asking the host government to allocate it free or subsidized space. For a host government, there are some obvious economic and reputational benefits attached to being the site of the headquarters of an international institution. The host country will also have a vested interest in making sure that security is adequate. The cost savings from making use of an accommodation by the host government might also extend to the cost of procuring furniture and equipment,[24]

[24] The IUSCT established a procurement system that consulted when necessary with the Rijksinkoopbureau, the Dutch government's central purchasing agency, in order to analyse competing bids (three were required).

which can be considerable and difficult to recoup by selling the equipment when the IMCC winds down.[25]

The location will also affect the ease of accepting claims, exchanging filings, lodging evidence and – if desired – holding hearings.[26] The decision to hold hearings adds an additional dimension of expense associated with housing and transporting commissioners and support staff (*e.g.*, transcription services and translators).[27] Security will always be a concern, but it may need to be more elaborate for an IMCC that wishes to be close to the potential claimant population and locates itself in a post-conflict situation.

Although an IMCC might in theory set up operations nearly anywhere, the decision will probably not be for the IMCC to make; location will likely already have been decided at the framework stage. The state parties will thus be in a position to satisfy themselves about the fairness of the location before they sign the agreement. The IUSCT and EECC, for instance, were required by their respective framework agreements to establish their headquarters in The Hague, a city that offers a number of obvious advantages. It is known as a center of international law. The city has a knowledgeable local talent pool, abundant facilities and functioning legal institutions (including the Permanent Court of Arbitration) with experience in getting an IMCC up and running quickly.

These same advantages make The Hague expensive. In addition to operating as an international-law hub, it is the seat of the Dutch government and parliament, Supreme Court and Council of State. Most foreign embassies in the Netherlands and 150 international organizations are located in the city. The Hague is one of the major cities hosting the United Nations. It is the headquarters of the International Court of Justice, the International Criminal Court and numerous *ad hoc* tribunals. There is keen competition for talent, space and resources.

The IUSCT began work in facilities provided by the Permanent Court of Arbitration in The Hague and later rented a permanent location from the Dutch government, two buildings with 2,500 square feet of space,

---

25 This is in some ways similar to the abandonment of capital assets by NGOs and the UN when they wind up a mission. It is common to leave vehicles and other equipment behind, which is sufficiently depreciated for accounting purposes that repatriation costs exceed its remaining value and which can be donated to the host state.

26 Whether a network of field offices is necessary or desirable is discussed in "Outreach" below.

27 This is in addition to similar costs incurred by the parties.

which it still occupies.[28] When originally rented, the IUSCT headquarters was empty except for carpet and draperies. The two buildings had to be fully furnished and built out to the particular specifications of the IUSCT, including a separate prayer annex and a fully functioning cafeteria able to prepare meals to accommodate the religious strictures of all personnel.[29] The EECC, which met infrequently and did not need a full-time headquarters, saved money by outsourcing its requirements to the Permanent Court of Arbitration. It used the PCA space for filings, hearings and the occasional meeting of the parties or the commissioners. The commissioners did the bulk of their work from home offices, communicating by telephone and email and sharing documents on a secure server that was provided by a commissioner's law firm.

Several other commissions chose or were required to locate in Geneva, which has an expense profile similar to The Hague. The IMCCs that established headquarters in Geneva were operated by or through entities with an established operation in the city.[30] The marginal cost of adding a claims-processing function to an existing entity, even in an expensive location, will almost certainly be less than attempting to set up the operation from scratch in a less-expensive location. Indeed, as the IOM became more experienced in handling Holocaust-era mass claims programs, the newer programs were outsourced to it, which drove marginal costs down further.

The CRPC, on the other hand, needed to operate near where the conflict occurred. The real-property assets and the associated records at the heart of the program were located there, as were a majority of the claimants. The CRPC began operations in temporary facilities provided by the IOM, but it quickly established a permanent headquarters at two separate locations in Sarajevo. It later set up a network of field offices throughout the affected area, which added to the cost of the program but was deemed necessary to reach potential claimants.

---

[28] Christopher Pinto, "Institutional Aspects of the Tribunal," in David D. Caron and John R. Crook (eds), *The Iran–United States Claims Tribunal and the Process of International Claims Resolution: A Study by the Panel on State Responsibility of the American Society of International Law* (ASIL, 2000), 100.

[29] Pinto, "Institutional Aspects of the Tribunal," 114.

[30] The UNCC was operated through the United Nations, CRT-I and CRT-II through Swiss banks, and the GFLCP through the International Organization for Migration.

Outreach

A commission must decide how it will give affected parties notice that claims are being accepted, provide claimants with information about eligibility and a way to submit claims, and notify claimants of the outcome. The greatest of these challenges is ensuring that an unknown population of potential claimants receives notice of the opportunity to request compensation. There are any number of ways to go about making the existence of a claims program known.

The simplest and least expensive way is to contact potential claimants directly, usually online or through the mail, and invite them to submit a claim (on paper or online). Direct solicitation is not feasible when claimants cannot be identified in advance and located with considerable precision. When the necessary information is unavailable, an IMCC should consider broadcasting through a variety of distribution channels. These can range from the very traditional (*e.g.*, notices in newspapers) to modern social media platforms. As the effort becomes less targeted and more channels are used, expense will rise. Whether the additional cost will yield sufficient incremental claims to justify the expense is difficult to predict. There is no question, however, that social media should be included in any outreach effort. Whether a particular social media campaign will gain traction depends to some extent on luck, but the cost is so low that the only conceivable disadvantage is an overly successful campaign that triggers a deluge of unqualified claims.

The IUSCT and UNCC are examples of situations where a large outreach effort was more a luxury than a necessity. The claimant pools were large, but publicity was abundant and mostly free. Each IMCC represented a high-profile resolution of events that had been front and center for protracted periods. The Iran Hostage Crisis, in particular, was inescapable; it lasted over a year and became the defining issue of a US presidential election. The claimant class was large, sophisticated and had substantial amounts at stake. Many of the claims were lawsuits that had been brought in US courts and were simply relocated to the IUSCT. The remaining claims came in without prodding. Indeed, the volume of claims submitted in the loss category under $250,000 was so large that it could not be handled by the IUSCT and was outsourced to the FCSC.[31]

The UNCC was the product of a war to drive Iraq out of Kuwait. Once the goal of liberating the territory was achieved, extracting reparations

---

[31] The program was completed in 1995. *See* Foreign Claims Settlement Commission of the US, Completed Programs: Iran, available at: https://www.justice.gov/fcsc/completed-programs-iran.

was the next logical step. The Gulf War coalition consisted of over 30 nations, all of whom were members of the United Nations. There was extensive cooperation among the nations affected by the invasion and their citizens to ensure that claims were filed and compensation was paid.

The CRPC relied on publicity but supplemented that channel with a comprehensive outreach campaign in the media and on the ground. The CRPC was concerned that a large population of rural residents who had been affected would not otherwise learn about the program and so took to print, broadcast advertisements on radio and television, and targeted mailings. The notification effort was augmented by 23 regional offices. Mobile teams of two to five members went to rural villages to inform residents about the commission's existence and to distribute and collect the completed claim forms. The CRPC also accepted claims online and established call centers to assist in completing and submitting the forms.[32]

The Holocaust-era programs had a more difficult task. The harms to be compensated had occurred 50 years earlier, and the claimant pool was dispersed and largely deceased. The IOM set up a large operation to discharge the responsibilities outsourced to it by the GFLCP. In addition to a publicity campaign, it set up special telephone helplines in 14 countries and equipped operators with guidelines and specialized training to assist claimants. At its peak, the GFLCP had operators in 46 field offices worldwide to assist with information requests received by letter, telephone, email, fax and personal visits.[33] The CRT-I and CRT-II took a similar approach, supplementing the Geneva headquarters with a global network of field offices rented from Ernst & Young. It used press releases, broadcast ads, established a rudimentary website and published lists of names of owners of dormant accounts. Despite having only 35,000 names on the list, CRT-II was inundated with claimants who were

---

[32] How the CRPC identified and overcame the many logistical challenges to identifying claimants and soliciting claims is covered in Commission for Real Property Claims of Displaced Persons and Refugees (CRPC): End of Mandate Report and Annexes A–G.

[33] German Forced Labor Compensation Program Holocaust Victim Assets Program (Swiss Banks), Activity Report July 2000 – December 20001, International Organization for Migration, Document No. MC/INF/248 (3 May 2002), at page 2. The IOM was also responsible for all property claims under the German Foundation without regard to the claimant's residence or whether or not Jewish; this program is not documented as comprehensively and therefore is not covered in this chapter.

undeterred by the absence of their names on the lists and claimed accounts for which there was no documentary evidence.

The EECC used a diplomatic representation model: state parties brought claims on behalf of individual citizens. This decision shifted the cost of locating claimants, completing claims and compiling evidence to the governments. Both governments had teams that went out to the conflict zones and interviewed local residents. The Eritrean legal team augmented these efforts with an online claims program to solicit evidence from the Eritrean diaspora. The Eritrean government was instrumental in making the existence of the online affidavit known to its expatriate nationals.

Processing

Once the outreach is complete and the claims begin to come in, an IMCC will need to be ready with a system to sort, enter and evaluate claims. Claims must be acknowledged, reviewed for defects that would preclude their being scheduled for filings and hearings, and entered into a tracking system that ensures that they continue to move through the process.

In a mass claims program, technology can ensure that preliminary processing does not become an expensive bottleneck. From a purely technological standpoint, an online claims submission process will be preferable. Online claim forms allow many tasks now done by humans to be automated. Validations can be built into the claim form to flag the most common mistakes so that claimants will have an opportunity to correct them. Documentary evidence can be uploaded. Attestations can be made using electronic signatures.

The practical reality, however, is that not all programs can be done online. The upfront cost may be prohibitive, and universal access to the internet cannot be assumed for a claimant class. While the EECC used an online program for evidentiary submissions, online claims were a small part of its overall evidence-gathering effort. It was, interestingly, the only IMCC reviewed in this chapter that had an online claims component. The remainder designed paper forms that were sent to a processing office and entered into a database.

That said, any IMCC with an eye on cost and a choice between online and paper should avoid paper where possible. Accuracy is the first casualty of a paper form process; repetitive data entry by fallible humans introduces error. Moreover, the processing of the paper forms can bog down easily if the volume is higher than expected. Even the GFLCP – which had engaged a third-party vendor to perform data entry in anticipation of high volume – was overwhelmed. The resulting delays rippled through the process, slowing acknowledgements of claims received and requiring the GFLCP to establish an additional interim pre-acknowledgement process in order not to sidetrack the processing effort.

Once claimant data has been entered into a tracking database, processing can begin. Claims can be examined for deficiencies and flagged for follow-up, or they can be cleared and sent on for processing. IMCCs that do not need to determine liability and are established solely to pay compensation can use a fast-track mechanism, which requires a claimant to make a *prima facie* showing of entitlement to compensation based on some harm or set of events. This fast-track mechanism will work best with claims that have a reliable set of third-party, ordinary-course documents that can be compared to the claimant's factual assertions. The GFLCP was able to use contemporaneous, historical records of individuals who had been used in a forced labor program. The UNCC Category "A" (involuntary departure from Kuwait) claims were compared to immigration records. The CRPC compiled a series of land records from various municipalities and government records into a comprehensive database. The CRT-I and CRT-II programs worked from records maintained by the Swiss banks. Because a fast-track mechanism requires a significant amount of upfront work and time to locate, analyse and compile the evidence into a usable, standardized format, it will be cost-efficient only where a large percentage of anticipated claims can be processed this way.

In addition to using fast-track processing, each of these IMCCs had a procedure to attempt to verify a claim that could not be externally validated or that was otherwise deficient. Claims would either be denied or they would be forwarded on to a decision maker for review and approval of payment. The review function can be the most costly and labor-intensive, since deficient claims will require individual attention. It helps reduce cost if these claims are exhaustively vetted up front by administrative personnel before being sent for individual reviews.

Because a technological process is only as good as the standardized guidelines that humans have formulated, it is wise to give an IMCC running a mass compensation program the flexibility to tweak its processing criteria and evidentiary presumptions in order to reflect ways in which the claimants' data diverge from initial assumptions.[34] Technology can also assist in detecting useful patterns in an otherwise large

---

[34] For instance, the CRPC revised its rules and regulations in light of evidentiary and legal developments, restructured its organization and certificate delivery system, and planned for and implemented the transfer of its functions to the Government of Bosnia–Herzegovina. See Commission for Real Property

and formidable dataset. For instance, calculating an average loss per similarly situated claimant and then continuously updating that average would allow a commission to create and adjust a standardized award above which losses would need to be documented. The GFLCP was constantly developing and refining sorting criteria that allowed its staff to reject or tentatively approve claims. The CRPC also revised its regulations "in light of evidentiary developments" in order to increase the pace of decision-making.

In cases where an award will be made on the merits of a contested claim, humans must step back into the process. IMCCs that exist solely to compensate an acknowledged harm can group together large numbers of similar claims for *pro forma* approval and payment, but IMCCs with a liability-finding component will issue written awards with factual findings and legal conclusions. Working with a large staff, the IUSCT has issued hundreds of individual decisions awarding hundreds of millions of dollars. This approach has yielded a large body of jurisprudence that comes closest to approximating the results of a more traditional litigation, with the attendant expense.

The EECC commissioners also resolved contested questions of law and fact and wrote their own awards and opinions. They were able to do this without employing a large legal staff because the commissioners issued fewer awards and covered more factual ground. The claims were stated in very broad terms that grouped together large numbers of factually and legally similar violations against individuals into a single award. The parties presented evidence that showed patterns of violations rather than attempting to prove every single allegation in detail. After the liability determinations were made, the EECC entered a damages phase, which took an additional two years.

Tracking claims

The volume of claims received by an IMCC and the related paperwork can be formidable. The UNCC remains the gold standard: nearly 30,000 square feet were necessary to store the files. Even if an IMCC elects not to use technology for claims processing, some sort of database software for tracking will be indispensable. Some of the older IMCCs managed without database software, but the modern cost-benefit calculation would

---

Claims of Displaced Persons and Refugees (CRPC): End of Mandate Report: Executive Summary (1996–2003).

favor technology over humans in all but the simplest cases.[35] Even the least expensive off-the-shelf software will facilitate claims intake, tracking and reporting.

The question is not whether a commission should use technology, but whether it will be worth the extra time and expense to have customized technology developed. The answer will depend to some extent on how sophisticated the claims reporting needs to be and how much flexibility will be needed to refine the technology over the life of the program. An IMCC that realizes too late that it should have invested more in technology will not be able to correct its course easily. A commission that is strapped for resources might consider seeking out a lower-cost partnership with a startup company that is looking to refine its technology and raise its profile.

Hearings

Hearings increase costs, and this is one category of expense that technology can do little to reduce. The parties to a contested proceeding – *e.g.*, the EECC and IUSCT – will often favor hearings, which allow parties a full opportunity to argue the merits of their cases. Hearings are time-consuming, logistically challenging and expensive. If hearings are to be held, the budget will need to provide for several additional categories of expense, including: securing a space to hold the hearings with separate working facilities for the parties, travel expenses for commissioners to attend, recording and transcription systems to provide a contemporaneous record of proceedings, translators to accommodate testimony in other languages, and a Secretariat qualified to manage the process.

Commissioners at the hearings rely on the parties to gather and present evidence. Unlike automated and standardized claims collections processes, where the cost of filing a claim is frequently borne by the program itself, the cost of creating the evidentiary record in advance of a hearing will most likely have been borne by the state parties. Depending on the sophistication of the material and the issues presented, an IMCC may need to retain legal, technical, historical, linguistic or forensic experts. Framework agreements frequently provide expressly for this possibility. An IMCC might also have the flexibility to conduct its own investigations. EECC commissioners briefly considered visiting both countries but eventually abandoned the idea.

---

35 The EECC would be a good example of an IMCC that might not benefit from any sort of tracking software. Ethiopia filed eight claims and Eritrea filed 26.

Staff

As in any commercial venture, personnel will be the largest line item in the budget. Although the non-profit sector pays lower compensation, an IMCC should still be prepared to budget a considerable amount to attract top talent to head up the legal and administrative functions. The largest per-employee expense will be salaries paid to the commissioners, who are frequently engaged part-time or as consultants. Equally important will be ensuring sufficient funds to recruit experienced senior management personnel to set up and oversee an efficient operation. They will, in turn, be managing a staff of full-time, permanent, administrative, financial, operational, technical, and legal professionals, all of whom will require the appropriate physical infrastructure augmented by whatever suite of benefits is required by the jurisdiction in which the IMCC is located.[36]

Recognizing that this may not always be possible, an IMCC should draw first on the local population and hold expatriate personnel to a minimum. The most obvious benefit is to permit payment in local currency and to hold down relocation and related expenses. In addition, if the commission is to be multilingual, the staff will need familiarity with one or more of the chosen languages. Should staff with the required skills and language ability be unavailable or prohibitively expensive, bringing in translators will add to cost and increase processing time.

There are additional indirect benefits to hiring local staff. The CRPC, based in Sarajevo, found national staff helped "facilitate local cooperation among disparate groups of claimants, and serve as local buy-in for decisions taken."[37] This local buy-in also assists in long-term institution building, which can be difficult to sustain after the international community departs.[38]

Stable funding and some up-front planning will be helpful in keeping personnel costs from spiraling. The CRPC, for instance, suffered chronic funding problems and had to resort to short-term contracts, which tend to be on less favorable financial terms and carry large opportunity costs. Professionals with training and experience can be more selective about choosing stable, fixed employment. This leaves an IMCC recruiting from a smaller pool of less experienced employees who will require training. Once the employees have been trained and brought up to speed, retention will become difficult if the offer is a short-term renewal. Employee

---

[36] These can include health and disability insurance, pensions, and indemnity payments upon early termination of employment.

[37] CRPC, End of Mandate Report: Executive Summary (1996–2003), 37.

[38] CRPC, End of Mandate Report: Executive Summary (1996–2003), 37.

turnover is expensive: it drives up training costs, requires more management oversight, deprives an organization of a tier of more-experienced personnel who can operate independently and mentor less-experienced employees, and impedes the creation of institutional knowledge.

Not all staff members need to be long-term or permanent. Some short-term contracts and outsourcing to experts could be desirable, and framework agreements make some provision for this. The EECC outsourced every function except commissioners to the PCA, with great success. The volume and/or complexity of claims might require bringing in lawyers or paralegals to present the commissioners with fully developed analyses for decision. The UNCC gives a sense of how expensive this can become. The UNCC had a governing council with permanent members that made policy decisions and was responsible for final approval of claims. The claims processing was initially done by panels of commissioners with subject-matter expertise brought in on temporary contracts. In 2001, a peak year for which we have relevant financial data, commissioners were employed as consultants under "special service agreements" at $8,920 per month. Stipend payments amounted to $8.8 million in the biennium 2000–2001.[39]

Temporary or part-time staff can also help with bureaucratic tasks. For instance, data entry staff can clear bottlenecks in processing. Some experts may come in on temporary contracts to deal with aspects of setting up operations, such as developing claims tracking or processing technology, or planning and implementing public outreach campaigns.

Appeals

Assuming that the infrastructure used for first-instance processing is adequate, the marginal operational cost of adding an appeals process will be small. The same software and staff can be used to help facilitate the appeals, which should be a fraction of the original claims. The additional workstream, however, is not cost-free. Appeals will generate additional correspondence, must be tracked, may require additional submissions and will require a second award confirming or amending the original decision, or – less likely – reopening issues for reconsideration.

All of this expense can theoretically be avoided by establishing at the outset that awards will be "final and binding," which does not necessarily mean there is no right of appeal. The CRPC framework document

---

[39] United Nations, Financial report and audited financial statements for the biennium ended 31 December 2001 and Report of the Board of Auditors, Vol. I, A/57/5, 29.

specified that decisions would be final and binding, but the CRPC was aware that the evidentiary database it used to process claims was imperfect. It therefore read this provision to preclude an appeal in domestic courts but allowed reconsideration by the CRPC. Eventually, 0.8 percent of all decisions requested reconsideration, of which 20 percent were reversed (0.12 percent of all CRPC decisions).[40]

The IUSCT, UNCC and EECC awards were final and binding and there was no appeal allowed beyond, in the case of the UNCC and EECC, a short interval to petition for correction of an obvious mistake in the award. All of the Holocaust-era programs allowed appeals and submission of new evidence when a claim was denied. The grounds for denial were very limited (failure to prove that account owner was a relative, evidence indicating that the claimant had already received the proceeds from the account). These were straightforward appeals and very simple to handle through correspondence.

Legacy

A commission should always be operating with its legacy in mind; its efforts at just and efficient dispute resolution will add, potentially, to the small but growing body of precedent and best practice. The principal objective should be to leave a comprehensive, searchable publicly available library of well-organized materials. Ideally this would be done by converting an existing online presence into a freely accessible repository and then paying whatever minimal hosting and periodic maintenance fees might be required to keep the site running. The first step is to agree how much information an IMCC will eventually make public and organize that information in a logical and accessible way. Sifting back through paper to locate and organize data to convert to an electronic archive is far less likely if that data was not captured as part of the process from the beginning.

The IMCCs reviewed here have a mixed record, which correlates in some degree to their financial resources. Of the mass claims programs, the CRPC has no website archive. Framework documents and the occasional report from the CRPC are available in scattered places on the internet, mostly the UN website. The Holocaust-era programs maintain as archives the websites used while the programs were active in the late 1990s and early 2000s. They are well-organized and easily researched. There is a general summary of the operations of the various programs,

---

[40] CRPC, End of Mandate Report: Executive Summary (1996–2003), 22.

but very little detail on specific decisions relating to cost or the costs themselves.

Of the individual commissions, the IUSCT has done perhaps the least to make its substantial and valuable body of work available online. The organization is still active and has a live website, but many important materials are protected by a login system that is available only to academics and does not permit new registrations. Accordingly, the best source for what is arguably the richest trove of primary documents from an international arbitration is scattered throughout the internet, available through commercial services, or published in books held by law libraries.

The PCA has an obvious stake in building resources to assist future generations and possesses the budget to do so. It maintains a public web archive that includes all decisions made by the EECC in interpreting its mandate, as well as the eventual awards. However, unless a user is familiar with the EECC claims structure, the taxonomy will not assist a researcher in quickly locating a relevant resource. (The PCA's website also hosts similar material for other cases handled by the PCA.)

The UNCC maintains a comprehensive website with all relevant documents. The designers have done what they can to establish a workable taxonomy, but attempting to navigate the thicket of decisions, reports, resolutions and other categories of documents without an encyclopedic understanding of how the UN operates is a formidable undertaking. Books written about the UNCC are helpful in creating an understanding of context without which the primary source material can be daunting.[41]

CONCLUSION

IMCCs are a valuable component of the international dispute resolution toolkit. Because they are still relatively rare and heterogeneous, no body of best practice has emerged to reduce the upfront time and attention that must be devoted to crafting the optimal structure. This is particularly true of the financial arrangements that will dictate whether the IMCC will fully discharge its mandate or whether it will be required to scale back its ambitions if funds run low.

An IMCC will only be as good as its funding, but planning for this upfront can reduce failure. State-parties should consider carefully how to

---

41 *See, e.g.*, Richard Lillich, *The United Nations Compensation Commission* (Martinus Nijoff, 1995) and di Rattalma and Treves, *The United Nations Compensation Commission.*

ensure secure funding that is calibrated to the scale of the enterprise. It will then be up to the commissioners and the Secretariat to budget carefully across the foreseeable categories of expense to make the funding last. A "thick" IMCC in this respect provides more cause for optimism than a "thin" one that would have only a minimalist funding structure, few employees, inadequate headquarters and a projected tenure inadequate to fulfill its mandate.

The financial opacity of most IMCCs – though understandable – makes this task harder than it should be. Were there a body of structured financial data available, future IMCCs would be able to plan more intelligently, and a best practice would emerge. Transparency here is more than a virtue, it is essential to advancing the state of the art and preventing unnecessary failure. Of course, this idea is counter to the attraction of an IMCC. IMCCs are, after all, *ad hoc* bodies that can be operated independently and adjusted on the fly.

Nevertheless, donors and other third-party sources of funding would do well to insist on auditing and financial accounting that would yield not only accountability but some rules of thumb. For instance, a standardized report detailing what percentage of an operating budget is devoted to particular expenses would eventually accrete sufficient data to yield averages or that could be isolated relative to variables such as location. A running list of categories of expense would allow planners to reduce "unknown unknowns" that could have been considered in planning.[42] These are but two examples of data that could usefully be made public without giving away sensitive financial data or numbers. More controversial data might include an efficiency ratio that expresses the ratio of award to expense or comparing the cost of outsourcing a function to creating it in house.

[42] For instance, salaries and employee benefits, accounting, outreach, office expenses, information technology, occupancy, legal compliance, travel, insurance, capital costs and maintenance.

6. Problems of proof and evidence

Few of the issues facing international mass claims commissions are of greater practical significance than problems of proof and evidence. Evidentiary rules matter greatly because they determine which of the materials that the parties provided in their written and oral submissions a tribunal can legitimately consider. Whole classes of otherwise probative evidence may be excluded from consideration by imposition of a restrictive standard; adoption of a lenient standard will have the opposite effect. IMCCs face a daily diet of contested factual assertions grounded on scanty factual support; evidentiary rules can easily alter the conclusions that a tribunal reaches on such assertions. These conclusions, in turn, can determine the legal viability of entire claims to recovery.

EVIDENTIARY ISSUES IN IMCCS

Much of the law of evidence, especially in common law countries, concerns itself with the standards for admissibility. Particular pieces of evidence may be excluded if they are taken to be hearsay, are not legally relevant, display bias or violate the rules of privilege. But there are other issues that are at least as significant. Two of these are burden of proof and standard of proof. "Standard of proof" refers to the rule dictating how much supporting evidence is required; "burden of proof" specifies which of the parties must produce it. Because they apply broadly, across all of the dispute's factual disagreements, these two elements can have widespread consequences for the tribunal's final awards.

This chapter starts by examining some of the characteristics of IMCC litigation that call for distinctive evidentiary treatment. The more general and fundamental questions of burden of proof and standard of proof are then addressed in light of these distinctive features. We examine, finally, the superficially plausible but erroneous intuition that where a dispute involves symmetric claims, any possible unfairness to one side is balanced out by unfairness to the other.

General Principles

There is no standard practice with respect to the rules of evidence in international adjudication.[1] However, two tendencies have fairly consistently characterized IMCC treatment of evidence. The first is that a tribunal is entitled to exercise great discretion in formulating a flexible approach to the law of evidence. The second is that a tribunal will ordinarily be quite lenient in its decisions whether evidence should be admitted. IMCC tribunals tend, in other words, to be both flexible and permissive in their treatment of evidence.

Tribunal discretion: flexibility and permissiveness

International tribunals ordinarily have great flexibility to make evidentiary decisions fit the particular context of the dispute at issue. They tend to exercise independent judgment rather than seek out rules and precedents for guidance. Traditionally, even permanent international institutions have avoided developing concrete rules of evidence, making each case "an incidental exercise bound by the circumstances."[2]

> [I]nternational tribunals have not committed themselves to the restrictive rules of evidence of municipal law. ... [In] the absence of the provision of a specific ground of exclusion in the arbitral agreements, there is no rule of law that can be invoked as binding a tribunal to exclude particular evidence.[3]

But international claims commissions are even less deferential to standard evidentiary conventions than other international tribunals.

Claims commissions generally hesitate to "constrain themselves by the authority of a given precedent or a given set of rules, in the absence of clear indications in their statutes."[4] A commission naturally will follow the provisions of its constituting instrument; if the commission is created by a treaty, for example, then any provisions of that treaty that deal with evidentiary matters will be authoritative. However, absent a provision in that constituting instrument, there are few – if any – outside rules that the

---

[1] Andrea Gattini, "Evidentiary Issues in the ICJ's Genocide Judgment," (2007) 5 *Journal of International Criminal Justice* 889.

[2] Gattini, "Evidentiary Issues."

[3] Mojtaba Kazazi, *Burden of Proof and Related Issues: A Study of Evidence before International Tribunals* (Springer, 1996), 184, citing Durward V. Sandifer, *Evidence Before International Tribunals* (University Press of Virginia, 1975).

[4] Gattini, "Evidentiary Issues," 889.

commission is bound to respect.[5] The evidentiary rules of other jurisdictions are of no particular relevance to the commission – another jurisdiction's evidentiary rules would have been written with its own circumstances in mind – and the commission is entitled to decide according to the needs of its own particular situation.

Lenient standards of admissibility – kinds of evidence

An IMCC's discretion is not ordinarily utilized to bar admission of evidence, but instead tends to *favor* admitting the evidence. As Kazazi notes, "[international tribunals] have found it justified to receive every kind and form of evidence, and have attached to them the probative value they deserve under the circumstances of a given case."[6]

One reason may be that the tribunal itself is the finder of fact. Some domestic legal systems depend on jurors to find the facts, and where that is the case, exclusion of inadmissible evidence is imperative. The rules of evidence allow a judge to keep the jury from hearing the challenged evidence until its admissibility is determined. Jurors (who are of course lay persons) must be shielded from inadmissible evidence because once they have heard the inadmissible evidence, they cannot be relied on to disregard it. Commissioners, in contrast, are assumed to be able to identify and disregard evidence that should never have been admitted in the first place.

Few IMCC awards go into any depth about the tribunal's reasons for admitting evidence. In many cases, a tribunal's right to accept or refuse evidence is simply taken for granted. For example, an award might simply mention that some piece of evidence supported its conclusions, without explicitly addressing the question of its admissibility. A commission's willingness to admit certain types of evidence may be inferred from the mention in its awards of the effect of particular pieces of evidence of that type. Even if the commission never discussed the matter explicitly in its awards, its position is clear because if it didn't think that the evidence was admissible, it would not have relied on that piece of evidence in writing its opinion.

---

[5] But note that if the Commission is bound by the treaty to follow international law then this might possibly contain rules of evidence that constrain the commission.

[6] Kazazi, *Burden of Proof and Related Issues*, 184.

For example, the EECC seems to have had almost a *per se* rule that testimonial evidence should be admitted without verification.[7] Testimonial evidence has its dangers; witnesses may be unreliable because they work for the defendant state or because they live in fear of it.[8] But testimonial evidence also provides information that cannot be obtained from any other likely sources. Thus, it is not surprising that EECC awards give no indication that exclusion of testimonial evidence in general was ever given serious consideration. Quite the opposite, the general silence on the matter suggests *per se* approval.

The same is true of documentary evidence.[9] The documentary evidence that the EECC admitted in the prisoner of war claims included "newspaper articles, public statements, medical and hospital records, and expenditure receipts," while in the war front claims both parties relied on "various pieces of documentary evidence, including military records,

---

7 Witness testimony is also frequently heard, of course, in other international tribunals. For example, the Inter-American Court of Human Rights has accepted "direct witness testimony" as "prima facie evidence demonstrating that a grave violation of human rights has occurred and that the state has failed to take steps to investigate and prosecute." Naomi Roht-Arriaza, "State Responsibility to Investigate and Prosecute Grave Human Rights Violations in International Law," (1990) 78 *California. Law Review* 451, 472 (discussing a case concerning an alleged crime by the Honduran government against a citizen).

8 Thus one author refers to "cooperation of … individuals who often may realistically fear terrible reprisals if they cooperate openly." Gian Luca Beruto (ed.), *Justice and Reconciliation: An Integrated Approach* (International Institute of Humanitarian Law, 2006), 21–22, available at: http://www.iihl.org/iihl/Documents/2bcb5426-3eac-48d4-9bd1-14e99e2b00aa.pdf. In addition to fear of reprisal, this source points out, witnesses may experience psychological trauma from testifying. In some cases, even where documentary evidence is available, it may be outweighed by testimony, as with the EECC: "Documentary evidence appears to have played a lesser, but still important, role than that played by testimonial evidence." Won Kidane, "Civil Liability for Violations of International Humanitarian Law: The Jurisprudence of the Eritrea–Ethiopia Claims Commission in The Hague," (2007) 25 *Wisconsin International Law Journal* 23, 78–79 (citing Eritrea–Ethiopia Claims Commission, Central Front, Ethiopia's Claim 2, ¶ 73(4) (2004)).

9 Entry 154, Docketed French Claims Against the US, Conventions of 1880, 1882 and 1883, French–US Claims Commission (1880–1884). Elsewhere, the commission described the evidence submitted by Eritrea as including, "hundreds of sworn affidavits, documents claims forms, expert reports, satellite imagery, photographs, charts, news reports, statements of officials, administrative and court documents and bomb fragments." Kazazi, *Burden of Proof and Related Issues*, 32–33.

photographs, and satellite imagery."[10] Documentary evidence is as nearly invaluable as testimonial evidence, particularly when it is produced by a neutral third party. At the EECC, "the Commission accorded the satellite imagery particularly strong probative value, mainly because it originated from a neutral source that was commercially available and showed the condition of buildings with a reasonable degree of clarity at specific dates."[11]

Uniquely, the UNCC also entertained many claims for monitoring and assessment (M&A) to (a) ascertain whether environmental damage or depletion of natural resources had occurred, (b) quantify the loss resulting from that damage or depletion and (c) assess the methodology to abate or mitigate the damage or depletion. M&A claims presented special problems because they had to be reviewed prior to any decision of compensability of the underlying claim, but were necessary for claimants to establish the existence of the damage and its compensability. The panel of commissioners did not require conclusive evidence of condition prior to environmental damage to compensate M&A. The establishment of a sufficient nexus between the activity and environmental damage or risk thereof attributable to Iraq's invasion was sufficient.[12]

Interestingly, to assist the Panel in evaluating the scientific and technical appropriateness of M&A claims, as well as the reasonableness of their expenses, the Commission *sua sponte* retained a multidisciplinary team of consultants, including experts in:

> chemistry; toxicology; biology (including microbiology, marine biology, biological oceanography, marine zoology and plant pathology); medicine; epidemiology; environmental, ecological and natural resource economics; geology (including geochemistry, hydrology, geo-ecology); atmospheric sciences; oil spill assessment and response; rangeland management; and accounting.[13]

---

10 Kidane, "Civil Liability for Violations of International Humanitarian Law," 78–79.

11 Kidane, "Civil Liability for Violations of International Humanitarian Law," 78–79.

12 United Nations Compensation Commission, *Report and Recommendations Made by the Panel of Commissioners Concerning the First Installment of "F4" Claims*, ¶¶ 28–35, UN Doc S/Ac.26/2001/16 (22 June 2001).

13 Framework agreements often explicitly authorize the tribunal to go outside the evidentiary record created by the parties and retain experts. See Chapter 3.

The Panel also requested information from a large number of international organizations, agencies and experts on a variety of issues, including:

> environmental damage and depletion of natural resources relevant to the claims including compensation for oil pollution damage; air quality monitoring and modelling; hydrogeology and groundwater pollution; soil remediation techniques; public health and epidemiology; and environmental and ecological economics.[14]

Claims commissions also frequently accept inferential and circumstantial evidence.[15] Indeed, it may be the commission's own inferences that are treated as relevant and admissible. For example, when one of the parties refuses to respond to the commission's request for information, the commission may treat this refusal as authorizing an adverse inference. The EECC, "owing to the nature of the proceedings and sensitivities of some types of evidence," adopted a "rule on adverse inference for failure to produce evidence" and specifically defined the conditions under which the Commission was to draw this adverse inference.[16] The rule stipulated that "the Commission may request the parties to produce documents, exhibits or other evidence within a specified time."[17] The EECC would "take note of any failure to do so, as well as any reason given for such failure," but "where circumstances warrant … may draw adverse inferences from any failure by a party to produce evidence."[18]

Likewise, commissions have been especially receptive to circumstantial evidence in cases involving uncooperative state actors or a general dearth of evidence. As Naomi Roht-Arriaza notes, "Where little direct evidence exists, parties should be permitted to submit circumstantial and inferential evidence sufficient to give rise to a presumption that the state is either supporting or tolerating" the alleged violation.[19]

---

[14] UN Doc S/Ac.26/2001/16, 44.

[15] *See, e.g.*, *Statute of the International Court of Justice* art. 49, 24 October 1945, 1 UNTS 993. There are instances in which producing evidence or allowing claimants to access records is a condition of broader cooperation.

[16] Kidane, "Civil Liability for Violations of International Humanitarian Law," 31 n40.

[17] Kidane, "Civil Liability for Violations of International Humanitarian Law."

[18] Kidane, "Civil Liability for Violations of International Humanitarian Law."

[19] Roht-Arriaza offers as examples, "Such evidence could include the frequency of similar violations, the impunity with which the perpetrators act, the lack of any investigation – or evidence of stonewalling in an investigation – and evidence showing that the violation at issue is part of a pattern and practice

Other evidentiary rules

This flexibility and permissiveness of IMCC evidentiary practice is not limited to challenges based on the type of evidence a party seeks to have admitted (*e.g.*, hearsay evidence). Other evidentiary rules are treated more or less identically. For example, claims commissions sometimes avoid setting strict deadlines and time frames for evidence submission. There is precedent for allowing late submissions and even the introduction of new evidence during claims proceedings. The IUSCT stated that "[t]he Tribunal is reluctant to permit an untimely filing to disrupt its proceedings. It is also reluctant to reject as untimely evidence which, while late, may be important for the fair resolution of the Claims involved."[20] Where restrictive filing periods could compromise fairness, claims commissions may create rules anticipating and regulating exceptions.[21]

IMCCs' Distinctive Attributes: Why Flexibility Matters

Although international tribunals generally tend to have more relaxed standards of admissibility than domestic courts, IMCC litigation calls for still greater flexibility. Flexibility is particularly important to IMCCs because of certain distinctive attributes characterizing IMCC litigation. The evidentiary needs of an IMCC tribunal are different from the evidentiary needs of most other sorts of courts and tribunals, in several respects.

First, IMCCs are *ad hoc* tribunals. Second, the amount of evidence that they generate makes the proceedings almost unmanageable by ordinary means. Third, their setting in international conflict interferes with evidence collection. The relative paucity of evidence must be understood, therefore, as a consequence of difficult circumstances rather than absence

---

initiated or tolerated by state authorities." Roht-Arriaza, "State Responsibility to Investigate and Prosecute Grave Human Rights Violations in International Law," 472.

20 *Islamic Republic of Iran v. United States of America*, Cases Nos. A3, A8, A9, A14 AND B61, Iran–US Claims Tribunal 8 at n24 (2011) (quoting Islamic Republic of Iran and United States of America, Cases Nos. A3, A8, A9, A14, and 861 (Apr. 2005)).

21 Chester Brown, *A Common Law of International Adjudication* (Oxford University Press, 2007), 171. Similarly, commissions have found reason to permit additional filing rounds. Kidane notes that the EECC "allowed a third round of filings for the rebuttal of evidence contained in the Counter-Memorials" for "the Central Front and Civilians Claims, and all other remaining claims." Kidane, "Civil Liability for Violations of International Humanitarian Law," 32.

of a meritorious claim. Tribunals must be free to assess the evidence in light of the atypical environments in which they find themselves.

Ad hoc versus standing tribunals

The first distinctive characteristic of IMCCs that shapes their treatment of evidence is that IMCCs are *ad hoc* tribunals. This has particular importance regarding the development of complex sets of rules, for at IMCCs there is no real vehicle for developing a body of rules over time.[22] Since the tribunal did not exist prior to the initiation of this case, there will be no body of precedent (or even persuasive authority) remaining from its own previous cases, and the tribunal is not bound to follow the evidentiary decisions of any other commission or court. Because it will have no standing body of evidentiary rules, or other procedural law, to fall back on when disagreements arise, flexibility is not optional; it is a necessity.

Sometimes commissions are charged with modeling their rules upon some other body of settled procedural law.[23] For example, United Nations Commission on International Trade Law (UNCITRAL) rules were the basis for rules adopted by the Iran–US Claims Tribunal. The UNCITRAL rules were a useful foundation at the Iran–US Claims Tribunal "because most of the claims [at that tribunal] have been of a commercial nature."[24]

The UNCITRAL rules were then used as a model in drafting the Permanent Court of Arbitration Optional Rules for Arbitrating Disputes Between Two States (PCA Rules).[25] For that purpose, the UNCITRAL rules were "modified to 'reflect the public international law character of disputes between States, and diplomatic practice appropriate to such

---

22 But note, as shown immediately below, that a tribunal may borrow extensively from other developed bodies of procedural rules.

23 As we touched on in Chapter 3, one of the unique legal characteristics of an IMCC is that its creators usually delegate to it the task of drafting and interpreting its own rules of procedure. This discretion may be limited to a standing body of model rules, but the IMCC will nearly always have some latitude to adapt those rules to the particular historical context presented by the dispute it is being asked to resolve.

24 Kidane, "Civil Liability for Violations of International Humanitarian Law," 28.

25 As Won Kidane notes, "The Iran–United States Claims Tribunal's rules of procedure are primarily based on the United Nations Commission on International Trade Law (UNCITRAL) rules." Kidane, "Civil Liability for Violations of International Humanitarian Law."

disputes'."[26] The PCA rules were, in turn, adapted by the Eritrea–Ethiopia Claims Commission under Article 5, paragraph 7 of the Algiers Agreement, which founded the EECC. But the peace treaty stated only that the Commission's rules should be "based on" the PCA rules; the Commission was not obligated to reproduce them in all their details.[27]

Size of the dispute: case management

IMCCs, as the name suggests, deal with masses of claims. Massive size is a challenge even in domestic judicial adjudication (*e.g.*, class actions), but the problem is more serious still for international claims. The cumbersome nature of IMCC litigation merely compounds the challenges otherwise present in large-scale disputes. For this reason, a commission may need special management techniques and specialized expertise.[28]

IMCCs must handle and dispose of large numbers of claims expeditiously, and that requires processing thousands of pages of documents. The practical difficulties that this presents – particularly for administrative efficiency and costs – are clear. To examine all of this material to determine evidentiary suitability is likely to be impossible. But inability to deal successfully with large amounts of evidence threatens the accuracy of a commission's awards and thus, potentially, the commission's legitimacy.

The most common solution is simply for the commission to accept and retain documents without any preliminary assessment of their relevance, admissibility or accuracy. At the point that a party relies on a document, that document might be challenged by its opponent. But the document will already be in the record. There is no way to test the tens of thousands of pages of material to determine whether they meet standards of admissibility.

At the UNCC, for example, Panels generally considered documents and other evidence sufficient to establish the facts of the claims and determine the existence of a direct loss warranting compensation. Any additional input of evidence by either the claimants or by Iraq "depended

[26] *See also* Eritrea–Ethiopia Claims Commission (EECC), Rules of Procedure art. 1, available at: http://www.pca-cpa.org/ENGLISH/RPC/EECC/Rules%20of%20Procedure.PDF.

[27] Agreement Between the Governments of the State of Eritrea and the Federal Democratic Republic of Ethiopia art. 5, ¶ 7, 12 December 2000 [hereinafter Algiers Agreement]. "The Commission shall adopt its own rules of procedure based upon the 1992 Permanent Court of Arbitration Optional Rules for Arbitrating Disputes Between Two States."

[28] Article 5 ¶ 7 Algiers Agreement 26.

on the extent to which the Panel found such input to be necessary" during the review process. Thus, in "unusually large or complex" claims, Panels could decide to make the files of the claims available to Iraq and to request additional written submissions by the parties. Panels could also invite claimants and Iraq to participate in oral proceedings.[29]

Conversely, the Governing Council of the UNCC decided to prioritize and treat on an urgent basis small claims of individuals who were forced to leave Iraq or Kuwait (Category "A" claims) and claims of individuals who suffered personal losses of up to $100,000 (Category "C" claims). These claims were small, but numerous, counting in the hundreds of thousands.[30] The Governing Council defined these claims as "small and urgent" and directed the Commission to grant priority for both for processing and payment. Given the urgency and the volume, the Commission found it impossible to review each claim individually. Thus, it adopted a number of internationally recognized techniques for mass claims processing, which included computerized matching of claims and verification information, sampling and statistical modeling.[31]

Hostile environment

IMCCs, by their very definition, involve post-conflict damages claims. Usually the conflict will be conventional international warfare, but domestic civil disturbance can necessitate formation of a claims commission as well. When operating in such an environment, the parties and the commission may have severe difficulties in obtaining evidence. The destruction of documentary records, as well as the displacement, incapacitation or death of potential witnesses may paralyze a commission if domestic evidentiary standards are applied. In such circumstances, rules of evidence may have to be modified to accommodate the fact that even the most diligent of advocates will otherwise be unable to present a convincing case.

In such situations, commissions may relax best evidence and authentication requirements.[32] As Bin Cheng noted in *General Principles of Law as Applied by International Courts and Tribunals*, "The general principle requiring the best available evidence is thus tempered by considerations

---

29 United Nations Compensation Commission, "What We Do – Claims Processing," available at: http://www.uncc.ch/claims-processing.

30 For example, there were 850,000 successful Category "A" claimants. *See* United Nations Compensation Commission, "What We Do – The Claims, Category 'A'," available at: http://www.uncc.ch/category.

31 UNCC, "What We Do – The Claims, Category 'A'."

32 *See, e.g.*, Fed. R. Evid. 901.

of possibility."[33] Neither "best" nor supplementary evidence may be required. The EECC, for example, accepted "ordinary photographs" and granted them "significant weight in establishing patterns of destruction" even though no special steps were taken to verify or authenticate them.[34]

What this evidentiary approach reveals

The approach to evidence that characterizes IMCCs suggests important (but usually implicit) assumptions about the function that they play in the enforcement of international law. Creation of an IMCC indicates a public interest in the historically accurate and legally appropriate resolution of the dispute. Especially where the dispute involves mass violations of human rights or humanitarian law, the international community benefits from a reliable statement of the historical facts to "set the record straight." Unpunished violations of human rights law impose a burden on the community and undermine the authority of human rights norms for the future. Because of this public interest, the dispute is not a purely private matter, of concern only to the parties.[35]

The commission is the only body well-positioned to consider the international interest surrounding an IMCC dispute. The parties are too involved in protecting their own situation to take on protection of the interests of the community. In doing so, the tribunal unavoidably relies on all available reliable sources of information. Restrictive rules of evidence threaten the commission's freedom to consider all facts, events, people and norms that it finds relevant from the international community's point of view. Permissive rules, which emphasize tribunal discretion and flexibility, encourage the widest possible consideration of factual evidence. The tribunal can exclude any evidence that it believes inappropriate but has complete latitude to consider any evidence it wishes.

Neutrality and ignorance

The significance of the difference between IMCCs and domestic courts is illustrated by comparing different legal positions on whether the finder of

---

33 Bin Cheng, *General Principles of Law as Applied by International Courts and Tribunals* (Cambridge University Press, 1987), 322.

34 Kidane, "Civil Liability for Violations of International Humanitarian Law," 78–79.

35 In the adversary system at use in the United States, in contrast, the parties have a monopoly of control over what evidence is admitted. If one party fails to submit evidence that would be helpful to his case, the tribunal is not empowered to help him out by proposing that evidence on its own.

fact may rely on material not in the record. In some legal systems, including the United States, elaborate precautions are taken to ensure that the finder of fact makes its decisions based only on evidence that has been properly determined to be admissible.[36] The "finder of fact" is ordinarily a jury.[37]

The rules relating to juror exposure to hearsay, prejudicial material and so on fall into this category; the judge makes admissibility decisions outside the hearing of the jury, in order to avoid prejudicing them. The rules for picking jurors in the first place display the same objective. During the voir dire process, a juror may be dismissed for cause if he or she has personal acquaintance with the participants or occurrences in the dispute.[38] The reasoning is that jurors who have personal knowledge of the events may have the tendency to rely on their personal experiences to decide the case, when they are legally obligated to decide the case on the facts presented at the trial – and nothing else.[39] As with disqualification

---

[36] *See Sheppard v. Maxwell*, 384 US 333, 351 (1966) ("The undeviating rule of this Court was expressed by Mr. Justice Holmes over half a century ago … '[t]he theory of our system is that the conclusions to be reached in a case will be induced only by evidence and argument in open court, and not by any outside influence, whether of private talk or public print'.") (quoting *Patterson v. State of Colorado ex rel. Att'y Gen.*, 205 US 454, 462 (1907)); *Singer v. United States*, 380 US 24, 35 (1965) ("[Trial by jury] has been surrounded with safeguards to make it as fair as possible – for example, venue can be changed when there is a well-founded fear of jury prejudice [under] Rule 21(a) of the Federal Rules of Criminal Procedure, and prospective jurors are subject to voir dire examination, to challenge for cause, and to peremptory challenge [under] Rule 24(a) and (b).").

[37] Jurors must undergo *voir dire* at the outset of the trial, to determine through questioning whether they have any conflict of interest or other reason that they are unsuitable to sit on the jury. Jurors who do not pass this test are disqualified "for cause." *See McCoy v. Goldston*, 652 F.2d 654, 657 (6th Cir. 1981) ("Though the Constitution guarantees only a fair and impartial jury, free from actual bias or prejudice, 'a juror's impartiality may not be assumed without inquiry.' The proper occasion for such determination is upon the voir dire examination.") (quoting *Kiernan v. Van Schaik*, 347 F.2d 776, 887 (3d Cir. 1965)).

[38] *See Miller v. Webb*, 385 F.3d 666, 675 (6th Cir. 2004) ("When a trial court is confronted with a biased juror … the judge must, either *sua sponte* or upon a motion, dismiss the prospective juror for cause.") (citing *Frazier v. United States*, 335 U.S. 497, 511 (1948)).

[39] *See, e.g., United States ex rel Bloeth v. Denno*, 313 F.2d 364, 372 (2d Cir. 1963) ("The reviewing court must determine, from a review of the entire voir dire, whether the extent and nature of the publicity has caused such a build up of prejudice that excluding the preconception of guilt from the deliberations would be too difficult for the jury to be honestly found impartial."); *see also* "Discovery of Prejudicial Pre-Trial Publicity on *Voir Dire*" (1965) 23 *Washington and Lee*

of individual jurors, the harm to be avoided is pollution of the finder of fact through exposure to non-record information about guilt or innocence.

For similar reasons, a criminal defendant is sometimes entitled to have his or her trial moved from a location where potential jurors may have already formed an opinion about the defendant's guilt.[40] Judges, also, are to disqualify themselves if they have personal knowledge about the "evidentiary facts" of the case.[41] Evidentiary facts are the circumstances of the dispute, the "who, how, where and why" of the legal problem between this defendant and this plaintiff.[42] These are contrasted with "legislative facts" – for example, the economic circumstances that motivated adoption of a particular piece of legislation – as to which the judge can take judicial notice.

The Code of Conduct for United States judges, accordingly, requires a judge to disqualify him or herself where "the judge has personal knowledge of disputed evidentiary facts concerning the proceeding":

> Judges' Ethical Obligations
>
> Canon 3: A Judge Should Perform the Duties of the Office Fairly, Impartially and Diligently …
>
> (C) *Disqualification.*
>
> (1) A judge shall disqualify himself or herself in a proceeding in which the judge's impartiality might reasonably be questioned, including but not limited to instances in which:

Law Review 230, 230 (1965) ("A major problem facing courts today is attainment of a fair trial with an impartial jury when pre-trial publicity has been sufficient so as to constitute 'trial by newspaper'.") (quoting *Sheppard v. Maxwell*, 231 F. Supp. 37 (S.D. Ohio 1964)).

40 "Petitioner relies heavily on our opinion in *Irvin v. Dowd,* 366 US 717, 81 S.Ct. 1639, 6 L.Ed.2d 751 (1961), to support his position. In that case, we held that pretrial publicity in connection with a capital trial had so tainted the jury pool in Gibson County, Indiana, that the defendant was entitled as a matter of federal constitutional law to a change of venue to another county." *Mu'Min v. Virginia*, 500 US 415, 427 (1991).

41 This rule does not apply to so-called legislative facts; as to those, the judge need not adhere to strict evidentiary rules.

42 Rule 201 of the US Federal Rules of Evidence addresses judicial notice of adjudicative facts: "[a] judicially noticed [adjudicative] fact must be one not subject to reasonable dispute in that it is either (1) generally known within the territorial jurisdiction of the trial court or (2) capable of accurate and ready determination by resort to sources whose accuracy cannot reasonably be questioned."

(a) the judge has a personal bias or prejudice concerning a party, or personal knowledge of disputed evidentiary facts concerning the proceeding.[43]

However, knowledge of "legislative facts" does not support a disqualification.[44]

This approach is quite different from the approach in international mass claims (and international adjudication generally). The fact that IMCCs are created to deal with violent conflict and serious upheaval means that IMCCs have a very public nature. Mass claims cases are typically disputes of great notoriety and the decision makers are recruited from a group most likely to have formed an impression about the facts: the international bar. Personal unfamiliarity with the facts of the case is not necessarily essential to a neutral and fair process, and, at any rate, would hardly be possible.[45]

BURDEN OF PROOF AND STANDARD OF PROOF

Burden of proof and standard of proof are related, but not identical, concepts. Both contribute to the resolution of claims that are based on a small amount of evidence. Using these tools, the commission will determine how thoroughly and persuasively a claim's support must be to meet the burden of proof. Many different standards have been used.

Burden of Proof versus Standard of Proof

Burden of proof refers to the designation of one party, Alpha, as the one that must move forward. If no evidence is presented in favor of Alpha's claim, then Alpha's claim must be rejected because Alpha has the burden

---

[43] Code of Conduct for United States Judges (2014), available at: http://www.uscourts.gov/judges-judgeships/code-conduct-united-states-judges#b.

[44] "Judicial notice of so-called legislative facts may exclude the application of burden of proof rules to a considerable extent in constitutional litigation. While fulfilling various functions in the United States legal system, the main result of the concept of judicial notice is to allow the judge to establish facts without adhering to the strict rules and requirements of the law of evidence." Juliane Kokott, *The Burden of Proof in Comparative and International Human Rights Law: Civil and Common Law Approaches With Special Reference to the American and German Legal Systems* (Springer, 1998), 30.

[45] Nevertheless, there are minimum ethical standards, some of which may be expressly incorporated into the arbitration agreement to ensure that commissioners are fair and impartial. These are discussed in Chapter 3.

of proof. Standard of proof, in contrast, refers to how much evidence Alpha must present to meet the burden of proof. If Alpha cannot produce enough evidence, then its claim fails as insufficiently proven. If Alpha is successful in producing that amount of evidence, then the burden of proof shifts to the defending state, Beta.

The commission will set the standard of proof to reflect its view of the circumstances of the case. Assume, for example, that Alpha has a claim that could be established easily with a few documents, such as letters, medical records, job applications or school transcripts. Alpha fails to introduce any documentary materials at all. The absence of evidence, if unexplained by the circumstances, seems like a telling indictment of Alpha's claim. But if Alpha provides reliable evidence that the country's public records were all destroyed in the course of the war when a particular document warehouse was bombed, then the absence of documentary evidence is less probative. The standard of proof may be lowered to accommodate the particular facts of the case.

As a basic matter, the burden of proof lies with the claimant; Alpha, in our example.[46] Difficulties in collecting evidence ordinarily do not shift the burden of proof, meaning it does not become incumbent upon Beta to prove its innocence. A commission may, however, lower the standard of proof when circumstances require.[47] Thus, according to the International Court of Justice, "the territorial exclusivity of one party over the possible evidence does not bring about a reversal of the burden of proof, although it can influence the standard of proof."[48] Only in an extreme scenario

---

[46] Note that even in proposals, such as that of Eyal Benvenisti, in which no proof of property ownership is required, claimants would still have to establish identity as a member of the group entitled to a standardized compensation – according to whatever standard the theoretical commission might establish. For a claims commission that addresses the claims of refugees, for example, the commission must set requirements for proving refugee status or, in the case of descendants, proving relationship to original refugee and/or the death of the original refugee. *See* Eyal Benvenisti, "Modalities for Processing Refugee Claims for Compensation" (April 2012) (unpublished paper) (on file with author).

[47] *See* "Evidentiary Issues" section above.

[48] Corfu Channel (*United Kingdom v. Albania*), 18 (1949) ICJ Rep. 4.

would the commission find support for shifting the burden of proof to the respondent,[49] as most literature finds no exceptions to *onus incumbit actori*.[50]

Setting the Standard of Proof

There is widespread agreement that the burden of proof will ordinarily fall on the party making the claim in question. But there is no settled standard of proof among international law tribunals and courts, much less a standard specific to claims commissions or claim types. In *Burden of Proof and Related Issues*, Mojtaba Kazazi, formerly a judge of the High Court of Tehran who also served as the executive head of the United Nations Compensation Commission (UNCC),[51] observed that the "exact meaning of [a] standard will eventually depend 'on how the particular tribunal views the matter and, hopefully, explains it'."[52]

While many courts and tribunals have used one of the recognized, traditional standards of proof, others seem to have created new standards or revised old ones: satisfactory proof, clear evidence, sufficient evidence of a reliable quality;[53] clear and convincing evidence in

---

49 Gattini, "Evidentiary Issues."

50 Kazazi, *Burden of Proof and Related Issues*, 230, (arguing that the rule on the duty to cooperate "does not generally affect the applicability of the rule *actori incumbit probatio* as a primary rule for allocating the burden of proof").

51 "Dr Mojtaba Kazazi, a former judge of the High Court of Tehran, served for many years as the Executive Head of the United Nations Compensation Commission (UNCC), and the Secretary of its Governing Council, with the Security Council membership, in Geneva, where he was instrumental in the setting up of the UNCC and in resolving 2.7 million claims from over 100 Governments. He also worked for several years as lead counsel and advocate, or as chief negotiator, on hundreds of arbitration claims before the Iran–US Claims Tribunal at The Hague; and more recently as arbitrator appointed by the ICC International Court of Arbitration." Tehran Regional Arbitration Centre, "About TRAC," available at: http://www.trac.ir/static.aspx?id=2.

52 Kazazi, *Burden of Proof and Related Issues*, 186.

53 Michael J. Matheson, *International Civil Tribunals and Armed Conflict* (Martinus Nijhoff, 2012) 153 (citing *Congo v. Uganda*, Judgment of 19 December 2005, ¶¶ 83, 123, 136, 146, 175, 208).

support;[54] beyond a reasonable doubt in civil contexts;[55] or indubitable proof.[56]

Scholars and practitioners alike have noted that the standard of "beyond a reasonable doubt" would be unmanageable in claims commission contexts.[57] This is the standard used for criminal cases in the US legal system. When too heavy a burden of proof is imposed, opponents argue, a claim may never get consideration: "reliance on heavy burdens of proof makes it more likely that the Court will not decide what actually happened in a case before it, but rather simply conclude that a burden has not been met."[58]

Some IMCCs have maintained a standard of proof comparable to international and domestic courts.[59] The EECC "adopted a high standard of evidentiary proof for the proceedings before it, concluding that the parties must establish facts with clear and convincing evidence based on the totality of the evidence and show that violations occurred in a frequent or pervasive manner."[60] The EECC stated that it "recognizes that this standard of proof and the existence of conflicting evidence may result in fewer findings of liability than either Party expects. The Awards

---

[54] "Particularly in the light of the gravity of some of the claims advanced, the Commission will require clear and convincing evidence in support of its findings … The Commission does not accept any suggestion that, because some claims may involve allegations of potentially criminal conduct, it should apply an even higher standard of proof corresponding to that in individual criminal proceedings. The Commission is not a criminal tribunal assessing individual criminal responsibility. It must instead decide whether there have been breaches of international law based on normal principles of state responsibility" *Id.* at 155 (quoting Prisoners of War (Eritrea), Partial Award of 1 July 2003, ¶¶ 44–47).

[55] Gattini, "Evidentiary Issues," 889.

[56] Gattini, "Evidentiary Issues." The authors note that some international courts and judicial bodies "have required an 'indubitable proof'" in all matters.

[57] Kazazi, *Burden of Proof and Related Issues*, 184, n 20 ("The standard of 'beyond a reasonable doubt' has been from time to time criticized in legal literature").

[58] Matheson, *International Civil Tribunals and Armed Conflict*, 154, n 47.

[59] The ICJ uses the "clear and convincing evidence" standard of proof. *See* Kidane, "Civil Liability for Violations of International Humanitarian Law," 74 ("the [EECC's] 'clear and convincing' standard appears to comport with the standard adopted by the International Court of Justice in the Congo case, where the ICJ stated that 'the Court must first establish which relevant facts it regards as having been convincingly established by the evidence.'").

[60] Kidane, "Civil Liability for Violations of International Humanitarian Law," 28.

on these Claims must be understood in that unavoidable context."[61] But both parties favored these heightened standards because they "took into account the seriousness of the violations at issue and the fact that states – not individuals or corporate entities – were parties to the proceedings."[62] The Commission settled on a "standard … somewhere between the standard of probability common in civil court proceedings in the United States and the standard of 'beyond a reasonable doubt' common in U.S. criminal proceedings."[63]

Some claims commissions appear to choose a "totality of evidence" standard to compensate for the difficulty of obtaining evidence under specific circumstances.[64] This choice may be most meaningful where a claimant needs to establish that "violations occurred not on an individual and isolated basis but in a frequent or pervasive manner."[65] Where a violation must be shown to be "frequent and pervasive," affecting a large number of victims, evidence supporting the claim of repeated transgressions must be provided.[66] However, in some cases, a commission may determine the violation is sufficiently serious for the commission to accept evidence supporting a single instance as adequate for a claim.[67]

---

[61] Kidane, "Civil Liability for Violations of International Humanitarian Law," 72.

[62] Kidane, "Civil Liability for Violations of International Humanitarian Law," 71.

[63] However, "[w]ith respect to one important set of claims, *i.e.*, allegations of rape, the Commission worked within this standard to produce a slightly altered approach that took into account characteristics of this violation that likely would not be accounted for under the general standard." Kidane, "Civil Liability for Violations of International Humanitarian Law."

[64] EECC, Eritrea's Claims 2, 4, 6, 7, 8 & 22, 39 (2004) (citing cultural reasons for low reporting rates and the difficulty of obtaining evidence in cases of sexual assault as cause to except rape from "frequent or pervasive" standard).

[65] Kidane, "Civil Liability for Violations of International Humanitarian Law," 73.

[66] "[T]he [EECC] stated that it d[id] not see its task to be the determination of liability of a Party for each individual incident of illegality suggested by the evidence. Rather, it is to determine liability for serious violations of the law by the Parties, which are usually illegal acts or omissions that were frequent or pervasive and consequently affected significant numbers of victims." *See* Kidane, "Civil Liability for Violations of International Humanitarian Law."

[67] "Rape, which by definition involves intentional and grievous harm to an individual civilian victim, is an illegal act that need not be frequent to support State responsibility." *See* Kidane, "Civil Liability for Violations of International Humanitarian Law," 75.

Fairness, Symmetry and Evidentiary Strategies

A final important consideration arises out of the symmetry of some IMCCs. Symmetry means that both sides are entitled to raise claims of the same sort, within the same jurisdictional time frame, subject to the same substantive law, and so forth. The EECC was completely symmetric while the UNCC was asymmetric because only one side was permitted to raise claims at all. The UNCC was predicated upon a threshold determination that Iraq (but only Iraq) was guilty and should pay reparations.

Given the difficulties in defining standards of proof, admissibility and other related issues, it would not be surprising if tribunals were somewhat uncertain about what formulation to adopt. The fact that in some commissions everything is symmetric encourages a rather relaxed attitude toward the possibility of inaccuracy. So long as both sides are treated equally, the argument goes, it would not matter too much whether the rules and decisions were adequately stated and explained in the commission's awards. If an evidentiary standard was too restrictive regarding Alpha's claims, it would be exactly as restrictive in regard to Beta's claims. Where the IMCC is symmetric, it might be argued, a commission need only concern itself with neutrality.

This is an attractive idea. The requirements for admission of evidence or for standard of proof are notoriously difficult – why not circumvent the whole problem just by engaging in some reasonable common sense when an evidentiary problem arises and then trying to do the same for both parties? Then, in calculating the final award, the "unfairness" will balance out.

The attractiveness of this intuition is not, however, justified. It might seem that Alpha and Beta would be indifferent toward systems in which the rules were strict and ones in which they were lenient. But this disregards the fact that some or all of the claims detail the victimization of the two state's nationals who are not indifferent: Changing the burden of proof will alter the likelihood that the individual victim will prevail. As we will show in Chapter 8, it makes a difference to the state's nationals whether the rule is restrictive, preventing the conclusion that the national has a cause of action, versus lenient, allowing greater recovery on both sides with the extra recovery on one side balanced out against the recovery on the other. Applying an unusually lenient, or unusually restrictive, standard neutrally to Alpha and Beta will "wash out" in the long run. However, applying an unusually lenient standard results in favoring victims over accused state perpetrators while applying an unusually restrictive standard has the opposite effect. And this will matter greatly to the states and individuals involved in IMCCs.

7. Remedies and compliance with claims commissions rulings

This chapter explores two related subjects: the remedies employed by international mass claims commissions (IMCCs) and the ways that commissions seek to ensure party compliance. The first of these is relatively straightforward. Although other remedies may be appropriate so long as they are consistent with the legal instrument that established the commission and with international law, monetary compensation is, by a wide margin, the remedy most commonly employed.

The second of these is considerably more difficult. In two of our illustrative examples of claims commissions – the Iran–US Claims Tribunal (IUSCT) and the United Nations Compensation Commission (UNCC) – special provisions were made for administering the commissions' awards. These administrative apparatuses were somewhat cumbersome, but compliance was general. However, not all IMCCs resemble the Iran–US Claims Tribunal and the UNCC in this respect. The Eritrea–Ethiopia Claims Commission (EECC) did not come equipped with an administrative structure comparable to the other two, and no special provision was made for administration of the awards. To this day, the parties have not made payment, reflecting perhaps the rough equivalence in value of the two sides' awards. Given this rough equivalence, neither state had much to gain. In such a situation of symmetric and roughly equal claims, a set-off might seem to be both the most obvious and least problematic of solutions – but, as we shall see, a set-off merely sweeps important difficulties under the rug.

The topic of compliance has an important theoretical dimension. International relations (as the "realists" tell us) take place in "a state of anarchy" in which enforcement is largely a matter of self-help.[1] Common

[1] "Right," Thucydides said, "as the world goes, is only in question between equals in power, while the strong do what they can and the weak suffer what they must." *Melian Dialogue* 352 (1996). *See also* E.H. Carr, *The Twenty Years' Crisis* (Macmillan, 1939); John J. Mearsheimer, *The Tragedy of Great Power Politics* (W.W. Norton, 2001); Hans Morgenthau, *Politics Among Nations* (Knopf, 1948); Kenneth N. Waltz, *Theory of International Politics* (McGraw-Hill, 1979).

sense, experience and legal theory all suggest that it is difficult – some might say impossible – to ensure compliance in a setting where effective third-party enforcement is lacking. This problem, unlike some others that IMCCs face, cannot be solved solely by more careful drafting of the underlying arbitration agreement. The parties cannot guarantee compliance by inserting assurances requiring compliance into the arbitration agreement because such assurances are as vulnerable to party defiance as any other of the agreement's provisions.

The logic of set-offs supports the non-payment of awards that come close to cancelling each other out. However, in the context of international mass claims commissions these responses are deeply problematic. Where the final award is carried out through set-offs, the end result is likely to be perverse: satisfaction of the interests of the defending state, the interests of the tribunal and the interests of the international community, but no satisfaction of the interests of the victims who have just proven their case to the commission's satisfaction and for whom the commission was supposedly created. This, surely, is exactly backwards.

REMEDIES

This chapter deals with the overlapping topics of remedies and compliance. Remedies are penalties imposed by the tribunal against one of the parties and to the benefit of the other, typically because of the first's failure to comply with relevant substantive or procedural norms. Part I of this chapter divides remedies into two categories, depending on whether they are imposed during the course of the proceeding or as a part of the final award. Compliance, which will be addressed in Part II, is the action that one or both parties takes in accordance with the tribunal's findings in the final award. The most important open issues about compliance concern how an international tribunal can maximize the probability that the losing party will comply.

Remedies in the Course of the Proceedings

For several reasons, potential weaknesses in the enforcement of remedies during the course of proceedings are less likely to be serious than deficiencies in the imposition of remedies at the stage of the final award. First, the stakes are higher at the end of the dispute than when dealing with decisions made during the proceedings. At the end of the dispute the final award decides the issues in the case and these are obviously the most important to the parties. Decisions about procedural matters are only a means to an end, and it is the end (that is, the content of the final award) that matters most. Second, a party may have additional opportunities to dissuade the commission of a procedural decision that the party disagrees with. But there are no opportunities to attempt to persuade the commission of errors in the final award. Third, with so much hanging in the balance in the final award, the parties are likely to be quite cautious about alienating the commission. Defying procedural orders carries with it a risk of losing much more than a procedural ruling.

Remedies during the course of the proceedings are, nevertheless, an important part of the commission's toolkit for managing the smooth conduct of the litigation. Generally, they are employed to induce party cooperation with the tribunal's procedural instructions.

Tribunals need effective remedies for disregard of its procedural rules because the parties cannot be counted on to automatically follow procedural rules contrary to their interests. Domestic courts need effective remedies for the same reason, but they are different in that they are supported by a domestic government and their rules thus have real bite. Contempt of court can mean jail time or large fines. Domestic arbitrations, like domestic courts, are supported by the domestic legal system. Their procedural rules must be loosely consistent with domestic law, including statutory or constitutional authority, but in exchange, domestic enforcement methods protect the authority of arbitration awards.

IMCCs have implied remedial authority for much the same reason: to devise reasonable, non-punitive responses to procedural violations. This much is uncontroversial. But most lack support from domestic enforcement institutions, and remedies for violations are left to the commission's own "self-help" devices. For certain sorts of procedural requirements, a commission will have little trouble devising an appropriate and effective remedy. For example, if one of the parties misses a filing deadline, a tribunal can simply refuse to accept the written pleading that is submitted late.

Another straightforward problem arises where one of the parties declines to produce a particular piece of evidence within its control in the face of a commission request. IMCCs are generally dependent on the evidence that the parties choose to produce and lack the practical capacity to directly compel the production of written materials from outside sources. They also cannot hold a party that refuses to supply the documents in contempt. But the tribunal can infer that the evidence is unfavorable to the party that refused to produce it. This is a reasonable response, which is employed at times in domestic courts as well; if the evidence was favorable, one assumes the party having that evidence in its control would produce it.

On other occasions formulation of a remedy is more challenging. What should be the remedy where one party violates a confidentiality order? If one party is found to have submitted fraudulent evidence, is it adequate for a tribunal to treat the evidence as withdrawn? Or is that too lenient for such a violation? It may be inadequate to deter future violations because the responsible party loses nothing by trying.

In some disputes, the arbitration agreement may contain indications of the appropriate penalty, removing the burden of devising a remedy from the tribunal. But creativity may be needed where the arbitration agreement is silent. For example, some sort of remedial order might be necessary where one of the parties falls behind in the payment of commission expenses. In such a case, the tribunal might hold up the issuance of that party's award until the assessment is paid. Likewise, although it is common to provide a right to challenge an arbitrator for bias, the agreement may inexplicably fail to say so. Where no power is specified to remove an arbitrator for cause, it may be inferred as a necessary condition for exercise of neutral judgment.

The power to devise procedural rules and remedies will almost certainly be specified in the underlying agreement, even if the specific remedies themselves are not. As a general matter, the tribunal should be able to exercise reasonable judgment in formulating a fair and effective remedy. A standing court will have procedural rules of some complexity and possibly a long line of precedents giving additional content to fill gaps where the procedural code is silent. But, unless the arbitration agreement adopts some pre-existing code (*e.g.*, the Permanent Court of Arbitration rules for state to state disputes, the UNCITRAL rules etc.), an IMCC is unlikely to have a comparable longstanding body of procedural rules and the tribunal must have reasonable discretion to deal with novel problems as they arise.

Remedies in the Final Award

IMCCs have a number of different remedies available to implement final awards. Although the claim for relief is generally focused on money damages, there is no categorical reason that a final award might not include, for example, declaratory relief or an apology.[2] The remedies that are available depend on two factors: which remedies are consistent with

---

2 For example, see EECC Final Award on Eritrea's Diplomatic Claim, recognizing apology as an adequate remedy for violation of diplomatic protections. Eritrea–Ethiopia Claims Commission, Final Award – Eritrea's Damages Claims (17 August 2009), 619–620.

general international law and which are consistent with the terms of the arbitration agreement.

Some of the difficulties that arise when calculating monetary compensation are virtually identical to difficulties that arise in garden variety domestic cases. For example, a commission may face the question of whether it should award pre-judgment interest, and, if so, how should it be calculated? The calculation of business losses can also be challenging.

Even something as apparently straightforward as the destruction of buildings and equipment raises serious issues of justice and policy. If an occupying army destroys a civilian hospital, should the measure of damages be the cost of rebuilding the hospital after the end of the conflict? Or should it include loss of civilian use as well, since making such destruction actionable was motivated by the civilian dependence on the hospital during the duration of the conflict?[3]

The calculation of compensation for intangible losses can be particularly difficult. The EECC, for example, had to determine the appropriate amount of compensation for deliberate destruction (by explosives) of a unique archeological monument.[4] A veterans' cemetery was also deliberately destroyed; graves were dug up and human bones were strewn around.[5] Commissions can be called upon to assign a dollar figure as compensation for an unlawful killing, or for torture or sexual violence, including rape. These issues raise important moral and policy questions. Is the life of someone in the third world worth less than the life of a Westerner? None of these questions have easy answers.

COMPLIANCE

Compliance is an issue for all international decision-making. A losing party's refusal to comply plagues international court decisions, including

---

[3] Lea Brilmayer and Geoffrey Chepiga, "Ownership or Use? Civilian Property Interests in International Humanitarian Law" (2008) 49 *Harvard Journal of International Law* 413.

[4] The conflict resulted in the destruction of the Stela of Matara, a 2,500 year-old stone obelisk, the only artifact of its kind in Eritrea. The EECC awarded Eritrea $50,000 to compensate for its destruction. Eritrea–Ethiopia Claims Commission, Final Award – Eritrea's Damage Claims (17 August 2009), 580.

[5] Eritrea was awarded damages for the looting and stripping of the Tserona Patriot Cemetery. The EECC awarded Eritrea $50,000 to compensate for its destruction. Eritrea–Ethiopia Claims Commission, Final Award – Eritrea's Damage Claims (17 August 2009), 48.

at the International Court of Justice[6] and in state-to-state arbitrations.[7] International compliance is addressed in a number of legal instruments. For example, Article 94 of the United Nations Charter assigns the responsibility of enforcing compliance with ICJ decisions to the Security Council, although Article 94 also provides that ICJ decisions are authoritative only against the parties to a case.[8] International commercial arbitrations are generally enforceable under the New York Convention on the Recognition and Enforcement of Foreign Arbitral Awards.[9]

The Many Faces of Compliance

Compliance is not monolithic; it is multifaceted. A number of different actors have a stake in the enforcement of a commission award. Although these interests operate more or less in tandem, they are not identical, and in situations where they diverge, conflicts arise.

The victim is the one with the most obvious interest in the commission's ability to compel compliance with the award ("the victim's interest"). This, clearly, is a legitimate interest as the commission has already concluded that the victim is legally entitled to an award in that amount. But there are at least three sets of additional interests.

The defending state has an interest ("the defending state's interest") in clearing its name of allegations that it believes to be unfounded. The defending state also has an interest in closure. The interest in closure is ordinarily supported by provisions in the arbitration agreement that designate the commission as the exclusive remedy, thereby imposing forfeiture of claims that are not filed in accordance with the commission's procedural requirements, and requiring the parties to respect the commission's awards.

The tribunal itself has interests ("the tribunal's interests") in successful resolution of the dispute, including pride in having contributed to the advancement of international law and concern for the integrity of its

---

6 *See*, for example, the *Case Concerning the Military and Paramilitary Activities in and Against Nicaragua* (*Nicaragua v. United States of America*) 1986 ICJ 14.

7 *See*, for example, the recent arbitration between the Philippines and China over the islands and maritime spaces in the South China Sea, *The Republic of the Philippines v. The People's Republic of China*, PCA Case Repository No. 2013–19 (2016); Eritrea–Ethiopia Boundary Commission, Decision Pursuant to Article 15B of the Commission's Demarcation Directions (2003).

8 UN Charter art. 94.

9 United Nations Convention on the Recognition and Enforcement of Foreign Arbitral Awards (10 June 1958).

decisions. Individual tribunal members may have professional reasons for wanting the tribunal to be seen as a success, including the desire to be considered for future arbitral commissions or other prestigious positions.

International community interests ("the community's interest") include support for law and order, deterrence of future wrongdoing and termination of potential threats to peace and security. International community interests in law and order are particularly important in the defense against the accusation that international norms do, indeed, constitute a legal system. The existence of conflict pressures onlooker states to choose between the different sides to the conflict, straining relations with the other side. Conflict between two particular nations is bad for their neighbors because fighting might spread over the border, create refugee flows and other issues.

These three sets of interests, together with the interests of the victim, are mutually reinforcing: compliance with the final award simultaneously promotes all of these interests. It is, therefore, usually not necessary to parse them out separately. But the interests of the defending state, of the tribunal and of the community sometimes seem to eclipse what should be the central objective – that is: providing adequate compensation for the victims whose injury was the commission's reason for coming into existence. It is important, for this reason, to identify the major situations in which interests conflict.

Overlapping but Distinct: Interests in Conflict

No two of the interests identified above are exactly identical. The victim's interests will sometimes conflict with the community's interests; the tribunal's interests will sometimes diverge from the victim's interests, and the defending state's interests may come into conflict with any one of these. In particular, the commission's and the international community's interests can be satisfied with a general *appearance* of regularity, accuracy and justice; the victim cares less about appearances and more about the actual sufficiency of the award.

The victim's legitimate interest in receiving the compensation it was awarded may get lost in a tangle of crosscutting interests; it may be unclear which interests should predominate when several different sets of interests come into conflict. But privileging community interests or tribunal interests only elevates the general appearance of justice. There should be a presumption, we believe, that the victim's interests come first, for there is little or no reason to invest heavily in *claims* commissions that do not seek first and foremost to compensate the victims with valid claims.

Competing interests of the international community

As a general matter, the international community is likely to have a strong interest in the peaceful resolution of disputes. This requires that there be general compliance with decisions arrived at peacefully. Where the decisions of adjudicative institutions are not respected, permanent and peaceful resolution is that much more difficult. And when it becomes clear that force is the only way to bring a dispute to a permanent resolution, the parties to a dispute may feel compelled to resort to force.

But although the international community has good reason to support the decisions of adjudicative tribunals, its interest in compliance may sometimes be sacrificed to other priorities. In certain circumstances, countervailing community interests that are in tension with the general interest in compliance are allowed to override the reasons for supporting a commission's award.

For example, the community may care more about having a co-operative relationship with one of the parties than pressuring it to comply. The defending state may be an ally, or the victim state may be an enemy. The victim may end up with more than the usual amount of international support for enforcement of its award, or the defending state may have less support than usual because it has angered strong states in the past.

One cannot fully appreciate the success of the UNCC without taking into account the international community's relationship with Saddam Hussein's Iraq. As will be discussed later in this chapter, the international community's unified disapproval of the Iraqi invasion of Kuwait, exemplified by a number of strongly worded Security Council resolutions, provided the necessary foundation for a suitable compliance regime. Had the situation been reversed, with Kuwait being the international pariah, the UNCC would quite possibly have looked rather different. Indeed, it might never have come into existence.

As the Iraqi invasion example illustrates, the victim may be disfavored by the international community for reasons having little or nothing to do with compliance with adjudicative decisions generally. In the Iraq invasion example, Saddam Hussein's pariah status rallied the international community behind the formation of a commission with real clout. But a state need not have been guilty of invasion to have forfeited the support of the international community. Stronger states may withhold support for an award as a way of pressuring the victim to step in line and support the stronger states' priorities. A victim that is unpopular (or considered less important than the defending state) may have a hard time forcing the defending state to comply with an award. Such examples are not uncommon.

Something similar can occur when the community wishes positively to support the wrongdoer for reasons completely tangential to the claims awaiting adjudication. Assume that the defending state is impoverished and threatened by drought and epidemic. If it pays a large judgment (its allies argue), it will only impoverish its nationals even more. What is the point of requiring payment of a large award if the result is even greater dependence on international aid and greater hardship to the country's nationals? Its allies may say that they do not want to pressure its fragile government, which has taken substantial steps toward building a democracy. While it would be difficult to rationalize these arguments as a principled position on the law of compliance with arbitral awards, they do illustrate how a genuine tension in the international community's legitimate policies can create difficulties for judgment compliance.

The community interest versus the victim's interest

In addition to tensions among the various interests of a single actor, the different actors in the system may have conflicting interests with one another. For example, the victim's legitimate interests are largely backward-looking; they concern returning the situation to the *status quo ante*, the state of affairs before the unlawful injury occurred. The community has an interest in deterring wrongful conduct in the future. An approach to compliance that promotes the former will not necessarily be the right approach to the latter.

A simplified illustration shows how the interests of the victim and the international community are not necessarily congruent. In deliberating about the claims, the tribunal might wrongly hold liable a state that did not actually cause unlawful injury, or it might wrongly excuse a defendant that should have been held responsible. If the community accepts and believes in the terms of the award, and the facts and law as the commission found them, then community members would assume that justice has been done. That is all that it takes to support an interest in deterrence. It undermines deterrence for individuals to believe that they can act unlawfully and escape punishment, but this is not the case where the commission's conclusions look convincing to an outside observer.

The same logic holds when the commission is correct in its conclusion of basic liability but mistaken in the amount of damage done to the victim. Awards of different sizes create different degrees of deterrence. If it were generally known that the wrongdoer was required to pay for only a fraction of the damage it caused, it would encourage unlawful behavior by states that were willing to take some risk that they might get caught. But if the inadequacy of the award is not generally known, then the deterrent effect of the award remains intact.

Assume that the commission determines, correctly, that a group of civilians was unlawfully injured. A final award is given, but, owing to commission error, it is for only half of what the claimants rightly demand. Looking at the award from the outside, onlookers are unlikely to know that the award is off by 50 percent. A false but sincere community-wide belief that the correct quantum of punishment was meted out may be enough to create a deterrent effect (thus satisfying the interest of the community at large) because individual actors are, mistakenly, convinced that if they violate international law they will have to compensate claimants for everything. If the members of the community believe – even falsely – that wrongdoers are punished appropriately, then they will be deterred. Thus an award may satisfy the community's interest in deterrence without necessarily being fair to the victims.

But, this would not and should not satisfy the claimants themselves.[10] They are most likely more aware than the community at large that the damages award was less than they deserved on the merits. They do not care whether the deterrent effect was enough to convince future wrong-doers that they will be caught and suitably punished. They are occupied, rightly, with the direct effects on their own claims.

The tribunal's interest versus the victim's interest

The same examples show a divergence between interests of the victims and the interests of the tribunal. The tribunal's interests may diverge from the victim's interests because the tribunal has an interest in making it look like they did a good job, and that the proceedings came out for the best, regardless of whether or not they really did. The best outcome, defined simply as the lawful resolution of the dispute, might be different from the most apparently successful outcome for the tribunal. Where such outcomes differ, the result is a distortion of incentives, which may be resolved in favor of the tribunal's or the international community's interests at the expense of the victim's.

Commissioners do not have life tenure, as do US federal judges; indeed, many appointments to claims commissions contemplate only part-time work for the commissioners. Thus, commissioners may not be as insulated from outside pressures and incentives as are life-tenured judges. Their professional abilities, as demonstrated in their work on one tribunal, make them more attractive as commission members in another.

---

[10] *E.g.*, the community needs to reserve pressure against the violator for other purposes.

Commissioners have professional interests in making it appear that their tenures are successful.

Thus, there could be strong motivations to make awards that are sufficiently satisfactory to the competing parties that the parties fully comply with them. In practical terms, this usually means a motivation to seek unanimity, often through compromise. Compromise provides the loser with a way not to look like a loser, thus providing some positive reason to accept the tribunal's judgment. It is often said that arbitrators (in contrast with judges) are likely to come to compromise verdicts. This is difficult to test as an empirical claim. But it does seem to be the case that a commission has an incentive to "balance" the awards. A remedy that, although factually and legally correct, is so large as to be unacceptable to the losing party runs the risk of being unsuccessful. Indeed, the losing party may choose not to comply with the award, leaving the impression that nothing at all has been accomplished toward the commission's mandate.

As has been recognized in both the arbitral and the judicial contexts, unanimous awards are more persuasive and generate more public confidence than ones that are sharply splintered.[11] The fact of unanimity suggests that both sides should be satisfied with the result. Arbitrators have professional reasons to look successful. A unanimous verdict seems to indicate mutual satisfaction – both sides can live with it. An arbitrator appointed by the prevailing state may therefore be willing to support a

---

[11] The connection between adjudicators' unanimity and the legitimacy of their decisions has long been pondered in legal commentary. Learned Hand, for example, argued that a dissenting adjudicator "cancels the impact of monolithic solidarity on which the authority of a bench of judges so largely depends." Learned Hand, *The Bill of Rights* (Harvard University Press, 1958), 72. For an opposing view, at least in the contemporary US domestic context, *see* M. Todd Henderson, "From Seriatim to Consensus and Back Again: A Theory of Dissent," (2007) *Supreme Court Review* 283, 339 ("Dissent is not only necessary to ensure the legitimacy of the Court, but also gives law the authority to resolve controversial social issues – it ensures a particular type of Court legitimacy. Just as the opinion of the court was necessary to increase the power of the Court during the Marshall era, dissent is the strategy that enables the Court and the law in general to maintain its institutional power given the highly political nature of the cases the Court decides today.") Nonetheless, Henderson agrees that unanimity was useful to the preservation of Court legitimacy in the nineteenth century. "Dissent ensures legal control over society just as the unanimity norm was necessary to achieve the same result in the early nineteenth century."

smaller award that is more acceptable to the opposing party, even if the arbitrator believes such a remedy to be too low to satisfy justice in the abstract.

For these reasons, the tribunal has an incentive to minimize any appearance of party non-compliance. Problems arise when it appears that the only way to achieve an appearance of complete compliance is by making substantive concessions. Rather than writing an award requiring the losing party to comply with an overwhelmingly unfavorable decision – an order that may be rejected and leave the dispute festering forever – that commission may bring the award and the defending state's response to it into sync by altering the terms of the award. We normally think of the defending state altering its conduct to conform to the award, but we should be also concerned about the drafters of the award altering its terms to conform to what they expect the defending state to do.

This is the problem of "direction of fit." If there is a discrepancy between the award necessary to satisfy the tribunal's interest and the interests of the victims, either side can be adjusted to meet the other. Either the losing party changes its behavior to "comply" with the award, or the commission (either anticipating resistance or maybe wishing to get a unanimous verdict) adjusts the award to be consistent with what the losing party is expected to do.[12] How ought the commission approach the question? Is adjusting the award to meet the intransigence of the more powerful party taking the easy way out? And if so, is that wrong?

It is arguable that the winning party might prefer to receive something rather than nothing, which would be the net result of a high award that the losing state refused to pay. Perhaps it is too invested immediately after the announcement of the award to make the politically unpopular decision to relinquish some of what it was just awarded, in which case the commission would be doing it a favor by announcing a reasonable compromise in the award itself.

In signing the agreement, the parties commit to abide by the commission's decision, not to the commission's decision if considered correct. There is no doubt that, even if the commission decides to compromise, or to tinker with the result to accommodate the interests of the defending state or to get a unanimous opinion, its decision is still binding. Of course, as the victim would point out, this logic applies to both parties, the winner and the loser. But the fact that the loser is also obliged to

[12] In IMCC processes, there is no obligation on third parties to support the arbitrator in enforcing the award. This makes the IMCC's enforcement powers comparatively weak.

honor a disappointing award is useless as a reason for the winner to declare that it was shortchanged. If the loser violates its obligations, the victim gains nothing from following suit.

The success incentive is perverse because, if the commission really wants to ensure compliance, it should just conform the award to the distribution that would result from the power differential between the competing parties. It would position the arbitrator as a kind of mediator looking for a result that both sides would accept without regard to international law. Or perhaps a better analogy would be a third-party negotiator, whose assignment would be to analyse power dynamics and determine an award accordingly. A very powerful state that violated the rights of citizens in a very weak state would, under this reasoning, always be made to pay only a negligible sum. Neither the gravity nor the extent of the powerful state's violations would be part of the arbitrator's reasoning process.[13]

We might wonder, then, the true purpose of IMCCs. Does such a "realist" adjustment violate the arbitrators' duties to remain neutral and to decide disputes on the merits? This depends on how the agreement establishing the arbitration is written; the parties themselves may care about a successful solution, rather than a decision on principle. If, for example, both parties' priority is to avert war or conflict, then both of them might prioritize success over truth.

"Compliance" sounds like an unalloyed benefit. But if wrongly applied, the concept can be the source of serious unfairness. Thus, one should reflect that valuing compliance above all else can bring closure for states, peace for the international community, respect for the tribunal and nothing for the victims.

The primacy of victim compensation

International mass claims commissions are expensive investments that often take years of written and oral filings and incur enormous costs. Although the monetary costs are the most obvious, the victims also pay emotionally and psychologically; in providing their testimony, they relive the pain, grief and anger of their experiences during the conflict. Thousands of hours of legal, administrative and substantive experts' time and energy are diverted to the project; especially in the developing world, such diversions cut into the limited pool of trained human resources that

---

[13] This follows the basic realist understanding of international relations, including the authors cited in note 1.

a state might otherwise have available to devote to development or other governance projects.

Such an investment is worthwhile only if the end result is a substantial achievement of the commission's reason for existence. A compensation commission's primary reason for existence is to compensate the victims of unlawful behavior. Although other values may be accomplished along the way, these (we believe) are secondary. Claims commissions are not set up when the sole achievement would be to effect closure for the parties. They are not set up to pursue the commission members' professional interests in effecting a successful outcome. They are not even established for the benefit of the international community's desire for peace and stability. These other objectives reinforce the primary objective: rightful compensation. For a *compensation* commission, victim compensation, usually expressed in monetary terms, should be the first priority. Successful provision of compensation is what justifies the large investment of financial and human capital.

How successful the commission is in providing compensation turns on two things: the degree to which the award reflects correctly the amount of compensation owed and the likelihood that the amount awarded will actually be delivered. The success of the tribunal therefore should be measured in terms of (1) whether the rightful amount of compensation (2) is actually provided to, and received by, the victims. Members of the tribunal should pursue strategies consistent with this understanding of "success."

Here, however, a problem arises. These two elements of a successful compensation commission are to some degree in tension. A tradeoff may in some disputes seem necessary. An arbitrator might face a difficult choice between correctly determining the victims' interests and maximizing the size of the compensation actually provided. Where the defending state is unwilling or unable to pay the entire award, a tribunal might accomplish more for the victims by reducing the amount awarded. The argument would be that the victims are better off, at the end of the day, with a compromise verdict than with a larger award on paper but less cash in hand.

This argument must be distinguished from a superficially similar one about the tension between the interests of the victim and the interests of the international community, the defending state or the tribunal. We recognized earlier that the interests of these other actors might in some cases come into competition with the interests of the victims. In such cases (we argue) the guiding principle should be the interests of the victim in achieving rightful compensation, which is the primary objective of a claims commission.

But this does not necessarily mean that the competing interests of the same actor, the victim, should not be taken into account. Whether to do so is a genuinely difficult question because it pits one of the victim's interests against another. All manner of arguments might be made about how best to calculate what is in the interest of the victim. If in favor of a compromise award, one might say that the victims would rather have some compensation rather than none; that the victims' interests are not served by prolonging the dispute (as would happen if the defending state defied the award); or that a compromise verdict is not too high a price to pay if that is what it takes for the award to be unanimous.

But a compromise award has its own disadvantages. The international community might be more likely to assist in pressuring the defending state if the tribunal took a stand on principle. A compromise award might be so low as to trivialize the victims' injuries. When in doubt it is always better to reason honestly and transparently. A compromise award will not be convincing; engaging in devious strategic calculations will likely backfire – or so it might be argued.

One might say that these two types of analysis, looking at the interests of the victims versus looking at the interests of the international community at large, hews to the traditional distinction between deontological and consequentialist ethics.[14] For our purposes, a deontological arbitrator would prioritize the rights of the victims, declining to consider the consequences for the international community at large except insofar as those consequences might impact the victims. This would reflect the view that the victims have rights that ought to be protected from the interests of the international community as a whole. By contrast, a consequentialist arbitrator would reason according to what she expected the aggregate benefits of the global consequences of her findings and compensation award to be. Our ideal arbitrator would be deontological towards the victims. To put it another way, success in arbitration should require consequentialist reasoning about international politics if and only if the victims' interests plainly require it.

---

[14] *Cf.* Lea Brilmayer, "Rights, Fairness, and Choice of Law" (1989) 98 *Yale Law Journal* 1277, 1278 ("Choosing to talk in terms of rights rather than policies or interests represents a fundamental jurisprudential commitment which is reflected in the way that concrete problems are resolved. Rights arise primarily in deontological theories while policies and interests are instrumental or consequentialist. Rights impose limits on state authority, protecting individuals from being forced to sacrifice for the good of society as a whole. They reflect a notion of individual desert that stands above the instrumental advantage to be achieved by the application of some particular state's substantive law.").

Our thesis is that in a mass compensation commission, the victims' interests should be taken as the most important. If the parties want otherwise, it would be possible to add a provision to the arbitration agreement stating, for example, that a decision should be made according to equitable principles rather than in accordance with international law.[15] Alternatively, if the victim would prefer immediate payment of a smaller award, it is always possible for the parties to negotiate to that conclusion after the award is announced.

Success, for our ideal arbitrator, would therefore entail placing greater value on determining the correct award based on international law, as the parties agreed at the outset. The likelihood of the losing party paying this award would be secondary to this first question. Redressing the injustice perpetrated against the victims would be the chief factor determining any award given. Because the victims' interests come first, closure for the states, peace for the international community, and respect for the tribunal should be discounted heavily.

Set-Offs: In Whose Interest?

Set-offs become an issue when the claims commission is structured symmetrically. For example, at the EECC each of the two state parties made claims against the other. Two final awards were issued, one in favor of Eritrea and the other in favor of Ethiopia. By set-off we mean a comparison between the two awards, with the "losing" party paying the "winning" party the difference between the amount owing to it and the amount it owed to the other side.

---

[15] Whether awards are made according to principles of law or equity depends on the agreement that establishes the commission. In the case of the EECC, for example, the peace agreement between Ethiopia and Eritrea that established the commission specified that the award would be made according to principles of law. "The mandate of the Commission is to decide through binding arbitration all claims for loss, damage or injury by one Government against the other, and by nationals (including both natural and juridical persons) of one party against the Government of the other party or entities owned or controlled by the other party that are (a) related to the conflict that was the subject of the Framework Agreement, the Modalities for its Implementation and the Cessation of Hostilities Agreement, and (b) *result from violations of international humanitarian law*, including the 1949 Geneva Conventions, or other violations of international law." Agreement Between the Government of the State of Eritrea and the Government of the Federal Democratic Republic of Ethiopia, art. 5, UN Doc A/55/686, 13 December 2000 (emphasis added).

At first glance, set-offs appear to be a useful approach to commissions with a symmetric structure. Particularly where the two final awards are fairly close in amount, no cumbersome transfer of money is necessary to comply with the awards. Of especial value, where the commission is symmetric and the awards are close in value, set-offs make concern about compliance unnecessary. However, set-offs are enormously problematic where the purpose of the commission is to determine compensation for individual victims of a state's unlawful conduct. In a claims commission, the purpose of the commission is to effect compensation for individual injured victims. Given that objective, set-offs undermine the most important reason that international mass claims commissions are created.

Statism versus individual rights of nationals

The question of set-offs must be understood in the context of an international legal system that for many years treated states as the only relevant actors in the international system.[16] From this point of view, an IMCC is a state-to-state arbitration, with the states making the decisions about which claims to file, when or if to settle, and what is to be done with any award money that it is paid. Set-offs are unobjectionable in the context of a world composed only of states.

But a potentially serious conflict of interest becomes evident when an attempt is made to accommodate the fact that the victims suffering the injury were the state's nationals. That conflict of interest arises because the state and the individual victim are competing for the same award money. The money paid pursuant to the award is paid as a consequence of the individual claim of the victim, whose case was strong enough to convince the tribunal to grant him or her relief. When the award money would be paid to the state, which will be driven by its own laws and policies – and needs for cash – in deciding how much to pass on, and to whom.[17] In these situations, the conflict of interest is that a dollar passed on to a victim is one dollar less for the state.

---

[16] See, for example, John J. Mearsheimer, "Structural Realism," in Tim Dunne, Milja Kurki and Steve Smith (eds), *International Relations Theories: Discipline and Diversity*, 3rd ed. (Oxford University Press, 2013), 77–93, who lays the foundation of Realism from the perspective of state actors; see also John M. Hobson, *The State and International Relations* (Cambridge University Press, 2000), who describes traditional International Relations as state-centered, with contemporary "vanguard" theorists in the field moving "away from the state."

[17] Note that both Iran–US Claims Tribunal and UNCC distinguished direct claims by individuals from claims by states. See Rudolf Dolzer, "The Settlement of War-Related Claims: Does International Law Recognize a Victim's Private

This can plausibly be characterized as the state stealing its nationals' money. But there are plausible reasons that the state might take some or all of those dollars. The state might feel that litigation costs should be paid out of the award money before it is passed on to the victims. Only a fraction of the state's population will benefit from the commission, but if it is financed out of general revenues, it is being paid for by all. The litigation, which was undertaken by the state on behalf of a small group of its nationals, should not be subsidized by their remaining countrymen and women. Or, the state may conclude that without its endeavors, the victims would have received nothing (surely they could not initiate international litigation on their own behalf), and so they are entitled to nothing.

Indeed, this position has merit; the state took some risks in order to make it possible for its victims to recover. By signing a framework agreement and by filing claims on behalf of the victims, the state placed its own interests at risk. It left itself open to liability for its own allegedly unlawful conduct, from which it otherwise would almost certainly have been immune since there was no other forum in which it could have been sued. It is not an exaggeration to say that it is only because the state agreed with its opponent to litigate the victims' claims that it must now pay the award.

Of course, we might respond that the state should not have violated the rights of the other state's nationals in the first place, and cannot blame its own innocent national victims for the fact that it was ultimately brought to justice. Moreover, the victim is not asking for a windfall. It is his (or her) claim based on unlawful treatment, which the tribunal has determined on the merits to deserve compensation. Further, as a result of the creation of the compensation commission, the victim will lose the opportunity to look for a more favorable forum, forever.[18] By agreeing to

---

Right of Action – Lessons after 1945" (2002) 20 *Berkeley Journal of International Law* 296, available at: http://scholarship.law.berkeley.edu/bjil/vol20/iss1/13.

[18] Generally, individual plaintiffs lack the ability to bring suits against states due to legal barriers such as the sovereign immunity doctrine. *See, e.g.,* Jasper Finke, "Sovereign Immunity: Rule, Comity, or Something Else?" (2010) 21 *European Journal of International Law* 853. Even where states provide statutory causes for action, such as the Alien Torts Statute, an unsatisfactory decision by an IMCC may preclude further litigation through the doctrines of *res judicata* or *collateral estoppel*, which prevent a claim or issue from being relitigated when such claims or issues have already received a final judgment on the merits.

set up the claims commission in the first place, the state foreclosed the victim from suing anywhere else.

There are compelling arguments on both sides. At any rate, the state will eventually have to decide whether to pass on to the victims the entire amount of the award, nothing or something in between. If the state is paid its award by the other state party, and uses those funds first to pay off the amount that it is out of pocket from paying its own legal liability (the award it must pay to the opposite side) then the state of affairs can roughly be assessed in the following terms:

- The international community's interests in deterrence are satisfied, because as a matter of public perception, the wrong-doer had to pay the consequences of its unlawful acts;
- The tribunal's interests in having brought the dispute to a successful conclusion are satisfied so long as the arbitrators were unanimous and the parties complied;
- The defending state's interest in closure – the termination of any future claims – are satisfied, because the IMCC gave everyone a chance to present his or her claim and the victims only get "one bite at the apple"; and yet,
- The victims' rights are foreclosed permanently; the victims cannot sue elsewhere.
- They receive at most a fraction of their rightful compensation even though the commission accepted their proofs of unlawful injury. Their share of the award was used to pay off the legal liability of their state, for its violations of human rights and international humanitarian law, for which the victims had no responsibility at all. The victim receives nothing or only a fraction of what it is entitled to and is precluded forever after from seeking redress in any other forum. Having lost his or her chance to sue forever, the victim is actually in a worse condition than if no litigation had ever occurred.

While somewhat contentiously expressed, the irony of such a final result is unavoidable. The only party whose interests are not fully recognized are the victims.

Five models of compliance

Mindful of the statist origins of international law, and of the effect that statism has on one's positions on the set-off problem, we can identify at least five different positions on what is the right approach to ensuring compensation. Each of these five models takes a position on whether the only relevant actors are states (the statist view) or whether a state's nationals have rights of their own (what we refer to as "the modern view"). A position is also taken on whether to provide for set-offs.

Table 7.1 Five models of compensation for international mass claims commissions

	Terms of Awards	Amount Paid	Ultimate Beneficiary
Purely statist model (historical version)	A owes $100k; B owes $90k	A pays B $100k; B pays A $90k	At discretion of the states
Modernized statist model	A owes $100k; B owes $90k	A pays B $100k and B pays A $90k	The states are expected to pass on to their nationals
Statist model (w/offset)	A owes $100k; B owes $90k	State A pays State B $10k	At discretion of the states
Purely vertical model (IHL, human rights)	A owes nationals of B $100k; B owes nationals of A $90K	A pays $100k directly to B's nationals; B pays $90k directly to A's nationals	Nationals of the two states
Domestic compensation model	A owes nationals of B $100k, B owes nationals of A $90k	State A pays its own nationals $90k, and pays $10k to State B. State B pays its own nationals $100k	A pays its nationals plus $10K to B; B pays its nationals

Table 7.1 summarizes the five general models of international claims compensation: the pure statist model; the modernized statist model; the statist model with off-set; the purely vertical model; and the domestic compensation model. We illustrate them in a hypothetical dispute in which two states (A and B) both filed claims against one another. Two awards were announced: A was awarded $90,000 for B's violations, and B was awarded $100,000 for A's violations.

The first model is the purely statist model and describes how monetary awards were treated historically. Reflecting the assumption that states were the only relevant actors, payments went directly from one state to another.[19] Whether the state that received the payment would use it to

[19] *E.g.*, in the American–Mexican Claims Commission. Howard F. Cline, *The United States and Mexico* (Cambridge University Press, 1961), 209.

compensate those of its nationals that had suffered injury was at the state's full discretion. This is the approach taken, for example, by the US Foreign Claims Settlement Commission.[20]

The second is the modernized statist model. It is "modernized" in the sense that modern international law broke with tradition and came to regard individual nationals of a state as worthy in their own right. Human rights and international humanitarian law violations are the claims of individual victims, not claims of the states themselves. This model differs from the first by including the expectation that the amount that the state receives should ultimately go to the citizens within State B who are entitled to such compensation. While this model secures the advantage of directing compensation toward the victims who have the strongest claim to it, it assumes that states will fully comply with such conditions. Often, there is no international enforcement mechanism to oversee the distribution of an award, and states can generally do as they like. A variation of this model was used by the UNCC to award individual claims. Yet, the UNCC, a modern claims commission, also ensured that mechanisms exist to verify the payments by the state to the specific person that was awarded the compensation.[21]

The third model is a statist model with set-off. This model occurs when both State A and State B have legitimate claims upon each other, such that both states owe each other a monetary sum. Under this model, the end payment is calculated by subtracting the lesser amount owed from the greater one, and then by awarding the net difference to the state who owed the least. In this case, the difference is $10,000, and only that amount need change hands from one state to the other. Once this net difference has been paid, the receiving state may do what it wishes with its final monetary compensation. Of our five, this model is the one closest to the structure of the EECC.

The fourth model is the purely vertical model, in the sense that it abandons the premise that states relate only to one another and individual victims are irrelevant. Instead, the relationship is conceptualized in law as between the state and the individual victim. This manner of understanding the problem requires State A to directly pay the victims within State B. Certain claims commissions have taken this shape, including the Iran–US Claims Tribunal.[22]

---

20 *See* US Foreign Claims Settlement Commission at https://www.justice.gov/fcsc.

21 *See* Chapter 4.

22 *See* Chapter 4, dealing with individual claims at the Iran–US Claims Tribunal.

This model has the advantage of bypassing State B as a middleman, remedying the uncertainty of the earlier models about whether the individual victims will ever actually be granted the compensation to which they are entitled. It has the disadvantage of lacking an administratively practicable enforcement mechanism by which State A may find and pay each victim within State B. Given the large numbers of victims and the sometimes dire conditions of post-war living, it may be no easy task to locate them and to ensure that direct payments are tailored to each individual's particular circumstances. Moreover, having a perverse incentive not to surrender the money that it has been ordered to pay, the paying state must also be monitored. Otherwise, payers can exploit the flexibility that they are given to undermine the compensatory regime (*e.g.*, through delays, diminished access to compensation via bureaucratic access points, etc.).

As depicted in the table, the purely vertical model does not provide for an off-set. The reason is that compensation to the ultimate beneficiaries is more difficult to achieve when off-sets enter into the calculations. Here, the offset would be \$10,000 (\$100,000–\$90,000). If State A were charged with distributing award money to the victims of B nationality under an off-set regime, it would at most be paying ten cents on the dollar.

The fifth compensation model we call the domestic compensation model. This model is similar to the statist model with off-set because it would be employed when both State A and State B owe each other payment. The loser pays the winner the difference between the two awards; in this case that means a payment of \$10,000. What is distinctive about this model is that, to the maximum degree possible, each state compensates its own citizens. For example, B's nationals proved claims of \$100,000. It would pay its own nationals \$90,000 of its own money and could then "top up" that amount with the \$10,000 it received from State A. Meanwhile, A would pay its nationals the award amount of \$90,000.

The end result is that A's claimants get \$90,000 and B's claimants get \$100,000; this is as it should be. In addition, A pays out a total of \$90,000 and B pays out a total of \$100,000; this also is as it should be. State A is responsible for paying its citizens what State B owes them, and vice-versa, with the net difference then being paid to the state which owed less. By requiring states to pay their citizens the amount that the other state owes, the domestic compensation model ensures that compensation flows to the victims, the essential goal of international compensation claim commissions. And by using states as the mechanism for providing compensation to their own nationals, this model places the responsibility for compensating victims in the hands of their own government. Admittedly, this model assumes that states will actually make such payments – and this is not always realistic. But at a minimum, a government is probably better informed and more trustworthy when it is compensating its own nationals than when it is compensating the nationals of its opponent.

Conditions of Compliance

The distinctive features of the three claims commissions that we have taken as examples reflect basic principles of international jurisprudence. They also differ greatly in the degree of centralization of authority, the extent to which the commission controls a fund formed of disputed assets, and the extent to which the international community is relatively unified and committed to the project. The UNCC might be called "the perfect storm" because the different elements all converge in the same direction. For all the reasons that the characterization of "anarchy" is inapposite, the UNCC was successful in effectuating policies of compensation. These claims commissions corroborate the argument that compliance is unreliable in a state of anarchy, but they also illustrate how "international" and "anarchy" are not synonymous.

Anarchy and reciprocity

These days, the standard answer to the question of how to achieve compliance in anarchy is borrowed from game theory: reciprocity.[23]

---

[23] The concept of reciprocity has some real challenges as an explanation for international agreements. As one of us has argued elsewhere, "tit for tat" is highly problematic where the substantive rights at stake are based on human rights law, IHL, or any other nonderogable individual rights. Lea Brilmayer, "From 'Contract' to 'Pledge': The Structure of International Human Rights Agreements" (2006) 77 *British Yearbook of International Law* 163, 181–183. This argument is grounded on the Vienna Convention on the Law of Treaties, the Geneva Conventions, as well as general principles of *jus cogens*. For example, while article 60(1) of the Vienna Convention generally treats a material breach of a bilateral treaty as a permissible ground for the non-breaching party to terminate and exercise a reprisal, Article 60(5) of the Vienna Convention makes an exception for human rights agreements, prohibiting one party's retaliation in response to another party's breach. Vienna Convention, Art. 60(1), 60(5). While this makes sense in advancing human rights, this prohibition of retaliation undermines the "tit for tat" model of compliance when retaliation is no longer permitted. *See* Yoram Dinstein, "Human Rights in Armed Conflict: International Humanitarian Law" in Theodore Meron (ed.), *Human Rights in International Law: Legal and Policy Issues* (Oxford University Press, 1984), 357–358. Article

Although originating in economics, political science and related disciplines, game theory and its fascination with "tit for tat" solutions to problems of behavior under situations of anarchy spread quickly to international law. Reciprocity is currently the favored analysis of legal academics seeking to explain whether international norms can really be called "law."[24]

The dominant model in applying game theoretical concepts to international law is a game known as the Prisoner's Dilemma. PD, as it is called, purports to demonstrate that two actors with competing interests can *both* increase their payoffs by adopting a strategy called "tit for tat," which is based on reciprocity. The standard PD model considers a hypothetical situation where two fellow gang members are caught, separated in individual interrogation rooms and cannot communicate. Each prisoner is given two choices: cooperate with the other, by staying silent, or defect to the authorities by ratting the other prisoner out. If both prisoners cooperate and stay silent, they both receive a lesser charge of a year in prison. If both prisoners defect, they both receive a greater sentence of two years in prison. However, if one prisoner stays silent and the other defects, the defector receives no punishment while the other prisoner receives the maximum punishment of three years in prison.

Assuming that both prisoners are self-interested, rational actors, the optimal strategy is to defect, because defecting risks either a two-year sentence (both prisoners defecting) or no sentence at all (the other prisoner staying silent). The result is an average outcome superior to staying silent, for remaining silent risks either a three-year sentence (if

---

13 of the Third Geneva Conventions expressly proclaims: "Measures of reprisal against prisoners of war are prohibited." Similar prohibitions of reprisals against protected persons appear in the other Geneva Conventions and in Protocol I; Theodor Meron, *Human Rights and Humanitarian Norms as Customary Law* (Oxford University Press, 1989), 238–239, citing Theodor Meron, *Human Rights Law-Making in the United Nations: A Critique of Instruments and Process* (Oxford University Press, 1986), 146–147; Bruno Simma, "Self-Contained Regimes" (1985) 16 *Netherlands Yearbook of International Law* 131.

[24] *See, e.g.*, Jens David Ohlin, *The Assault on International Law* (Oxford University Press, 2015) ch. 4; Robert O. Keohane, "Reciprocity in International Relations" (1986) 40 *International Organization* 1; Andrew T. Guzman, "A Compliance-Based Theory of International Law" (2002) 90 *California Law Review* 1823, available at: http://scholarship.law.berkeley.edu/californialaw review/vol90/iss6/2. See also Harold Hongju Koh, "Why Do Nations Obey International Law?" (1997), Yale Faculty Scholarship Series, Paper No. 2101, available at: http://digitalcommons.law.yale.edu/fss_papers/2101.

the other prisoner defects) or a one-year sentence (if the other also cooperates).

This simplest version of the Prisoner's Dilemma game leads to the paradoxical conclusion that both should defect, even though both prisoners know that they will do better overall if neither defects. But the calculation changes when the prisoners know that they will continue to play the game over and over. If they know that they will continue to play indefinitely, they must take into account the consequences of defecting in one round on the players' strategy in the next round. Because each actor recalls the previous decisions made by the other, reciprocating the other actor's decisions becomes the best strategy because both actors reward each other's cooperation while punishing the other actor if they choose to defect.[25]

Application to the present context is not difficult to imagine. Here we would make the states the players, and treat it as a compliance game. Each state has the choice of cooperating, by complying with the terms of the IMCC, or defecting, by reneging on the terms of the agreement. Under the game theoretical model, theorists who favor reciprocity would suggest that self-interested and rational states will opt to cooperate because states will continue to have future interactions with each other, meaning that there will be further iterations of the compliance game. Thus, states would have an incentive to cooperate because defection creates the risk that states will punish the defecting state in future agreements.

Neoconservatives agree that reciprocity is key, but they interpret its importance differently. Their argument is that if there exists an explanation other than centralized enforcement that could account for the apparent convergence of state behavior in international affairs, then it is erroneous to characterize that convergence as law. That other explanation, they argue, is reciprocity; and since that alternative explanation is based on self-interest rather than coercive enforcement of international norms, calling it "law" is a mischaracterization.

Despite this fundamental difference in perspective, for our purposes the commonalities are more significant. What appears to be accepted by both sides is that PD models how actors with inconsistent or competing interests, acting in anarchy, must behave cooperatively to maximize net gains. They may disagree about the consequences of finding oneself in a situation of "anarchy," but both seem to assume that the label "law" and

---

[25] Robert Axelrod, *The Evolution of Cooperation* (Basic Books, 1984), 31–32.

the phenomenon of "compliance" are relatively unproblematic *outside of anarchy*. Compliance in anarchy takes special efforts to explain; compliance cannot be taken for granted.

The perfect storm

The concept of anarchy sheds a certain amount of light on why some final awards face compliance problems while others do not. Consider the UNCC: it is a success story of compliance.[26] Most importantly, its formation and subsequent conduct do not seem to be taking place in a situation of anarchy.

For present purposes, what matters is the empirical question of the degree of cohesion on the particular issue in the particular international community – the degree of power that the community, acting together, can exercise. Thus, the more an IMCC represents the unified will of the community of states, the more that compliance with its orders can be taken for granted. The UNCC is instructive in this sense. As we will explain in Chapter 8, the UNCC was a "thick" IMCC because of the density of the institution – its strong foundation of procedural rules, its careful attention to the practicalities of payment, the adequacy of its staffing and the extent to which it was anticipated as having an expansive time of operation.

Decisions of the UNCC achieved a very high degree of compliance. As explained above, the international community was united in the condemnation of Iraq's invasion of Kuwait. Thus, the creation of a mechanism, the UNCC, to compensate individuals and states that suffered the consequences of that invasion received vast support by actors of the international community.

In addition, under the complex regime that created the UNCC,[27] the establishment of a funding mechanism deserves particular attention. Not only did the funding mechanism allow for almost full compensation of the awards issued by the UNCC, but it also allowed for the smooth conduct of the operation of the UNCC, by funding both personnel and location.

The special Compensation Fund was created in accordance with UNSC Resolution 687 (1991). It operated under the financial rules of the United Nations, and the UNCC administered the Fund under the authority of the

---

[26] As should be clear, not all IMCCs look like this. The EECC possessed vague community support, but not a real adequate force. These concerns can become particularly exacerbated when IMCCs attempt to establish compliance between state entities that were very recently enemies or in conflict.

[27] *See* Chapter 1.

Security Council.[28] A percentage of the proceeds of the sale of Iraqi petroleum and petroleum products funded the Compensation Fund. The level of Iraq's contribution to the Fund varied over time and took into account "the requirement of the people of Iraq" as well as "Iraq's payment capacity as assessed in conjunction with the international financial institutions," taking into consideration the servicing of external debt and the need of the economy of Iraq.[29] In 1991, the Security Council determined that the compensation to be paid by Iraq "shall not exceed 30 percent of the annual value of the experts of petroleum and petroleum exports from Iraq." The percentage decreased to 25 percent in December 2000,[30] and to 5 percent in 2003.[31]

Initially, Iraq resisted the creation of the Fund. Revenues from the sale of Iraqi's oil only began to come into the Fund in 1996, after the creation of the Oil-for-Food program.[32] In the interim, the Security Council urged all Member States to fund the Compensation Fund.[33] Once the money started flowing, however, the Fund arrangement allowed the UNCC to employ numerous staff for several years in its headquarters in Geneva

---

[28] UNSC Res 692 (1991). In general, see Timothy J. Feighery, "The United Nations Compensation Commission" in C. Giorgetti (ed.), *The Rules, Practice, and Jurisprudence of International Courts and Tribunals* (Brill, 2013), 518–520.

[29] UNSC Res 687 (1991), para. 19. This aspect of the funding was criticized: see UN, Office of the Iraq Program, Oil for Food, at http://www.un.org/Depts/oip/.

[30] UNSC Res 1330 (2000), para 12 ("Decides that the effective deduction rate of the funds deposited in the escrow account established by resolution 986 (1995) to be transferred to the Compensation Fund in the 180-day period shall be 25 per cent.").

[31] UNSC Res 1483 (2003), para 21 ("Decides further that 5 per cent of the proceeds … shall be deposited into the Compensation Fund established in accordance with resolution 687 (1991) and subsequent relevant resolutions" and also decided that "this requirement shall be binding on a properly constituted, internationally recognized, representative government of Iraq and any successor thereto.").

[32] UNSC Res 986 (1995) (The Security Council, acting under Chapter VII of the Charter of the United Nations authorizes states "to permit the import of petroleum and petroleum products originating in Iraq" to "(d) … meet the costs to the United Nations of the independent inspection agents and the certified public accountants and the activities associated with implementation of this resolution" paras 1 and 8(b)(d)).

[33] UNSC Res 778 (1992) (deploring Iraq's refusal to cooperate and recalling Iraq's liability for all direct damages resulting from the invasion and the requirement that Iraq contributed to the Compensation Fund and urging "all States to contribute funds" to the escrow account, preamble and para. 3).

and to award a total of $52.4 billion (of which about $47.8 billion has been paid out) to approximately 1.5 million successful claimants.[34]

The existence of funds to compensate for damages does not explain completely the success of the UNCC, but goes a long way toward doing so. In addition, the fact that the UNCC was a multilateral commission, which heard cases from a variety of individuals, states and international organizations, also explains its success. The UNCC enjoyed wide support from many different actors of the international community and there was little opposition to it.

When an IMCC is essentially bilateral, as occurs in most cases, incentives to comply may differ. The agreement that created the Iran–US Claims Tribunal, for example, was more polarized and less unanimous and did not enshrine one "common will" of the community of states. Yet, the Iran–US Claims Tribunal is also generally regarded as a successful example of a claims commission and its awards have been complied with. In situations as the Iran–US Claims Tribunal, the creation of a fund for the payment of any compensation prior to or in conjunction with the creation of the claims commission is even more important. Specifically, under paragraph 7 of the 1981 General Declaration that created the Tribunal, Iran was required to place $1 billion into a security account to ensure payment of any award rendered by the Tribunal against Iran, and was also required to continue replenishing the account to a minimum balance $500 million until all awards against Iran had been satisfied. The existence of the Security Fund has allowed all awards issued against Iran to be fully paid, even when the interest of the international community in the compliance with awards has moved on.

Like the Iran–US Claims Tribunal, the EECC was also a bilateral commission. Differently from the UNCC, however, its creation never resulted in decisive and unanimous support by the international community. In contrast with the Iran–US Claims Tribunal, as well, there were no built-in incentives for compliance. This lacuna, coupled with the indifference of the international community, helps to explain the lack of compliance with the decisions of the EECC, regardless of their modest amount.

In sum, the more centralized, powerful and effective the IMCC is, the less it has to concern itself with compliance. The more that it enjoys the unified will of the community of states, the more that compliance with its orders can be taken for granted. In contrast, when an IMCC lacks that power and effectiveness, only a well-funded mechanism may help assure

---

[34] UNCC, Home, available at: http://www.uncc.ch/home.

compliance with its decisions. But of course it is the tribunals that lack power and influence that are the least able to ensure adequate outside funding. This is a problem that no amount of clever drafting of an agreement to go to arbitration can address with complete confidence.

8. Conclusions

International mass claims commissions are increasingly the vehicle of choice for settling scores legally after an episode of violent conflict. Those optimists among us who believe in international peace through international law attribute almost supernatural powers to this form of dispute resolution. IMCCs compensate the injured; preserve a group's history for future generations; provide innocent victims with a chance to tell their story; punish evil doers; and deter evil wrongdoing in the future.

They do so in the most difficult of circumstances. Timing is one difficulty – this legal activity gets underway while memories of violent conflict are still raw and available resources are all being directed to reconstruction and peace building. The large number of alleged unlawful incidents creates massive difficulties in corroboration of claims, both documentary and testimonial. Yet, there may be no other international legal institution for which proponents claim to see so much potential.

Faced with a document tsunami of our own – the number and complexity of different IMCCs that we could study is daunting – we selected three to take as our chief examples: The Iran–US Claims Tribunal, the United Nations Compensation Commission and the Ethiopia–Eritrea Claims Commission. These examples are sufficiently different from one another to illustrate the wide range of compensation mechanisms, while simultaneously revealing the shared assumptions that make the IMCC model uniquely valuable.

This book is designed to analyse the fundamental procedural and substantive characteristics of IMCCs with two aims in mind. The first is to provide a critical appraisal of past claims commissions in general, and the second is to offer some observations about the creation of IMCCs that are still in the making. This final chapter therefore contains an in-depth study of one possible claims mechanism now under discussion: a "loss and damage" provision for a treaty addressing global climate change.

No single book is likely to be comprehensive and deep enough to identify and resolve all the ups and downs, the plusses and minuses, the nuances and tensions – "the good, the bad and the ugly"[1] – of international mass claims commissions. The future of IMCC legal scholarship is bright; IMCCs will continue to puzzle, dazzle, challenge and frustrate academic writers and legal practitioners alike for the foreseeable future. Before leaving the subject to other lawyers and legal academics, however, we wish to revisit a few of our conclusions from earlier chapters as some of those conclusions can be better appreciated now that the full argument has been laid out.

SUMMARY OF BASIC POINTS

We started by defining IMCCs as *ad hoc* binding international dispute mechanisms established to consider claims resulting from significant international war-related and traumatic historical events.[2] IMCCs are constituted under international law and (in some respects) are modeled on and act like judicial bodies. But they are *ad hoc* bodies whose structure, jurisdiction, procedure and ability to remedy vary considerably. Parties that choose IMCCs to address a particular political, legal and factual context often do so because of the extraordinary flexibility obtainable by *ad hoc* mechanisms – a level of flexibility that is rarely available in any existing standing court system.

Pros and Cons of *Ad Hoc* Institutions

Proponents have good reasons to place their hopes on claims commissions. Consensual and flexible by nature, IMCCs can be configured to undertake whatever assignment the opposing parties have in mind. For it is the parties who bring IMCCs to life and provide them with a source of legal authority.

Considering the variety of situations that give rise to the desire to adjudicate, it is not surprising that flexibility is so highly valued. When an IMCC is created, the entire legal edifice is constructed from the ground up. Every new IMCC requires starting from nothing in the way of procedural rules, practical support and staffing (both legal and administrative). Even the members of the tribunal are, at the outset, unknown.

For every advantage obtained by being consensual and flexible, however, advocates of international courts cite the problems that these

---

1 The reference, of course, is to the 1966 "Spaghetti Western" starring Clint Eastwood and Eli Wallach, and directed by Sergio Leone.

2 *See* Chapter 1.

characteristics create. Starting from a *tabula rasa* provides freedom of choice, but also a complete lack of guidance. Courts, both international and domestic, build on precedent – the practice of other courts in previous generations. International courts have a structure that transcends the resolution of any particular dispute; the litigants start with a model that defines the court's method of operation and fit their case into that existing mold.[3] IMCCs, in contrast, are a form of "build-it-yourself" justice.

In the case of the massive disputes at issue here, the practical burden of "build-it-yourself" justice is substantial. Chapter 2 argued that new and different procedural rules may be needed to accommodate the large amount of new and different evidence. A tribunal may need to hire experts knowledgeable in up-to-date techniques of statistical sampling, data searching or document processing. Monumental amounts of translation may be required. The practical burden imposed on all participants is sufficiently substantial as to discourage all but the most determined.

Are the benefits achieved worthwhile? The parties apparently think so; otherwise they would not choose to go ahead. Both sides must agree, in effect, that a claims commission is better than whatever alternatives are available – otherwise they would not have reached agreement. If only one of the parties is willing to litigate, then the matter is moot.

Now, that much might also be said about standing institutions such as the International Court of Justice. Where the parties agree to submit their case to the ICJ, this can be taken as a clear sign that the ICJ seems to the parties to be an improvement over military conflict or, for that matter, rolling dice. But although this inference is true for both courts and IMCCs, it is more true for the latter than the former. The single most important benefit following from the choice of an IMCC rather than a judicial model may be that it may be easier to induce the other party to agree to the former than the latter. Where the range of permissible choices is limited only by the parties' imagination, the likelihood of reaching agreement to adjudicate peaceably is higher. Flexibility increases the chance that the parties will be able to agree; and when it comes to flexibility, IMCCs are preeminent.

3 IMCCs (it might be said) write the legal world's free verse when everyone else is penning sonnets.

Basic Issues for the Drafters of the Arbitration Agreement

The process of establishing a successful IMCC begins by understanding the unique needs and characteristics of the dispute that the IMCC is meant to resolve. Drafting the international agreement that creates the IMCC requires careful attention to the human context in which the IMCC will operate. Several questions are immediately apparent.

Qualifications for the tribunal members

Chapter 3 argued that specific guidance on how to choose decision makers (arbitrators, panelists or commissioners) should be included in the agreement. This should include both desired and necessary qualities for decision makers.

All parties involved should consider their decision makers qualified, unbiased and balanced. Thus, it is important to include in the rules of procedure some guidance about composition, appointment and leadership of the commissioners, as well as guidance on how they will make decisions. For example, the agreement might prohibit choice of a commissioner who is a national of the state that appoints him or her. It is also advisable to include rules on how to challenge and remove commissioners and arbitrators and how to fill vacancies, should one arise. Related to the issue of who the decision makers should be, is the issue of secretarial and registrar support. It is desirable, although not strictly speaking necessary, that the arbitration agreement already designates the registry.

Which claimants to include?

As Chapter 4 details, the most difficult choice involves the identity of the claimants. Ordinarily, the designation of claimants is a straightforward matter of identifying the people who believe that their rights have been violated and who are tied together – and to the dispute – by nationality or some other immutable criterion such as religion or ethnicity.

In international cases, ordinarily the claimant must be a national of the state party; this requirement is a consequence of the concept of "diplomatic representation." Indeed, claimants were required to have been nationals of that state at all times, starting at the outset of the dispute and continuing through the adjudication of the case. Claims by states are still the most common form of claims submitted to an IMCC and are probably the easiest to administer procedurally.

Such contemporary discussion about whether a particular state can represent a particular victim in international adjudication is important, so far as it goes. But of greater importance is whether a state party will speak for the victims, or will the victims themselves present their claims with the necessary supporting documentation? Historically, international law treated the state as the only entity that could be a party to an international court case. More recently, certain claimants have been able to access claims commissions directly, for example in the IUSCT. So, we cannot assume in international compensation cases that state representation will continue to be the standard.

Practice at the UNCC, the IUSCT and the EECC The three commissions studied here all took different paths. All three proceeded in ways that reflected the circumstances of their particular dispute; all three, therefore, are examples of how the flexibility of IMCCs can be put to good use.

The path taken by litigants at the EECC was unconventional because the arbitration agreement specifically made exceptions to the normal rule of diplomatic representation. Normally, a state would have no right to present the claims of persons who are not nationals.[4]

At the time of drafting of the EECC, Eritrea claimed a strong basis for bringing to the commission claims made by persons of Ethiopian nationality but Eritrean national origin.[5] This deviation from usual practice was necessitated by the claim that Ethiopia had unlawfully deported tens of thousands of Ethiopian citizens and deprived them of their citizenship because of their Eritrean national origin. Under conventional notions of diplomatic representation, there would have been no way to bring such claims before the tribunal. For, the very offense of which Ethiopia was accused was *altering* their nationality; and diplomatic representation would have required their being Eritrean nationals at all times.

Under the IUSCT, individual claimants could submit claims directly to the tribunal, though Iran and the United States agreed to litigate small claims on behalf of their nationals. And at the UNCC, governments submitted millions of claims on behalf of their nationals. Those were named claims and they were submitted on behalf of their nationals. Governments then had a responsibility to deliver any awarded sum to

---

4 In addition, at the EECC, the two states had the option to submit claims on behalf of their nationals, but chose to submit most claims on their own behalf. Only Eritrea filed claims on behalf of named individuals, and it filed only four.

5 Agreement Between the Governments of the State of Eritrea and the Federal Democratic Republic of Ethiopia art. 5, ¶ 7, 12 December 2000 [hereinafter Algiers Agreement].

their nationals, and this responsibility included a duty of reporting and returning any amounts that could not be so delivered.

Pointing out the important role that individuals have to play in modern international litigation is not the same as saying that the states no longer had any role to play when their nationals are victims. At the tribunals just described, certain kinds of claims were only to be presented by states, and there were others in which the state was the victim (*e.g.*, destruction of public property). Moreover, the role of the state in drafting the agreements constituting the commission was still central; authority to represent themselves was delegated to the individual victims only by consent of the states. The model was not the conventional historic one of "states only" but rather a hybrid model of "states as parties, victims as claimants."

States as parties; victims as claimants: a "hybrid" model At least two of our exemplary tribunals heard a mixture of state claims, individual claims and claims in which states represented individual claims. The most important lesson to come out of this pattern is that the states that are setting up these commissions do not seem obliged to conform to some standard out of the historical past. The drafters charged with creation of an IMCC, one must conclude, can define the claimants in any reasonable way that fits their convictions and interests.

What claims to include?

Chapter 4 also addressed the thorny question of what claims should be included. Certainly, relevant claims must be somehow linked to the events that resulted in the creation of the IMCC and the types of losses and injury suffered. But are there other limitations? What considerations should be taken into account in defining the jurisdiction of an IMCC?

Set-offs and the effect of symmetry A successful IMCC must be able to resolve a sufficient number of claims to justify its creation. It should resolve claims that can be finally and fully compensated with the funds that are available. It must also have jurisdiction over the appropriate number of claims to ensure that its decisions create a sense of justice, and thus also foster the reconciliation process for which it was created. It is desirable, if possible, to group them in a way that will allow easier and more expedited proceedings, and to categorize them in readily understandable categories.

The question of what sort of claims to allow has in one important aspect been misunderstood. An argument might be made that the importance of identifying specific claims in the arbitration agreement has been overstated. At least where the dispute is symmetric (meaning that both sides are permitted to file the same sorts of claims, and the two sides have similar claims against one another) the ultimate judgments will be two dollar figures; one will be the amount that Alpha owes Beta, and the other the amount that Beta owes Alpha. These can be offset to produce a single dollar figure which contains the final amount owed.

Furthermore, if the dispute is symmetric, then adding or subtracting another claim will not make much difference. Any new claims added to the previous list of permissible claims may add to the total amount due to one state, but at the same time it will add to the total amount due to the other state. When the two final awards are set off against one another, the end result will not be substantially different from the result of the set-off before the new claim was added.

This logic has an important oversight, however.[6] It fails to account for the interests of the injured victims who are hoping for compensation. With the two parties, each plays the role of the defendant sometimes and the role of the plaintiff at others. Thus, changing the legal standard for recovery will lower the amount of recovery (if the standard of proof is raised) and will raise the amount of recovery (if the standard of proof is lower).

This does not happen when the claimants' interests are accounted for. The claimants have interests only as plaintiffs; they are never defendants because violations of human rights and humanitarian law are committed by states – not by individual citizens.

If the legal standard for committing a violation is lowered, this has a benefit for claimants (because it will be easier to prove the case) but no corresponding detriment. They are plaintiffs, but not defendants. Conversely, if the legal standard for some violation is raised to make it stricter, this change in the law will detract from a plaintiff's ability to make his or her case, but will not convey any corresponding advantage. The decision to alter the included substantive claims, in other words, impacts the amount that Alpha owes to Mr. B (a national of Beta). It affects, as well, the amount that Beta owes to Ms. A (a national of

---

[6] For one thing, there may be different proportions of the cases in the population of disputes with which the IMCC must deal. Assume that Alpha and Beta are equally subject to a particular standard of proof (say, "clear and convincing evidence"). Alpha may have a higher percentage of cases that are based on inadequate amounts of evidence than Beta does. Therefore, even if the standard applies equally to them, Alpha will have more problems dealing with it and will lose more cases because of it.

Alpha). Put another way, changing the substantive law will change the balance of payments between plaintiffs and defendants.

If one cares only about the respective rights of state parties, then it makes a certain amount of sense to say that altering the substantive standard would not (over the long run) alter the rights between Alpha and Beta. But, as Chapter 7 concluded, such an account focuses solely on the rights of states – and this sort of statism is outmoded and contrary to the reasons for setting up individual compensation schemes in the first place.

Taking implementation seriously A central issue for all claims commissions is and remains the ability to ensure payments of any awarded sum. The importance of having a mechanism that ensures and oversees payments of claims cannot be overestimated. A commission will and should be judged by how well it is able to compensate those who deserved compensation. In the case of IMCCs, this means the mass of individual victims whose narrative international law recognizes as unlawful and compensable. This is not simply an idealistic (naïve?) critique from the ivory tower. It is also a very practical argument to the effect that the terms of the arbitration agreement will inevitably have consequences for the success of the IMCC in fulfilling its mandate. In particular, the degree to which implementation problems are carefully thought through may indicate the commission's long-run success. And it is sometimes not difficult to determine the degree of careful advance planning simply by examining the arbitration agreement's provisions for implementation.

While some commissions have established rather detailed systems for the funding and payment of awards, others have elected to provide more generic – and more terse – instructions. This point can be illustrated by reference to the arbitration agreements of our three illustrative cases.

The Algiers Agreement of December 2000 established the EECC, but it has almost nothing to say about making sure that the actual victims of unlawful state action will receive any money from the awards. The entirety of its discussion of implementation is a two-sentence provision on the payment of awards: "Decisions and awards of the commission shall be final and binding. The parties agree to honor all decisions and to pay any monetary awards rendered against them promptly."[7] Nothing further is mentioned regarding the modality for payment or the consequences for failure to pay an award.

---

[7] Agreement Between the Government of the Federal Democratic Republic of Ethiopia and the Government of the State of Eritrea (2000), Art. 5(17).

The result could be that all interests are accommodated except for the victims'; the victims' interests are simply made available to the state to set off its own liability. Thus, a thoughtful and deliberate choice of the kinds of claimants and types of claims is essential to the project's success. It is fundamental to the credibility of the IMCC as a dispute resolution mechanism, its feasibility as a compensation project and its ability to provide satisfactory justice and closure.

The UNCC and the IUSTC, on the other hand, established detailed systems for funding and facilitating award payments. The UNCC established a Compensation Fund to finance both the operations of claims processing and the payment of awards. The funds for the Compensation Fund were derived from a percentage of Iraqi petroleum exports, with due consideration given to the needs of the Iraqi people and the Iraqi economy.[8] If Iraq failed to comply with its funding obligations, the UNCC could take alternative means, such as freezing assets derived from Iraqi oil sales in particular states.[9] The Oil-for-Food Program was also later introduced to ensure that Iraq contributed the necessary payments to the Fund.[10] Similarly, the Algiers Accords, establishing the IUSCT, provided that a "mutually agreeable [c]entral [b]ank" was to be established as the depositary of funds to facilitate the transfer of financial assets between Iran and the United States.[11] The escrow account that was created in the Central Bank was also the conduit through which Washington returned all remaining Iranian assets in the United States.[12] Half of these assets went into a special interest-bearing security account that

[8] UN Security Council Resolution 687 (1991), UN Doc. S/Res/687, ¶¶ 18–19 (8 April 1991), available at: http://www.un.org/Depts/unmovic/documents/687.pdf; see also UNSC Res 692 ¶ 6 (20 May 1991).

[9] *See* UN Security Council Resolution 1483 (2003), ¶ 23, UN Doc S/Res/1483 (22 May 2003); UNSC Res 1546 (2004), UN Doc S/Res/1546, ¶ 29 (8 June 2004).

[10] The "Oil-for-Food" Program automatically allocated a certain percentage of Iraq's annual revenues from oil exports to the Fund. *See* UN Security Council Resolution 986 (1995), UN Doc S/RES/986 (14 April 1995) (originally allocating up to 30% of annual oil revenues to the Fund); *see also* UN Security Council Resolution 1360 (2001), UN Doc S/RES/1360 (3 July 2001), ¶ 9 (decreasing the annual allocation to 25% of oil revenues); Resolution 1483 (2003), UN Doc S/RES/1483 (22 May 2003), ¶ 21 (decreasing the percentage yet further to 5% of annual oil revenues).

[11] Declaration of the Government of the Democratic and Popular Republic of Algeria, Algiers Accord, ¶ 2 (19 January 1981).

[12] Declaration of the Government of the Democratic and Popular Republic of Algeria, Algiers Accord, ¶ 6 (19 January 1981).

was to be used solely for the purpose of paying claims against Iran. Whenever the balance in the security account fell below the mandated $500 million limit, the Central Bank would then turn to Iran and require that it supply additional funds.[13]

Chapter 6 focused on the final, and obviously important, question of the availability of funds. Only IMCCs that have available funds will be able to issue payments. In this instance, the examples of the IUSCT and the UNCC are once more instructive. The 1981 General Declaration that created the tribunal specified that Iran was required to place $1 billion into a security account to ensure payment of any award rendered by the tribunal against Iran. Iran was also required to continue replenishing the account to a minimum balance of $500 million until all awards against Iran had been satisfied. The existence of the Security Fund has allowed all awards issued against Iran to be fully paid, even when the interest of the international community in the compliance with awards has moved on. The creation of the UNCC also included mechanisms that diverted parts of the revenue from the sale of Iraqi oil to a fund exclusively created for the payment of UNCC awards. Conversely, the EECC never had such a mechanism, and indeed the final awards of the EECC have never been paid.

While looking purely at the level of detail in these provisions is not the only metric by which to assess a commission's commitment to compliance, it is telling that the awards issued by the EECC continue to go unpaid, whereas the UNCC and IUSCT have seen far higher levels of compliance. As the purpose of an IMCC is often not only to evaluate claims but also to ensure that those harmed are properly compensated, a failure to create strong compliance provisions *ex ante*, or a failure to fortify – through actions or text – more ambiguous provisions *ex post*, largely undermines a commission's basis for existence.

[13] Declaration of the Government of the Democratic and Popular Republic of Algeria, Algiers Accord, Points II and III, ¶ 7.

TOWARD A CLIMATE CHANGE COMPENSATION MECHANISM: LESSONS FROM INTERNATIONAL CLAIMS COMMISSIONS[14]

In December 2015, the international community reached a new agreement to govern the international response to climate change – "the Paris Agreement." In the Paris Agreement and its associated texts, collectively known as the "Paris Package," the wealthy and powerful states conceded in principle the desirability of a "loss and damage" mechanism to increase support for unavoidable damages resulting from climate change. This concession acknowledged the growing evidence that developing nations will suffer the greatest impacts of climate change even though they are least responsible for the phenomenon.

Neither the Paris Agreement nor its accompanying documents specifies what "loss and damage" claims would qualify a state for relief or what sort of procedural mechanism should be adopted to implement the claims that qualified. These matters were left for subsequent discussions of the parties to the agreement. Since the Paris Agreement, parties have struggled to further shape and define an adequate mechanism for "loss and damage."

What Do We Mean by "Climate Change"?

Climate change refers to statistically identifiable changes in average weather conditions over an extended period of time – typically decades or longer.[15] Climate change is distinct from changes in weather, which concern differences in temperature, clouds, precipitation, humidity and wind over the short-term – usually over days or months. It is also distinct from "global warming" or "sea level rise," terms that have acquired a

---

[14] This section is informed by fieldwork conducted in Belize in April 2016. Research consisted of interviews with individuals, government officials, tourism officials and others with direct knowledge of the effects of climate change on the country. The three authors of the ensuing report (Dena Adles, John Giamatteo and Melissa Legge) are grateful for the guidance and time interviewees provided. The authors of this book wish to thank them for making the report's empirical conclusions and legal analysis available for discussion in this chapter.

[15] "Annex II: Glossary" in K.J. Mach, S. Planton and C. von Stechow (eds), *Climate Change 2014: Synthesis Report. Contribution of Working Groups I, II and III to the Fifth Assessment Report of the Intergovernmental Panel on Climate Change* (IPCC, 2014), 117–130.

certain popular currency but which are not technically accurate.[16] The international scientific community continues to strengthen its climate change consensus that the "warming of the climate system is unequivocal, and since the 1950s, many of the observed changes are unprecedented over decades to millennia."[17] Further, the build-up of anthropogenic greenhouse gas emissions in the atmosphere is "extremely likely" to have been the dominant cause of the observed warming since the mid-twentieth century.[18] Humans produce greenhouse gas emissions through the burning of fossil fuels, deforestation, land-use changes, livestock farming and use of fertilizer. These human-caused or "anthropogenic" emissions then trap heat in the atmosphere through a process known as the greenhouse effect.

The United Nations Framework Convention on Climate Change (UNFCCC), the basis for an international response to climate change, defines "climate change" to reference only climate change caused directly or indirectly by humans. Since the Paris Agreement was adopted under the umbrella of the UNFCCC, this definition is similarly in force for a "loss and damage" mechanism; for this reason, we also focus specifically on anthropogenic climate change and compensation for its damages.

Dangers Likely to Result from Climate Change

Damages from climate change are difficult to measure due to uncertainties in the attribution of events, indirect impacts and the range of future emissions scenarios. Climate change leads to several ocean impacts, including sea level rise, increased storm surge, coastal erosion, submergence, coastal flooding, ocean acidification, coral bleaching and added pressure on fisheries.[19] Sea level rise contributes to coastal erosion and larger storm surges that damage infrastructure and ecosystems. Ocean

---

16 "Global warming" is inaccurate because increases in average temperature in one location are likely to be met with decreases in other areas. "Sea level rise" is imprecise because many phenomena other than increase in sea level are likely to occur – *e.g.*, increased frequency of extreme weather events.

17 IPCC, 2014: "Summary for Policymakers," in R.K. Pachauri and L.A. Meyer (eds), *Climate Change 2014: Synthesis Report. Contribution of Working Groups I, II and III to the Fifth Assessment Report of the Intergovernmental Panel on Climate Change* [Core Writing Team] IPCC, (Geneva, IPCC, 2014), 2.

18 "Summary for Policymakers," 4.

19 P.P. Wong et al., "Coastal Systems and Low-lying Areas," in *Climate Change 2014*, 361–409.

changes negatively impact fisheries and the communities that depend on them for sustenance, industry, and tourism.

Climate change further impacts freshwater hydrology and weather. Melting ice and changes in precipitation, for instance, negatively impact the quantity and quality of freshwater resources.[20] In polar latitudes, thawing permafrost might cause trillions of dollars in damages.[21] Climate change can cause more intense precipitation events, flooding, drought and heatwaves.[22]

Climate change can also have a range of negative health impacts including heat-influenced mortality, increases in water-borne illnesses, shifting of insect vectors and worsened health conditions from poor air quality.[23] Changes in weather and pests negatively impact agriculture, contributing to food insecurity, increased food prices and loss of livelihood.[24] Infrastructure damage results from extreme weather events and sea level rise. Additionally, climate change also causes a range of "non-economic" costs including lost heritage, sovereignty and traditional knowledge, which should be included in a loss and damage framework.[25]

The impacts of climate change vary in severity depending on the resilience and adaptation actions taken by communities. Many populations in developing countries are especially vulnerable to climate change due to non-climatic factors and multidimensional inequalities.[26] The

---

20 "Summary for Policymakers."

21 Puneet Kollipara, "Climate Change Could Cost Trillions More in Damages, Because of Thawing Arctic Permafrost," *Science News* (21 September 2015), DOI: 10.1126/science. aad1787.

22 N.L. Bindoff et al., "2013: Detection and Attribution of Climate Change: from Global to Regional," in *Climate Change 2013: The Physical Science Basis. Contribution of Working Group I to the Fifth Assessment Report of the Intergovernmental Panel on Climate Change* (2013), 871, 910–916.

23 *See e.g.*, G. Luber et al., "Human Health," in J.M. Melillo, Terese Richmond and G.W. Yohe (eds), *Climate Change Impacts in the United States: The Third National Climate Assessment* (US Global Change Research Program, 2014), 220–256.

24 J.R. Porter et al., "Food Security and Food Production Systems," in *Climate Change 2014*, 485–533.

25 *See e.g.*, UNFCCC (2013), "Non-economic losses in the context of the work programme on loss and damage: technical paper", FCCC/TP/2013/2.

26 "Summary for Policymakers," 6.

United Nations Environment Programme estimates that developing countries could need to spend $500 billion per year by 2050 to adapt to climate change.[27]

The Paris Agreement and the Emergence of a "Loss and Damage" Solution Space

The United Nations Framework Convention on Climate Change (UNFCCC) dates to 1992. It entered into force in 1994, with near universal participation of 196 parties. The parties to the UNFCCC meet annually for a Conference of the Parties (COP), of which the most recent, COP 21, was held in Paris in December 2015. The Paris Agreement, adopted at COP 21, ushers in new workability to the UNFCCC by requiring climate action from developing countries. It recognizes that developing nations need financial and technical support in taking on these new commitments. The Paris Agreement's "loss and damage" provision is designed to help meet that need.

Overview and history behind "loss and damage"

In 1993 at COP 19, the Warsaw International Mechanism for Loss and Damage Associated with Climate Change Impacts ("The Warsaw Mechanism) acknowledged that loss and damage "includes at least, and in some cases more than, that which can be reduced by adaptation."[28] While the UNFCCC uses the terms "loss" and "damage" interchangeably, some have suggested that "loss" signifies irrecoverable costs – such as lost heritage from a sacred site washed away – while "damage" represents recoverable costs – such as infrastructure damages.[29]

The Warsaw Mechanism itself focuses specifically on "loss and damage associated with the impacts of climate change in *developing countries* that are *particularly vulnerable* to the adverse effects of climate

[27] The United Nations Environmental Programme, *The Adaptation Finance Gap Report* (2016), available at: http://www.un.org/sustainabledevelopment/blog/2016/05/unep-report-cost-of-adapting-to-climate-change-could-hit-500b-per-year-by-2050/.

[28] UNFCCC (2013), Decision 2/CP.19. ("Warsaw International Mechanism").

[29] Ainun Nishat et al., "A Range of Approaches to Address Loss and Damage from Climate Change Impacts in Bangladesh," *Loss and Damage* (June 2013), 7, available at: http://www.loss-and-damage.net/download/7069.pdf, accessed 27 December 2015; "Framing the Loss and Damage Debate," *Loss and Damage* (August 2012), available at: https://germanwatch.org/fr/download/6673.pdf, accessed 26 December 2015.

change."[30] The Warsaw Mechanism also sets out some parameters on the range of impacts it will consider. The UNFCCC definition of "loss and damage" explicitly recognizes that "these adverse effects include those related to extreme events and slow onset events such as sea level rise, increasing temperatures, ocean acidification, glacial retreat and related impacts, salinization, land and forest degradation, loss of biodiversity and desertification."[31] The UNFCCC also considers both economic as well as non-economic costs (*e.g.*, loss of culture and sovereignty, loss of biodiversity or decline in indigenous knowledge) in its loss and damage framework.[32]

The Paris Agreement's commitment to help particularly vulnerable states challenged by global climate change

At COP 21 in Paris, the parties agreed to continue the Warsaw Mechanism beyond its anticipated review in 2016. They also requested that the executive committee establish a clearing house to develop and implement comprehensive risk management strategies. Importantly, however, it explicitly stipulated "that Article 8 of the Agreement does not involve or provide a basis for any liability or compensation." This language reveals the strong position of several developed countries to not be put on the hook for liability or compensation under the agreement.

The development of Article 8, however – an entire Article for the loss and damage mechanism – signifies a victory for vulnerable countries. Under Article 8, Parties agreed to "recognize the importance of averting, minimizing and addressing loss and damage associated with the adverse effects of climate change, including extreme weather events and slow onset events, and the role of sustainable development in reducing the risk of loss and damage." They made further stipulations for Parties to "enhance understanding, action and support" which was defined to include: (a) early warning systems; (b) emergency preparedness; (c) slow onset events; (d) events that may involve irreversible and permanent loss and damage; (e) comprehensive risk assessment and management; (f) risk insurance facilities, climate risk pooling and other insurance solutions;

---

30 UNFCCC (2013), Decision 2/CP.19 ("Warsaw International Mechanism") (emphasis added).

31 UNFCCC (2013), Decision 2/CP.19 ("Warsaw International Mechanism").

32 UNFCCC (2013), "Non-Economic Losses in the Context of the Work Programme on Loss and Damage," FCCC/TP/2013/2, available at: http://unfccc.int/resource/docs/2013/tp/02.pdf.

(g) non-economic losses; and (h) resilience of communities, livelihoods and ecosystems.[33]

Since the close of the Paris negotiations in December 2015, the Executive Committee has met twice. Much still remains to be fleshed out, however.[34] Comparison between the Paris and Warsaw Mechanisms and commissions such as the three that we have been studying provides some objective encouragement, but it must be conceded that the challenges in the climate change context are even greater than those facing the EECC, the IUSTC and the UNCC. There are no IMCC precedents that more nearly resemble the proposed climate change loss and damages mechanism than these three. We set out to examine the likely analogies and dis-analogies with guarded optimism.

Institutional Design and Procedural Frameworks

Climate change differs in significant ways from the subject matter of other IMCCs. First, climate change is a global phenomenon with global effect, while past claims commissions have dealt with territorially limited conflicts. The global scope of the problem will entail increased administrative and bureaucratic costs, complicating the collection of evidence and making it difficult to ensure quality and standardization of claims across a massive pool of putative claimants. Any commission created to deal with the problem of climate change will very likely find itself in an environment of continuing crisis. Finally, international law on climate change is far less certain than international law on most of the topics that have hitherto been adjudicated before an international mass claims commission. Much of international humanitarian and human rights law has been fairly stable for decades; the law of international climate change is still in flux, and the science on which it is based is to a certain extent still unfolding. Causation, in particular, is not always easy to determine. To reach a considered conclusion about disputed issues such as causation, for example, a commission would have to sift through large amounts of technical data involving whether, for instance, an individual incidence of coastal erosion was due to climate effects, like sea level rise, or other anthropogenic causes, like poor watershed management upriver or mangrove deforestation along the coast.

---

[33] UNFCCC (2015), Decision 1/CP.21, Annex ("The Paris Agreement"), Article 8.

[34] A. Petherick, "Loss and Damage Post Paris," *Nature Climate Change* (August 2016), available at: http://www.nature.com/nclimate/journal/v6/n8/pdf/nclimate3090.pdf.

With these daunting challenges in mind, the task ahead should not be underestimated. The strength of a claims commission model is that it allows an opportunity to construct an adjudicatory framework that is at once unique, adaptive to the specific circumstances, yet also draws from the successes of past commissions. We will examine only a few of the evident difficulties that would face such a commission.[35]

Party structure

Consider party structure: who would, in the instant case, have standing to submit a claim before the commission? The UNCC, the EECC and the IUSCT provide useful models. The simplest option would have states collect claims and bring them before the commission on behalf of those within their territories. Such a party structure has clear precedent. At the EECC, for instance, the two governments served as the parties before the commission.[36] Ethiopian claims were filed "by and on behalf of" the Ethiopian government; Eritrean claims were primarily filed "by and on behalf" of the Eritrean government. Several individual claims were also transmitted through the Eritrean government. This method has a certain clarity: the parties are limited in number and sophisticated in their understanding of international legal processes. A second option might allow designated international organizations to bring claims before the commission. The rules of procedure for the UNCC, for instance, allowed that "governments and international organizations are entitled to submit claims to the Commission."[37] For claimants unable to submit claims through their governments – such as stateless individuals – the UNCC rules provided that "an appropriate person, authority, or body appointed by the Governing Council may submit claims on behalf of persons who are not in a position to have their claims submitted by a Government."[38]

---

[35] For in-depth treatment of each of these Commissions, *see* George H. Aldrich, *The Jurisprudence of the Iran–United States Claims Tribunal* (Clarendon, 1996); Sean D. Murphy, Won Kidane and Thomas Snider, *Litigating War: Mass Civil Injury and the Eritrea–Ethiopia Claims Commission* (Oxford University Press, 2013); Cymie R. Payne, *Gulf War Reparations and the UN Compensation Commission: Environmental Liability* (Oxford University Press, 2011).

[36] For a description of the party and claim process at the EECC, *see* Murphy, Kidane and Snyder, *Litigating War*, 57.

[37] Article V (1). Decision Taken by the Governing Council of the United Nations Compensation Commission at the 27th meeting, Sixth Session held on 26 June 1992. S/AC.26/1992/10 (26 June 1992).

[38] Article V (3). Decision Taken by the Governing Council of the United Nations Compensation Commission at the 27th meeting, Sixth Session held on 26 June 1992. S/AC.26/1992/10 (26 June 1992).

These organizations included the United Nations High Commissioner for Refugees (UNHCR), the United Nations Development Programme, and the United Nations Relief and Works Agency for Palestine Refugees in the Near East.[39] In the climate context, the commission might designate regional organizations – like the Caribbean Community Climate Change Center[40] – to collect claims on behalf of residents.

Third, individuals might bring claims directly to the commission. While this would be challenging administratively, it could be made easier based on the UNCC's model to expedite claims. At the UNCC, for example, the Secretariat helped facilitate claims and administration.[41] The commissioners then resolved the individual claims. The whole process would be *quasi-judicial*, "a partial recognition that a process to resolve over 2 million claims could not involve individualized adjudication of claims or the expectations of due process that ordinarily accompany such adjudication."[42] The Governing Council set policy, stipulated evidentiary standards and procedural frameworks that were then followed in the adjudication of individual claims by panels composed of commissioners. This structure allowed the commissioners to move quickly in processing the claims using the guidelines set by Governing Council decisions. A similar structure could aid in the climate context: a governing council could dictate policy, claim amounts, evidentiary standards, which could then be applied to individual claims on a regional or sub-regional basis. Such a system would be more efficient, timely, and sidestep critiques of a state-party structure.

Causation, evidence and efficiency

As addressed above, causation might be especially difficult to evaluate, given the complex nature of climate phenomena. However, past claims commissions have also had to carefully consider causation requirements as part of their mandates.

---

[39] *See* United Nations Claims Commission, "The Claims," http://www.uncc.ch/claims.

[40] The Caribbean Climate Change Centre, http://caribbeanclimate.bz/.

[41] *See* Frances E. McGovern, "Dispute System Design: The United Nations Compensation Commission" in Feighery, Gibson and Rajah, *War Reparations and the UN Compensation Commission*, 29, 37–40.

[42] David Caron, "Introduction," in Feighery, Gibson and Rajah, *War Reparations and the UN Compensation Commission*, xxiii, xxviii.

The EECC saw its role as judicial, with responsibility for applying and interpreting international law.[43] Therefore, the commission adopted "the commonly used nomenclature of 'proximate cause'" as its causation standard.[44] The EECC chose the standard after examining, and eventually dismissing, a reasonableness standard and a standard based on direct and indirect causation.[45] The Commission went on to note that it would also use foreseeability as a yardstick by which to measure proximity. If the "particular damage should have been foreseeable to an actor committing the international delict in question," then the agent's actor's behavior was likely to be a proximate cause and meet the causation standard.

The UNCC's mandate was for "direct" claims arising from the Iraqi invasion of Kuwait. While injuries sustained directly from military personnel might be easily seen as direct, "the direct link between the invasion and a serious personal injury or death is not so clear in other instances."[46] The UNCC considered different standards in each of the categories of claims, with increasingly strict standards of evidence to prove causation. For instance, for personal injury claims – Category "B" Claims – a causal link could be established between health effects and the invasion by submitting a personal statement linking the injury to the conflict, and by further confirmation by the Commission's medical examiner. For claims for damages exceeding $100,000, the Commission considered "whether the act of a State was the 'proximate cause' of the loss suffered, or whether the act was too remote to create liability."[47] The UNCC's Governing Council also established different evidentiary standards to accompany the causality requirements. For Category "A" claims – those of individuals fleeing opposing forces – the UNCC only required

---

43 *See* Eritrea–Ethiopia Claims Commission Decision Number 7, Guidance Regarding *Jus ad Bellum* Liability. Decided 27 July 2007, available at: https://pcacases.com/web/sendAttach/749.

44 EECC Decision Number 7, Guidance Regarding *Jus ad Bellum* Liability, 4.

45 EECC Decision Number 7, Guidance Regarding *Jus ad Bellum* Liability, 4.

46 Recommendations Made by the Panel of Commissioners Concerning Individual Claims for Serious Personal Injury or Death (Category "B" Claims), S/AC.26/1994/1, 26 May 1994.

47 Report and Recommendations Made by the Panel of Commissioners Concerning Part One of the First Instalment of Individual Claims for Damages above US$100,000 (Category "D" Claims) S/AC.26/1998/1 3 February 1998, available at: http://www.uncc.ch/sites/default/files/attachments/documents/r1998-01.pdf.

evidence of a flight or travel during a set time period.[48] Claimants did not have to show that they left *because* of the conflict, merely that they left *during* the conflict. For the Commission, such a relaxed standard was acceptable because "[t]he evidentiary standard set by the Governing Council for departure claims is to a large extent explained by the modest level of compensation."[49]

Substantive Difficulties in the Creation of a Commission

Obtaining agreement on the substantive rules for resolving "loss and damage" claims arising from greenhouse gas emissions and climate-related harms will be another challenge. One of the advantages of creating a claims commission, of course, is that the commission can establish rules particularly suited to the problem of climate change, rather than having to shoehorn the claims into an established framework or existing body of law. Many have noted that the traditional legal standards, especially those from tort law, are a poor fit for climate change claims. As Professor Douglas Kysar once observed, "[a]t each stage of the traditional tort analysis – duty, breach, causation, and harm – the climate change plaintiff finds herself bumping up against doctrines that are premised on a classical liberal worldview in which threats such as climate change simply do not register."[50]

Duty and breach

A loss and damage compensation mechanism will have to determine *ex ante* what sorts of claims the mechanism will redress and establish legal rules to do so. The commission will have to determine what conduct establishes liability; in other words: what duties do international actors have and what behavior constitutes a breach of that duty.

A related question that must be resolved is *when* a duty to avoid emissions inhered. In the climate change context, liability would stem from the breach of a duty not to harm others by emitting greenhouse gases, but only once the duty existed. The commission's determination, or prior decision by the creators of the commission, of the date on which

---

48 Report and Recommendations Made by the Panel of Commissioners Concerning the First Instalment of Individual Claims for Departure from Iraq or Kuwait (Category "A" Claims), S/Ac.26/1994/2, 21 October 1994, available at: http://www.uncc.ch/sites/default/files/attachments/documents/r1994-02.pdf.

49 Report and Recommendations on Category "A" Claims, 10.

50 Douglas A. Kysar, "What Climate Change Can Do About Tort Law" (2011) 41 *Environmental Law* 2, 9–10.

the duty to avoid greenhouse gas emissions inhered will have a dramatic effect on the apportionment of liability.[51]

As an alternative, the commission might want to avoid the question of historical liability by only looking at future climate liability. The date of the commission's inception might be considered the date that a duty to avoid emissions is established, in which case the commission would only determine liability for a country's emissions after the formation of the commission. This would differ from the traditional model of a claims commission, formed to address past rather than future violations.

The liability standard

To reduce the complexity and expense of determining liability for climate negligence, the commission might opt for a strict liability standard. Treating greenhouse gas emissions as a strict liability tort would greatly simplify the commission's adjudicatory task because the commission would not have to engage in any analysis of the reasonability of the emissions and the negligence of a country or emitter. After the date that the duty inhered, simple proof of emissions would establish a country's liability.

However, the parties may decide not to assign liability at all. The process of assigning liability is politically unwieldy, and calculating payment obligations based on past harmful acts by climate polluters may not be the appropriate or even desired approach. Some parties, including US negotiators, have indicated that creation of liability would be a deal breaker for any loss and damage mechanism.[52] A commission could avoid assigning liability by encouraging emitter countries to contribute to a fund for compensation of climate harms on a voluntary basis.

---

[51] Total emissions from developing countries surpassed developed countries in 2007. Thus, if the duty to avoid emissions only inhered when the Kyoto Protocol went into effect in 1995, developed countries will have considerably less liability than if a more historical date is determined. *See* Johannes Friedrich and Thomas Damassa, "The History of Carbon Dioxide Emissions" *World Resources Institute* (21 May 2014), available at: http://www.wri.org/blog/2014/05/history-carbon-dioxide-emissions.

[52] US Secretary of State John Kerry discussed the political difficulties of establishing a loss and damage mechanism in an interview with *Rolling Stone* magazine, in anticipation of the climate negotiations in Paris: "We're in favor of framing [the loss and damage mechanism] in a way that doesn't create a legal remedy, because Congress will never buy into an agreement that has something like that." Jeff Goodell, "John Kerry on Climate Change: The Fight of Our Time," *Rolling Stone* (1 December 2015), available at: http://www.rollingstone.com/politics/news/john-kerry-on-climate-change-the-fight-of-our-time-20151201.

Harms

Perhaps the most important substantive decision to be made in the creation of a climate compensation commission as a "loss and damage" mechanism is determining what principles will guide compensation. The concept of "loss and damage" could follow one of several substantive models:

Compensation of harms: "loss and damage" A model based on "compensation of harms" would most nearly resemble the conventional legal approach to determining loss and damage, as that concept has been developed in both domestic law and international law. "Loss and damage" is consistent with the compensation of harms approach traditionally taken in tort, in which a wrongdoer, found liable, compensates a wronged person retroactively for the value of the harm done to him or her.

Adaptation costs An approach based on adaptation costs would necessarily award less funding than a "loss and damage" approach because countries would be still left bearing the cost of loss and damage, i.e., the residual damage cost of whatever warming they would still experience after the implementation of adaptation measures.[53] Adaptation costs include the costs of preparing existing institutions to endure climate change, such as new infrastructure to protect existing settlements from sea-level rise, as well as the cost of developing new institutions and ways of life to respond to the changing climate, such as changes in subsistence livelihood practices to respond to loss of biodiversity.[54] Adaptation funding to avert future climate damage is much needed in the short term to avert damages in the long term. In fact, these adaptation funds may be more needed than a backward-looking payment for harms experienced already or to be experienced in the future.[55] A compensation commission might add the adjudication of liability to the approaches of existing voluntary adaptation finance mechanisms such as the Adaptation Fund,

---

[53] *See* United Nations Environment Program, *The Adaptation Finance Gap Report* (May 2016), 5, available at: http://web.unep.org/adaptationgapreport/sites/unep.org.adaptationgapreport/files/documents/agr2016.pdf (including both costs of adapting existing institutions and costs of resiliency). Adaptation costs are still significant. For developing countries, the cost of adaptation alone could reach $500 billion by 2050. UNEP, *The Adaptation Finance Gap Report*, xii.

[54] For a list of examples of adaptation initiatives by region, *see* IPCC, Fourth Assessment Report: Climate Change 2007 § 17.2.2 (2007), https://www.ipcc.ch/publications_and_data/ar4/wg2/en/ch17s17-2-2.html.

[55] UNEP, *The Adaptation Finance Gap Report*.

so that emitter countries' contributions to the fund became mandatory in proportion to their contributions to climate change.

Costs of small-state mitigation The commission could narrow its focus even further and only consider compensation for climate change mitigation. This would be the most forward-looking remedy. It would ask that developed nations, in addition to mitigating their own climate pollution through deployment of renewable energy and efficiency measures, also pay for the costs of mitigating emissions from developing states. This would likely entail investment in similar renewable energy and efficiency solutions in the developing world, as well as economic development to prevent land use changes like deforestation that also heavily contribute to the carbon footprint of developing nations. However, such a fund would not necessarily channel resources to the countries experiencing the greatest effects of climate change, where adaptation to a drastically changed future may be a more crucial need than mitigation.

Unjust enrichment Another approach to compensation could apportion liability on the basis of unjust enrichment. This legal concept, recognized in both international and domestic law, "provides that an unjust benefit must be restored if it has been acquired at the cost of another."[56] In the climate change context, this would require climate polluters to repay an amount equal to the economic benefit they received from the use of fossil fuels and/or uncontrolled emission of greenhouse gases into the atmosphere. This option has been discussed little in international negotiations and is seldom mentioned in the academic literature,[57] no doubt because the potential award amounts would be astronomical. Yet the example of unjust enrichment demonstrates the full range of possible methods for calculating compensation.

Lastly, an insurance model for climate compensation is emerging as a potential mechanism for developed countries to help developing countries as they manage their climate risk. Termed "InsuResilience," this insurance model aims to reduce financial risk to those most vulnerable to climate change by making insurance against climate damages available to

---

[56] Charles Manga Fombad, "The Principle of Unjust Enrichment in International Law" (1997) 30 *Comparative and International Law Journal of South Africa* 120, 120.

[57] One exception is a student comment on the subject. *See* Aura Weinbaum, "Comment: Unjust Enrichment: An Alternative to Tort Law and Human Rights in the Climate Change Context?" (2011) 20 *Pacific Rim Law and Policy Journal* 429.

them.[58] Following the Paris talks, the US government pledged $30 million to subsidize climate insurance for developing nations, to support an initiative by the G7 countries to increase by 40 million the number of people insured against climate risk in the most vulnerable countries.[59] It is possible to construe such proposals as a means for developed countries to compensate for loss and damage without admitting liability.

A FINAL WORD: LESSONS LEARNED

Enough has been said about the different types of IMCCs to support some preliminary observations about how a climate change compensation mechanism might be structured. Recognizing that different constituencies may have different objectives for a climate change IMCC, the points below are more in the nature of questions that ought to be considered than instructions about what must be done. They draw on the experience of previous IMCCs, especially the three that this book takes as exemplifying modern IMCCs' special roles in, and contributions to, contemporary international litigation.

We start by outlining the different objectives that proponents of IMCCs may be entertaining. These are not inconsistent in any strong sense – a single person or state might pursue all of these objectives at once – but there are situations where they do not all point in the same direction and in these, they are in competition. For any given IMCC, one or two of these basic objectives will likely dominate the others. To the extent that one or two of these basic objectives do dominate, they will shape profoundly the contours of the adjudicative institution which results.

Basic Objectives

What do we want out of an institution such as the IMCCs described above? Regardless of which side wins, the economic and human costs of years of litigation are substantial. What anticipated gains would make the financial, political and psychological risks of an unfavorable award worth taking? In Chapter 7 we teased apart a variety of basic objectives

---

[58] *See* G7, "Joint Statement on InsuResilience: The Initiative on Climate Risk Insurance" (5 December 2015), available at: http://www.bmz.de/g7/includes/Downloadarchiv/G7_Joint_Statement_InsuResilience.pdf.

[59] Megan Rowling, "Obama Unveils $30 Mln for Climate Risk Insurance to Protect Poor," *Reuters* (1 December 2015), available at: http://www.reuters.com/article/climatechange-summit-insurance-idUSL8N13Q3S320151201.

underlying creation of a claims commission, recognizing these as overlapping but not identical – often supporting one another but sometimes in tension.

The most obvious objective, certainly, is recovery of an award for compensation. IMCCs are "mass compensation" commissions; the motivation for establishing one is to return the innocent injured person to his or her condition prior to the unlawful injury. A commission is more or less a success to the extent that it accomplishes that goal.

But there are also other objectives. One is to help cement peaceful relations between the parties by providing a forum for lawful interaction. Both the UNCC and the EECC have this objective. The EECC was an element of a comprehensive peace agreement between Ethiopia and Eritrea at the end of a brutal war. The IUSCT was an integral part of an attempted restoration of friendly (or, at least, friendlier) relations between the United States and Iran.

The objective of the defending state is likely to be to obtain closure – relief from the prospect of further litigation. A claims commission may be a more attractive forum for mounting a defense than any of the alternatives, such as defense in a US domestic court. US courts provide extensive rights of discovery; are often not reliably confidential; and might possibly lead to a jury trial or an award that includes attorneys' fees. Litigation before an international claims commission, as we observed in Chapter 7, is likely to be a more attractive alternative than that, and where the arbitration agreement provides that it is the claimant's exclusive remedy the commission will provide security from multiple lawsuits in a variety of different forums.

Truth telling – setting the historical record straight for future generations – is another basic objective. Where the recent conflict was psychologically particularly damaging, individual victims may want a chance to tell their stories. Absent some sort of corrective measures, it is likely to be the victor to a conflict whose views dominate the narrative. A neutral forum can hopefully separate historical facts from propaganda.

Another basic objective is deterrence. Requiring the guilty party to pay for loss or damage caused by its unlawful conduct is not only morally appropriate but also practically sound. Since there is at present no international criminal court set up to determine "unlawful aggression" generally, and no international police force to apprehend violators of international law, claims commissions can play an important role in discouraging unlawful conduct of similar kinds in the future.

Finally, the dominant reason for establishing a claims commission may simply be to satisfy one of the parties and induce it to put an end to whatever conflict is causing the damage in question. The objective in agreeing to establish a commission may be nothing more complicated than the expected peace dividend.

This is only a rough list of some of the many reasons that a claims commission may be brought into existence. They are overlapping and interrelated; but logical tidiness is not important for present purposes. What matters here is that the eventual shape that the IMCC takes is likely to be a function of which basic objectives are considered to be most important in the particular context. Certain basic objectives require the construction of "thick" IMMCs while others can be satisfied with "thin" ones.

"Thick" and "Thin" IMMCs

In Chapter 7 we showed that the different objectives of different participants in the claims commission led to different demands on what the institution would eventually look like. The different shapes that IMCCs take will appeal to a greater or lesser extent to different constituencies. The different participants, that is to say, are satisfied in rather different ways.

For example, the interests of the individual claimant in being awarded legally accurate compensation for his or her injury require accuracy of determination of the surrounding facts, and of the lawfulness or unlawfulness of the defendant's activity. To achieve this objective requires a substantial administrative apparatus that remains in place for a considerable length of time. It also requires continued emphasis on the individual (as opposed to the state). It does not sit squarely with traditional statist assumptions; these would divert all recovery to the state, to handle as it saw fit. Where states are permitted to use their nationals' recovery as a set-off to their own liability, the individual claimants are likely to get no recovery at all.

The interests and objectives of other constituents do not so strongly require that the actual compensation be correctly determined and paid to the injured victim. Neither the defending state, the tribunal nor the international law community has any interest *per se* in awarding the right amount of compensation and ensuring that it reaches the hands of the individual victim. To the contrary, their interests are satisfied in other ways. Satisfaction of the interests of the members of the tribunal depends on the public confidence that is generated by the *appearance* of accuracy and justice. The international lay community prioritizes the termination of hostilities that may generate suffering for the international community at large. The defending state has an interest in closure – once it defends the case before the IMCC and is absolved, it will not need to put in another appearance before another forum.

These other interests emphasize different structural needs for IMCCs striving to achieve different objectives. This is clearest with regard to IMCCs that are dedicated to the provision of accurate compensation into the hands of the individual victims. In the mass claims context, it is no easy trick to determine accurately the compensation needed by each claimant and to deliver it to that right person accurately. It cannot, certainly, be done by anything other than a five-person commission with support from a registry and perhaps some individual research assistants. The costs of such an undertaking are substantial, and the guarantees of accurate accomplishment are minimal.

Some IMMCs might be characterized as "thick" while others might be characterized as "thin." The former are robust institutions with large staff, extensive administrative responsibilities, guaranteed sources of funding, adequate resources to deal directly with large numbers of individual claimants and long term expected time in existence. Their institutional presence is so secure and longstanding that they almost approach the solidity of a standing body such as a court.

The latter – the "thin" ones – are minimalist. Limited in staff to hardly more that their (usually part-time) commission members, thin IMCCs have no secure funding and must request money for costs from the parties when they need it. They may rely on services of an external registry such as the Permanent Court of Arbitration, rather than hiring their own administrative staff. The agreement that sets them in motion may specify only a short period of time in which to finish their work, after which they are authorized to take additional time only if necessary. Perhaps most important for present purposes, they deal largely with states as claimants. Thin IMCCs lack the support structure to take on the time consuming and error-prone task of making individual determinations of large numbers of claims.

The EECC and the IUSCT Compared

Contrast the structure of the Eritrea–Ethiopia Claims Commission to the structure of the Iran–US Claims Tribunal. The administrative side of the EECC was as thin as the IUSCT's was thick. Almost nothing was said in the arbitration agreement about any mechanism for ensuring that awards would be paid. Throughout the proceedings, part time support was obtained from the PCA (which acted as the registry) but there were no full-time staff, no dedicated building for office space, and almost no indication that the Commission would identify particular victims to take particular shares in the awards.

The drafters of the agreement establishing the IUSCT took a maximalist position. Most obviously, they took care to create a system in which awards would be paid. As described in Chapter 3, the agreement that established the Tribunal specified that Iran would create a fund from which judgments would be paid. When the amount in the fund fell below a certain amount Iran was required to "top it up" so that there would always be enough to pay a judgment. This arrangement was more focused on compensation for individuals than on the rights of the two states (Iran and the United States) against one another.

Several decades after its creation, the IUSCT is still at work deciding disputes, arranging the payment of awards and creating a rich jurisprudence of international law that has made it one of the preeminent sources of international arbitral practice and international substantive law. The Tribunal is almost a standing court, with its turnover and replacement of judges and, in particular, its publication of legal awards – a system of precedent. The Tribunal has taken on a presence and a persona that verge on an identity above and beyond what the parties created with their initial agreement. The UNCC is, in many respects, in the same position. Upon its creation, it hired staff and arranged dedicated office facilities; it drew on a source of guaranteed funding; and it still remains, though much reduced, at work after some two decades of operation.

When the EECC is compared with the other two illustrative commissions, it is easy to conclude that the UNCC and the IUSCT were really set up to award compensation. This is less the case with the EECC. There are several different possible explanations for this. For one thing, if the EECC had conceived of its responsibility solely in terms of granting individual awards to be paid directly to victims, the job would have been entirely cost prohibitive. The EECC dealt with impoverished African countries that could not have found the means to pay the awards other than by set-off. On a per capita basis, it would have cost more to determine who was entitled to compensation, and how much, than the award was likely to be worth. The EECC was expensive enough viewed as a state-to-state arbitration. But it would have been crushingly impractical to conceive of it as anything else.

Moreover, objects other than individual compensation were important at the EECC. Its establishment in Article 5 of the Algiers Agreement was important as an inducement to one or both of the parties to sign the Algiers Agreement as a whole, thereby putting a definitive end to the countries' border war. Management of the claims of unlawful behavior during the war was shown to be possible through exemplary peaceful means. Truth telling was an ostensible objective of one party (Ethiopia) to the degree that it was able to convince the Tribunal to take on the responsibility of determining the cause of the war (which, it claimed, was an Eritrean war of aggression). These objectives might have been adequate motivation to form a commission even had there been no indication at any point that compensation would be distributed at the end of the day. The same cannot be said of the UNCC and the IUSCT, both of which seemed genuinely focused on monetary compensation.

Implications for a Possible Climate Change Commission

These thoughts have implications for what a climate change commission might look like, and they raise questions that call out for thoughtful consideration before steps are taken to devise a mechanism to remedy the injury suffered by innocent low-lying states that face the wrath of rising waters or extreme weather conditions.

First, and most important, clarity is needed about the objectives underlying this compensation project. The most obvious objective is, of course, to make the injured victims whole for the loss that they have suffered. But to what extent is that possible? If the commission that is created is seriously intent upon providing compensation, then will a procedural apparatus be created that has enough resources to actually carry out this difficult task?

What other objectives might also contribute to the project? It is unlikely that the powerful states will recognize deterrence as an objective; they have insisted that willingness to create a mechanism cannot be understood as an admission of legal responsibility. Truth telling as an objective is uncertain for the same reason; the parties who would contribute to a fund for the awards are unlikely to create a system intended to expose the unlawful conduct that they have engaged in for years. All in all, the posture that they have adopted suggests that compensation is the only viable public rationalization for a climate change commission. Yet without a very thick structure – an IMCC comparable at least to the IUSCT or UNCC model – such an aspiration is entirely impractical. The international community must be willing to set up a system that works, and resist the temptation to establish a sham mechanism that wastes resources and accomplishes nothing more than kicking the can down the road.

A final difficult – but unavoidable – consideration is the position to be taken on how much the new commission would perceive itself as deciding compensation for individuals and how much as deciding compensation for the involved states. Will the commission stick close to the statist paradigm or will it reinforce the contemporary trend to devise mechanisms for individual protection also? We think the latter would be a welcome development.

Index